Vergil
Aeneid Book 5

The Focus Vergil Aeneid Commentaries

For intermediate students
  Aeneid 1 • Randall Ganiban, editor • Available now
  Aeneid 2 • Randall Ganiban, editor • Available now
  Aeneid 3 • Christine Perkell, editor • Available now
  Aeneid 4 • James O'Hara, editor • Available now
  Aeneid 5 • Joseph Farrell, editor • Available now
  Aeneid 6 • Patricia Johnston, editor • Available now

For advanced students
  Aeneid 1–6 • Available now (Single volume. Contributors as listed above)
  Aeneid 7–12 • Available 2015 (Single volume. Contributors as listed below)
  Contributors:
  Randall Ganiban, editor • Aeneid 7
  James O'Hara, editor • Aeneid 8
  Joseph Farrell, editor • Aeneid 9
  Andreola Rossi, editor • Aeneid 10
  Charles McNelis, editor • Aeneid 11
  Christine Perkell, editor • Aeneid 12

Vergil

Aeneid Book 5

Joseph Farrell
University of Pennsylvania

Focus Publishing
R. Pullins Company
Newburyport, MA
www.focusbookstore.com

Vergil Aeneid 5

© 2014 Joseph Farrell

Focus Publishing / R. Pullins Company
PO Box 369
Newburyport MA 01950
www.focusbookstore.com

ISBN 13: 978-1-58510-229-7

Library of Congress Cataloging-in-Publication Data

Virgil, author.

   [Aeneis. Liber 5]

   Vergil, Aeneid book 5 / Joseph Farrell.

      pages cm   (The Focus Vergil Aeneid commentaries for intermediate students)

   ISBN 978-1-58510-229-7

   1. Virgil. Aeneis. Liber 5. 2. Latin literature—History and criticism. I. Farrell, Joseph, 1955– II. Title. III. Series: Focus Vergil Aeneid commentaries for intermediate students.

   PA6803.B25F377 2014

   873'.01—dc23   2014034848

All rights are reserved. No part of this publication may be reproduced, stored in a retrieval system, or transmitted in any form or by any means, electronic, mechanical, by photocopying, recording, or by any other means without the prior written permission of the publisher. If you have received this material as an examination copy free of charge, Focus Publishing/R. Pullins Company retains the title to the material and it may not be resold. Resale of any examination copies of Focus Publishing/R. Pullins Company materials is strictly prohibited.

Printed in the United States of America

10 9 8 7 6 5 4 3 2 1

1014V

Table of Contents

Preface	vii
Introduction to Vergil's *Aeneid*	1
Vergil's lifetime and poetry	1
Vergil and his predecessors	6
The *Aeneid*, Rome, and Augustus	9
Introduction to book 5: Its role in the *Aeneid*	11
Latin text and Commentary on *Aeneid* 5	17
Appendix A: Vergil's Meter	109
Appendix B: Stylistic Terms	119
Works Cited	133
Vocabulary	141
Index	187

Preface

This volume contains a text and commentary of *Aeneid* 5 intended for use at the intermediate level or higher. It is substantially the same as the one contained in the multi-author Focus commentary on *Aeneid* 1–6, but it contains somewhat more grammatical explanation, and it has been rewritten to be more nearly self-sufficient. When one of the companion volumes in this series contains a note that is pertinent to a passage in book 5, I repeat or adapt it rather than simply citing it (as is the general practice in the 1–6 commentary). In addition, like the other single-book commentaries in this series, this volume contains a vocabulary to assist the reader in construing Vergil. Definitions specified within the commentary itself are keyed to this vocabulary, which in turn cites the relevant sub-headings of the *Oxford Latin Dictionary (OLD)* and Lewis and Short's *A Latin Dictionary* (L&S) where this seems necessary. Explanations of grammar and syntax refer to the relevant sections of Allen and Greenough, *A New Latin Grammar* (AG). The point of such specificity is to assist students and their teachers in understanding Vergil's Latin according to a traditional, clear, comprehensive, and widely available point of reference. Most of what Vergil writes can easily be explained in these terms, but one does not have to read far before noticing that he occasionally strains the resources of the language, sometimes in ways that AG regard as standard "poeticisms," but at other times in ways that go beyond what any reference work sanctions as "normal." This is a useful thing for students of Vergil to notice. His influence on later poets was so great that his style quickly became a kind of standard; but in his own day, he was recognized as, and sometimes criticized for being too experimental. Realizing that Vergil's Latin does not always conform to expectations will help even first-time readers to understand its impact on Latin literature.

The commentary takes as its starting point the perennially valuable school edition of *Aeneid* 1–6 by T. E. Page (1894), although Page's notes have been extensively revised, whether by expansion, paring down, or omission, while numerous new notes and introductory material have been inserted. In addition, I have tried to be more explicit than Page in commenting on the structure of the book, which I regard as an outstandingly clear and elegant example of an area of poetics in which Vergil particularly excelled. Where I substantially reproduce one of Page's notes in its original form (or, indeed, where I follow the note of some other commentator), I have cited my source, although I have not fully collated all of the many commentaries that have been written on Vergil, so that there may be cases in which I cite a relatively recent commentator withing having traced a particular note to its ultimate source. In addition, the general introduction and the appendices on meter and style, which are the work of series editor Randall Ganiban (the appendices as they appear here having been adapted to the needs of book 5 by me), as well as the bibliography and the general index, are all new.

The Latin text used here is based on that of F. A. Hirtzel (Oxford, 1900) with the following differences in readings:

	Focus	**Hirtzel**	**Mynors**
29	demittere	demittere	dimittere
112	talenta	talentum	talenta
162	gressum	gressum	cursum
317	signant,	signant.	signant,
347	reddantur	reddentur	reddentur
505	micuitque	timuitque	micuitque
512	alta	alta	atra
520	contendit	contorsit	contendit
551	discedere	discedere	decedere
649	qui	quis	qui
777–8	777 *post* 778	778 *post* 777	777 *post* 778
825	tenent	tenent	tenet
851	caeli	caelo	caeli

This edition places the Latin text and the commentary on the same page. Nevertheless, readers may find it helpful to have a complete text of *Aeneid* 5, or indeed of the entire poem, ready to hand either for individual study or for classroom use, and such materials have therefore been made available for download on the publisher's website, along with information and updates on this commentary and others in the series (at http://www.focusbookstore.com).

It is my pleasure to thank those who have helped me in various ways as I worked both on this edition and on the version that appears in the one-volume commentary on books 1–6. I am most grateful to my four colleagues on this project, Randy Ganiban, Pat Johnston, Jim O'Hara, and Christine Perkell, for the example that they set, for their acumen, and (not least) their patience. To Christine I owe a special debt for having invited me to take part as visiting professor in an exceptionally rewarding NEH summer institute held at Emory University in 1994. The plan of that seminar was to bring in visitors to work with the other participants on one book of the *Aeneid* for several days at a time. When Christine asked me which book I would like, I told her, truthfully, that it did not matter, because I regard every word of the poem as solid gold. In the event, she asked me to do book 5, which was apparently not in much demand; doing so, and then working up my contribution on the same book for the volume of essays that Christine later edited, were indirectly responsible for determining my contribution to the Focus project and directly responsible for furthering my already great admiration for this book. Particular thanks are also owed to Randy, who has contributed in many ways to the betterment of this volume, as has Jim, especially since joining Randy as co-editor of a second series of commentaries on books 7–12. Damien Nelis, as he has many times in the past, has been a timely source of good advice and much-appreciated encouragement. I would also like to thank for their contribution to my appreciation of this book the students whom I had the good fortune to teach in a pair of courses at the University of Pennsylvania, the first in 2010 on Latin poetry concerned with the Argonautic tradition, and the second in 2013 on the poetry of Vergil as a whole. As always, I am immensely grateful to my wife, Ann de Forest, my daughter, Flannery, and my son, Kai, who have always helped me find the time to work on this project (and others) over the years and have not been fazed by those occasional periods when I was unable, even during what ought to have been family time, to free my mind completely from *Aeneid* 5.

Joseph Farrell
University of Pennsylvania

Introduction

Vergil's lifetime and poetry

Publius Vergilius Maro (i.e. Vergil)[1] was born on October 15, 70 BCE near the town of Mantua (modern Mantova) in what was then still Cisalpine Gaul.[2] Little else about his life can be stated with certainty, because our main source, the ancient biography by the grammarian Donatus (fourth century CE),[3] is of questionable value.[4] The historical and political background to Vergil's life, by contrast, is amply documented and provides a useful framework for understanding his career. Indeed, his poetic development displays an increasing engagement with the politics of contemporary Rome, an engagement that culminates in the *Aeneid*.

Vergil lived and wrote in a time of political strife and uncertainty. In his early twenties the Roman Republic was torn apart by the civil wars of 49–45 BCE, when Julius Caesar fought and defeated Pompey and his supporters. Caesar was declared *dictator perpetuo* ("Dictator for Life") early in 44 BCE but was assassinated on the Ides of March by a group of senators led by Brutus[5] and Cassius. They sought to restore the Republic, which, they believed, was being destroyed by Caesar's domination and intimations of kingship.[6]

---

1   The spelling "Virgil" (*Virgilius*) is also used by convention. It developed early and has been explained by its similarity to two words: *virgo* ("maiden") and *virga* ("wand"). For discussion of the origins and potential meanings of these connections, see Jackson Knight (1944) 36–7 and Putnam (1993) 127–8 with notes.

2   Cisalpine Gaul, the northern part of what we now think of as Italy, was incorporated into Roman Italy in 42 BCE. Mantua is located ca. 520 kilometers north of Rome.

3   This biography drew heavily from the *De poetis* of Suetonius (born ca. 70 CE).

4   Horsfall (1995: 1–25; 2006: xxii–xxiv) argues that nearly every detail is unreliable.

5   Kingship was hateful to the Romans ever since Brutus' own ancestor, Lucius Junius Brutus, led the expulsion of Rome's last king, Tarquin the Proud, in ca. 509 BCE, an act that ended the regal period of Rome and initiated the Republic (cf. *Aeneid* 6.817–18). In killing Caesar, Brutus claimed that he was following the example of his great ancestor—an important concept for the Romans.

6   For the reasons behind Caesar's assassination and the fall of the Republic, see the brief accounts in Scullard (1982) 126–53 and Shotter (2005) 4–19.

The assassination initiated a new round of turmoil that profoundly shaped the course of Roman history. In his will, Caesar adopted and named as his primary heir his great-nephew Octavian (63 BCE–14 CE), the man who would later be called "Augustus."[7] Though only eighteen years old, Octavian boldly accepted and used this inheritance. Through a combination of shrewd calculation and luck, he managed to attain the consulship in 43 BCE, though he was merely nineteen years of age.[8] He then joined forces with two of Caesar's lieutenants, Marc Antony (initially Octavian's rival) and Lepidus. Together they demanded recognition as a Board of Three (*triumviri* or "triumvirs") to reconstitute the state as they saw fit, and were granted extraordinary powers to do so by the Roman senate and people. In 42 BCE they avenged Caesar's murder by defeating his assassins commanded by Brutus and Cassius at the battle of Philippi in Macedonia, but their alliance gradually began to deteriorate as a result of further civil strife and interpersonal rivalries.

Vergil composed the *Eclogues*, his first major work, during this tumultuous period.[9] Published ca. 39 BCE,[10] the *Eclogues* comprise a sophisticated collection of ten pastoral poems that treat the experiences of shepherds.[11] The poems were modeled on the *Idylls* of Theocritus, a Hellenistic Greek poet of the third century BCE (see below). But whereas Theocritus' poetry created a world that was largely timeless, Vergil sets his pastoral world against the backdrop of contemporary Rome and the disruption caused by the civil wars. *Eclogues* 1 and 9, for example, deal with the differing fortunes of shepherds during a time of land confiscations that resonate with historical events in 41–40 BCE.[12] *Eclogue* 4 describes the birth of a child during the

---

7   See below.

8   By the *lex Villia annalis* of 180 BCE, a consul had to be at least forty-two years of age.

9   Other works have been attributed to Vergil: *Aetna, Catalepton, Ciris, Copa, Culex, Dirae, Elegiae in Maecenatem, Moretum,* and *Priapea*. They are collected in what is called the *Appendix Vergiliana* and are generally believed to be spurious.

10 This traditional dating, however, has recently been called into question through re-evaluation of *Eclogue* 8, which may very well refer to events in 35 BCE. See Clausen (1994) 232–7.

11 Coleman (1977) and Clausen (1994) are excellent commentaries on the *Eclogues*. For a discussion of the pastoral genre at Rome, see Heyworth (2005). For general interpretation of the *Eclogues*, see Hardie (1998) 5–27 with extensive bibliography in the notes, Volk (2008a), and Smith (2011) 40–74.

12 Octavian rewarded veterans with land that was already occupied.

consulship of Asinius Pollio (40 BCE) who will bring a new golden age to Rome.[13] By interjecting the Roman world into his poetic landscape,[14] Vergil allows readers to sense how political developments both threaten and give promise to the very possibility of pastoral existence.

The *Eclogues* established Vergil as a new and important poetic voice, and led him to the cultural circle of the great literary patron Maecenas, an influential supporter and confidant of Octavian. Their association grew throughout the 30s.[15] The political situation, however, remained precarious. Lepidus was ousted from the triumvirate in 36 BCE because of his treacherous behavior. Tensions between Octavian and Antony that were simmering over Antony's collaboration and affair with the Egyptian queen Cleopatra eventually exploded.[16] In 32 BCE, Octavian had Antony's powers revoked, and war was declared against Cleopatra (and thus in effect against Antony as well). During a naval confrontation off Actium on the coast of western Greece in September of 31 BCE, Octavian's fleet decisively routed the forces of Marc Antony and Cleopatra, who both fled to Egypt and committed suicide in the following year to avoid capture.[17] This momentous victory solidified

---

13 This is sometimes called the "Messianic Eclogue" because later ages read it as foreseeing the birth of Christ, which occurred nearly four decades later. The identity of the child is debated, but the poem may celebrate the marriage between Marc Antony and Octavian's sister Octavia that resulted from the treaty of Brundisium in 40 BCE; this union helped stave off the immediate outbreak of war between the two triumvirs. For more on this poem, see Van Sickle (1992) and Petrini (1997) 111–21, as well as the commentaries by Coleman (1977) and Clausen (1994).

14 In addition to the contemporary themes that Vergil treats, he also mentions or dedicates individual poems to a number of his contemporaries, including Asinius Pollio, Alfenus Varus, Cornelius Gallus, and probably Octavian, who is likely the *iuvenis* ("young man") mentioned at 1.42 and perhaps also the patron addressed at 8.6–13.

15 For the relationship between Augustus and the poets, see White (2005). White (1993) is a book-length study of this topic. For an overview of literature of the Augustan period from 40 BCE–14 CE, see Farrell (2005).

16 In addition to the political conflicts, there were also familial tensions: Antony conducted a decade-long affair with Cleopatra, even though he had married Octavia, Octavian's (Augustus') sister, as a result of the treaty of Brundisium in 40 BCE (see n. 13 above). Antony divorced Octavia in 32 BCE.

17 For the history of the triumviral period, see the brief accounts in Scullard (1982) 154–71 and Shotter (2005) 20–7; for more detailed treatments, see Syme (1939) 187–312 and Pelling (1996). For discussion of the contemporary artistic representations of Actium, see Gurval (1995).

Octavian's claim of being the protector of traditional Roman values against the detrimental influence of Antony, Cleopatra, and the East.[18]

Vergil began his next work, the *Georgics*, sometime in the 30s, completed it ca. 29 BCE in the aftermath of Actium, and dedicated it to Maecenas. Like the *Eclogues*, the *Georgics* was heavily influenced by Greek models—particularly the work of Hesiod (eighth century BCE) and of Hellenistic poets[19] such as Callimachus, Aratus, and Nicander (third–second centuries BCE). On the surface, it purports to be a poetic farming guide.[20] Each of its four book examines a different aspect or sphere of agricultural life: crops and weather signs (book 1), trees and vines (book 2), livestock (book 3), and bees (book 4). Its actual scope, however, is much more ambitious. The poem explores the nature of humankind's struggle with the beauty and difficulties of the agricultural world, but it does so within the context of contemporary war-torn Italy. It bears witness to the strife following Caesar's assassination, and sets the chaos and disorder inherent in nature against the upheaval caused by civil war (1.461–514). Moreover, Octavian's success and victories are commemorated both in the introduction (1.24–42) and conclusion (4.559–62) of the poem, as well as in the beginning of the third book (3.1–39). Thus once again, the political world is juxtaposed against Vergil's poetic landscape, but the relationship between the two is not fully addressed.[21]

Octavian's victory represented a turning point for Rome's development. Over the next decade, he centralized political and military control in his hands. He claimed to have returned the state (*res publica*) to the senate

---

18   This ideological interpretation is suggested in Vergil's depiction of the battle on Aeneas' shield (8.671–713).

19   See discussion below.

20   Recent commentaries on the *Georgics* include Thomas (1988) and Mynors (1990). For interpretation, see the introduction to the *Georgics* in Hardie (1998) 28–52 with extensive bibliography in the notes, Volk (2008b), and Smith (2011) 75–103. Individual studies include Wilkinson (1969), Putnam (1979), Johnston (1980), Ross (1987), Perkell (1989), and Nappa (2005). For allusion in the *Georgics*, see Thomas (1986), Farrell (1991), and Gale (2000).

21   The overall meaning of the *Georgics* is contested. Interpretation of the *Georgics*, like that of the *Aeneid* (see below), has optimistic and pessimistic poles. Otis (1964) is an example of the former; Ross (1987) the latter. Other scholars, such as Perkell (1989), fall in between by discerning inherent ambivalence. For discussion of these interpretive trends, see Hardie (1998) 50–2.

and Roman people in 27 BCE.[22] His powers were redefined, and he was granted the name "Augustus' ("Revered One") by the senate. It is true that he maintained many traditional Republican institutions, but in reality he was transforming the state into a monarchy. So effective was his stabilization and control of Rome after decades of civil war that he reigned as *Princeps* ("First Citizen") from 27 BCE to 14 CE, creating a political framework (the Principate) that served the Roman state for centuries.[23]

Vergil wrote his final poem, the *Aeneid*, largely in the 20s, during the first years of Augustus' reign, when the Roman people presumably hoped that the civil wars were behind them but feared that the Augustan peace would not last. The *Aeneid* tells the story of the Trojan hero Aeneas. He fought the Greeks at Troy and saw his city destroyed, but with the guidance of the gods and fate he led his surviving people across the Mediterranean to a new homeland in Italy.[24] As in the *Eclogues* and *Georgics*, Vergil interjects his contemporary world into his poetic world. In the *Aeneid*, however, the thematic connections between these two realms are developed still more explicitly, with Aeneas' actions shown to be necessary for and to lead ultimately to the reign of Augustus. (See below for further discussion.)

Vergil was still finishing the *Aeneid* when he was stricken by a fatal illness in 19 BCE. The ancient biographical tradition claims that he traveled to Greece, intending to spend three years editing his epic there and in Asia, but that early on he encountered Augustus, who was returning to Rome from the East, and decided to accompany him. Vergil, however, fell ill during the journey and died in Brundisium (in southern Italy) in September of 19 BCE. The *Aeneid* was largely complete but had not yet received its final revision. We are

---

22   Augustus, *Res Gestae* 34.

23   For general political and historical narratives of Augustus' reign, see the relatively brief account in Shotter (2005); longer, more detailed treatments can be found in A. H. M. Jones (1970), Crook (1996), Southern (1998), and Everitt (2006) 186–320. A classic and influential book by Syme (1939) paints Augustus in extremely dark colors. For broader considerations of the Augustan age, see the short but interesting volume by Wallace-Hadrill (1993) and the more comprehensive treatments by Galinsky (1996, 2005). For the interaction of art and ideology in the Augustan Age, see Zanker (1988).

24   For general interpretation of the *Aeneid*, see the recent overviews provided by Hardie (1998) 53–101, Perkell (1999), Anderson (2005), Johnson (2005), Fratantuono (2007), Ross (2007), and Smith (2011) 104–49. For the literary and cultural backgrounds, see Martindale (1997), Farrell (2005), and Galinsky (2005).

told that Vergil asked that it be burned, but that Augustus ultimately had it published. While such details regarding Vergil's death are doubted, the poem clearly needed final editing.[25] However, its present shape, including its sudden ending, is generally accepted to be as Vergil had planned.

Vergil and his predecessors

By writing an epic about the Trojan war, Vergil was rivaling Homer, the greatest of all the Greek poets. The *Aeneid* was therefore a bold undertaking, but its success makes it arguably the quintessential Roman work because it accomplishes what Latin poetry had always striven to do: to appropriate the Greek tradition and transform it into something that was both equally impressive and distinctly "Roman."

Homer's *Iliad* tells the story of the Trojan war by focusing on Achilles' strife with the Greek leader Agamemnon and consequent rage in the tenth and final year of the conflict, while the *Odyssey* treats the war's aftermath by relating Odysseus' struggle to return home. These were the earliest and most revered works of Greek literature,[26] and they exerted a defining influence on both the overall framework of the *Aeneid* and the close details of its poetry. In general terms, *Aeneid* 1–6, like the *Odyssey*, describes a hero's return (to a new) home after the Trojan war, while *Aeneid* 7–12, like the *Iliad*, tells the story of a war. But throughout the *Aeneid*, Vergil reworks ideas, language, characters, and scenes from both poems. Some ancient critics faulted Vergil for his use of Homer, calling his appropriations "thefts." Vergil, however, is said to have responded that it is "easier to steal his club from Hercules than a line from Homer."[27] Indeed, Vergil does much more than simply quote material from Homer. His creative use and transformation of Homeric language and theme are central not only to his artistry but also to the meaning of the *Aeneid*.

Though Homer is the primary model, Vergil was also influenced by the Hellenistic Greek tradition of poetry that originated in Alexandria, Egypt in the third century BCE. There scholar-poets such as Apollonius,

---

25 We can be sure that the poem had not received its final revision for a number of reasons, including the presence of roughly fifty-eight incomplete or "half" lines. See commentary note on line 294.

26 These poems were culminations of a centuries-old oral tradition and were written down probably in the eighth century BCE.

27 ... *facilius esse Herculi clavam quam Homeri versum subripere* (Donatus/Suetonius, *Life of Vergil* 46).

Callimachus, and Theocritus reacted against the earlier literary tradition (particularly epic which by their time had become largely derivative). They developed a poetic aesthetic that valued sophistication in meter and word order, small-scale treatments over large, the unusual and recherché over the conventional. Hellenistic poetry was introduced into the mainstream of Latin poetry a generation before Vergil by the so-called "neoterics" or "new poets," of whom Catullus (c. 84–c. 54 BCE) was the most influential for Vergil and for the later literary tradition.[28]

Vergil's earlier works, the *Eclogues* and *Georgics*, had been modeled to a significant extent on Hellenistic poems,[29] so it was perhaps a surprise that Vergil would then have turned to a large-scale epic concerning the Trojan war.[30] However, one of his great feats was the incorporation of the Hellenistic and neoteric sensibilities into the *Aeneid*. Two models were particularly important in this regard: the *Argonautica* by Apollonius of Rhodes, an epic retelling the hero Jason's quest for the Golden Fleece, and Catullus 64, a poem on the wedding of Peleus and Thetis.[31] Both works brought the great and elevated heroes of the past down to the human level, thereby offering new insights into their strengths, passions and flaws, and both greatly influenced Vergil's presentation of Aeneas.

Of Vergil's other predecessors in Latin literature, the most important was Ennius (239–169 BCE), often called the father of Roman poetry.[32] His

---

28 Clausen (1987, 2002), George (1974), Briggs (1981), Thomas (1988, 1999), and Hunter (2006) display these influences, while O'Hara (1996) provides a thorough examination of wordplay (important to the Alexandrian poets) in Vergil.

29 The *Eclogues* were modeled on Theocritus' *Idylls*; the *Georgics* had numerous models, though the Hellenistic poets Callimachus, Nicander, and Aratus were particularly important influences. See above.

30 For example, at *Eclogue* 6.3–5, Vergil explains in highly programmatic language his decision to compose poetry in the refined Callimachean or Hellenistic manner rather than traditional epic. See Clausen (1994) 174–5.

31 On the influence of Apollonius on Vergil, see the important book by Nelis (2001).

32 Ennius introduced the dactylic hexameter as the meter of Latin epic. Two earlier epic writers were Livius Andronicus who composed a translation of Homer's *Odyssey* into Latin, and Naevius who composed the *Bellum Punicum*, an epic on the First Punic War. Both Naevius and Livius wrote their epics in a meter called Saturnian that is not fully understood. For the influence of the early Latin poets on the *Aeneid*, see Wigodsky (1972).

Annales, which survives only in fragments, was an historical epic about Rome that traced the city's origins back to Aeneas and Troy. It remained the most influential Latin poem until the *Aeneid* was composed, and provided a model not only for Vergil's poetic language and themes, but also for his integration of Homer and Roman history. In addition, the *De Rerum Natura* of Lucretius (ca. 94–55/51 BCE), a hexameter poem on Epicurean philosophy, profoundly influenced Vergil with its forceful language and philosophical ideas.[33]

Finally, Vergil drew much from Greek and Roman[34] tragedy. Many episodes in the *Aeneid* share tragedy's well-known dramatic patterns (such as reversal of fortune), and explore the suffering that befalls mortals often as a result of the immense and incomprehensible power of the gods and fate.[35] As a recent critic has written, "The influence of tragedy on the *Aeneid* is pervasive, and arguably the single most important factor in Virgil's successful revitalization of the genre of epic."[36]

The *Aeneid* is thus a highly literary work. By considering its interactions with these and other models, or, to put it another way, by examining

---

33 See Hardie (1986) 157–240 and Adler (2003). The influence of the Epicurean Philodemus on Vergil (and the Augustans more generally) is explored in the collection edited by Armstrong, Fish, Johnston, and Skinner (2004). For Lucretius' influence on Vergil's *Georgics*, see especially Farrell (1991) and Gale (2000).

34 The earliest epic writers (Livius, Naevius and Ennius; see above) also wrote tragedy, and so it is not surprising that epic and tragedy would influence one another. Latin tragic writing continued into the first century through the work of, e.g., Pacuvius (220–ca. 130 BCE) and Accius (170–c. 86 BCE). Their tragedies, which included Homeric and Trojan War themes, were important for Vergil. However, since only meager fragments of them have survived, their precise influence is difficult to gauge.

35 Cf., e.g., Heinze (1915, trans. 1993: 251–8). Wlosok (1999) offers a reading of the Dido episode as tragedy, and Pavlock (1985) examines Euripidean influence in the Nisus and Euryalus episode. Hardie (1991, 1997), Panoussi (2002, 2009), and Galinsky (2003) examine the influence of tragedy, particularly in light of French theories of Greek tragedy (e.g. Vernant and Vidal-Naquet (1988)), and draw important parallels between the political and cultural milieus of fifth-century Athens and Augustan Rome. On tragedy and conflicting viewpoints, see Conte (1999) and Galinsky (2003).

36 Hardie (1998) 62. See also Hardie (1997).

Vergil's use of "allusion" or "intertextuality," [37] we can enrich both our experience of his artistry and our interpretation of his epic. However, no source study can fully account for the creative, aesthetic, and moral achievement of the *Aeneid*, which is a work until itself.

The *Aeneid*, Rome, and Augustus

While Aeneas' story takes place in the distant, mythological past of the Trojan war era, it had a special relevance for Vergil's contemporaries. Not only did the Romans draw their descent from the Trojans, but the emperor Augustus believed that Aeneas was his own ancestor.[38] Vergil makes these national and familial connections major thematic concerns of his epic.

As a result, the *Aeneid* is about more than the Trojan war and its aftermath. It is also about the foundation of Rome and its flourishing under Augustus. To incorporate these themes into his epic, Vergil connects mythological and historical time by associating three leaders and city foundations: the founding of Lavinium by Aeneas, the actual founding of Rome by Romulus, and the "re-founding" of Rome by Augustus. These events are prominent in the most important prophecies of the epic: Jupiter's speech to Venus (1.257–96) and Anchises' revelation to his son Aeneas (6.756–853). Together these passages provide what may be called an Augustan reading of Roman history,

---

[37] See Farrell (1997) for a full and insightful introduction to the interpretive possibilities that the study of intertextuality in Vergil can offer readers. For a general introduction to intertextuality, see Allen (2000). For the study of intertextuality in Latin literature, see Conte (1986), Farrell (1991) 1–25, Hardie (1993), Fowler (1997), Hinds (1998), and Edmunds (2001). For Vergil's use of Homer, see Knauer (1964b), Barchiesi (1984, in Italian), Gransden (1984), and Cairns (1989) 177–248. Knauer (1964a), written in German, is a standard work on this topic; those without German can still benefit from its detailed citations and lists of parallels. For Vergil's use of Homer and Apollonius, see Nelis (2001).

[38] Augustus' clan, the Julian *gens*, claimed its descent from Iulus (another name for Aeneas' son Ascanius) and thus also from Aeneas and Venus. Julius Caesar in particular emphasized this ancestry; Augustus made these connections central to his political self-presentation as well. See, e.g., Zanker (1988) 193–210 and Galinsky (1996) 141–224.

one that is shaped by the deeds of these three men and that views Augustus as the culmination of the processes of fate and history.[39]

This is not to say that the associations among Aeneas, Romulus, and Augustus are always positive or unproblematic, particularly given the ways that Aeneas is portrayed and can be interpreted.[40] To some, Vergil's Aeneas represents an idealized Roman hero, who thus reflects positively on Augustus by association.[41] In general this type of reading sees a positive imperial ideology in the epic and is referred to as "optimistic" or "Augustan." Others are more troubled by Vergil's Aeneas, and advocate interpretations that challenge the moral and spiritual value of his actions, as well as of the role of the gods and fate. Such readings perceive a much darker poetic world[42] and have been called "pessimistic" or "ambivalent."[43] Vergil's portrayal of Aeneas is thus a major element in debates over the epic's meaning.[44]

Randall Ganiban, *Series Editor*

---

[39] See O'Hara (1990), however, for the deceptiveness of prophecies in the *Aeneid*.

[40] For general interpretation of the *Aeneid*, see n. 24 (above).

[41] This type of reading is represented especially by Heinze (1915, trans. 1993), Pöschl (1950, trans. 1962), and Otis (1964). More recent and complex Augustan interpretations can be found in Hardie (1986) and Cairns (1989).

[42] See, e.g., Putnam (1965), Johnson (1976), Lyne (1987), and Thomas (2001). Putnam's reading of the *Aeneid* has been particularly influential. Of the ending of the poem he writes: "By giving himself over with such suddenness to the private wrath which the sight of the belt of Pallas arouses, Aeneas becomes himself *impius Furor*, as rage wins the day over moderation, disintegration defeats order, and the achievements of history through heroism fall victim to the human frailty of one man" (1965: 193–4). For a different understanding of Aeneas' wrath, see Galinsky (1988).

[43] For a general treatment of the optimism/pessimism debate, see Kennedy (1992). For a critique of the "pessimistic" view, see Martindale (1993); for critique of the "optimistic" stance and its rejection of "pessimism," see Thomas (2001). For the continuing debate over the politics of the *Aeneid* and over the Augustan age more generally, see the collections of Powell (1992) and Stahl (1998).

[44] Indeed some readers also question whether it is even possible to resolve this interpretive debate because of Vergil's inherent ambiguity. See Johnson (1976), Perkell (1994), and O'Hara (2007) 77–103. Martindale (1993) offers a critique of ambiguous readings.

Introduction to Book 5: Its Role in the *Aeneid*

In *Aeneid* 5, the Trojans sail from Carthage to Italy by way of Sicily, where they mark the anniversary of Anchises' death. This observance takes the form of offerings at Anchises' grave followed by the athletic contests that comprise the central episode of the book. During these contests the Trojan women, left to mourn for the dead hero, reflect gloomily upon their own sufferings and so fall under the influence of Juno's agent Isis, who causes them to set fire to the Trojan ships. As a result, Aeneas leaves the women behind in Sicily, together with anyone else who is unable or unwilling to continue the journey to Italy. The main themes of the book — sacrifice, leadership, family, and cultural inheritance — are central to the poem as a whole. This thematic economy contributes to the highly symmetrical structure and strong narrative movement of what Montaigne (*Essays* 2.10) perceptively called "the most perfect" book of the poem.

A relatively placid surface narrative masks difficult pyschological and social issues, which are prefigured by the storm that drives the Trojan ships back to Sicily and by many aspects of the athletic contests, before these issues eventually break through to the surface in the burning of the ships. The crisis thus precipitated makes it clear that Aeneas cannot succeed simply by enduring the many physical tests that stand in his way. He must also at last face up to the inner challenges of leadership and humanity represented by the loss of his father and the death of Dido. How well he succeeds can be judged only from his experiences in the books that follow.

More than an expedient response to immediate circumstances, Aeneas' return to Sicily can be read as a journey back in space and (wishfully, perhaps) in time: the Trojans return to the very place where they found themselves before Juno's storm blew them off course to Carthage one year earlier. But even if the place is the same, time has not stood still: Aeneas has spent the year since his father's death at Carthage with Dido in a love affair that ended disastrously. The reader must assume that Aeneas is truly unaware that Dido has taken her own life. But as the book opens, the Trojans gaze from the open sea back upon a fire in Carthage, brooding uncomfortably on what it means and nearly bridging the gap between the hero's ignorance and the reader's knowledge of what has just happened (5 n.). It is therefore powerfully ironic that Aeneas mourns not for Dido but only and instead for his father. The hero is selective in what he remembers and what he does not; and in any case his mourning, while it is motivated by *pietas*, is also a sign that he continues to look backwards rather than to the future.

Book 5, especially in the episode of the games, is a famous instance of Vergil's intertextual engagement with Homer. This engagement is itself often figured as involving a paternal and a filial relationship, much like that of Aeneas and Anchises. But Richard Heinze shows how Vergil, even when he is at his most "Homeric," brings to bear quite different and more exacting principles of formal artistry than he found in his model; while Brooks Otis is particularly good at revealing the psychological qualities of Vergilian narrative, what he calls Vergil's "subjective style" (in contrast to Homer's comparative "objectivity"). In structural terms, we are still in the "Odyssean" half of the *Aeneid* (books 1–6), and elements of Vergil's games are borrowed from the contests held at the court of Alcinous (*Od.* 8); but the games are obviously indebted to an Iliadic episode as well, the Funeral Games of Patroclus (*Il.* 23). For G. N. Knauer such passages prove that the traditional idea of an "Odyssean" *Aeneid* 1–6 followed by an "Iliadic" 7–12 is too simple; instead, he argues, Vergil's plan was to demonstrate through analysis and recombination the fundamental similarity of the Homeric poems to one another at the level of plot and to fashion his *Aeneid* as a simultaneous imitation of the *Iliad* and *Odyssey* in their entirety. This double imitation extends beyond structural to thematic concerns: notably, the games in both the *Iliad* and the *Odyssey* occur at the point when Achilles and Odysseus emerge from isolation and begin to reintegrate themselves into society, much as Aeneas must do in the wake of his ill-fated sojourn in Carthage.

Critics have also explored the ways in which Vergil incorporates other poetic voices into his intertext, turning what is often conceived as a dialogue into something much more polyphonic. The most important contribution of this kind comes from Damien Nelis' study of Vergil and Apollonius (2001), which shows that Apollonius' influence extends throughout the *Aeneid* in much the same way as Homer's. Thus Aeneas' voyage from Carthage to Sicily and the events that take place there in book 5 correspond to Jason's voyage from Colchis to Aeaea and the events that take place there in *Arg.* 4. (Both episodes mark the westernmost points reached in the two heroes' voyages.) Here again a narrative congruency points to a similarity of theme, in this case ritual purification. Jason, of course, has escaped from Colchis with Medea's assistance: in particular, Medea has gone so far as to help Jason murder her own brother, Apsyrtus; and it is the pollution that the couple have incurred that must be expiated when they reach Aeaea, home of Circe, Medea's aunt. Reference to Apollonius, then, confirms that the games in *Aeneid* 5 are a symbolic "expiation" of Aeneas' failure to bring Anchises with him to Italy (as he did in, for instance, Naevius' *Bellum Punicum*, an early Roman epic that was an important model for Vergil in other respects). But Aeneas did not murder Anchises or leave him unburied; and Vergil's reference to the *Argonautica* reminds the reader of an "absent presence" in his narrative. For if we ask who the Medea of the *Aeneid* is, the obvious answer is Dido.[45] It is thus (from the reader's point of view) the more immediate pollution brought upon Aeneas by Dido's death of which the hero must be purified. But, as was noted above, Aeneas is either unaware of this necessity or he suppresses such awareness. In these ways, Vergil's intertextual program powerfully reinforces the psychological element of his narrative.

Expiation frequently takes the form of sacrifice, a motif that permeates this book (Putnam (1965)), in both the literal form of animal sacrifice, a fundamental element of Roman religion, and the metaphorical form of human sacrifice. The two aspects are repeatedly joined through symbol and metaphor (e.g. 327–38 n., 483–4 n.) until, at the end of the book, we encounter an actual human sacrifice when Neptune demands (814–15) and obtains (827–71) one life as payment for his guarantee of safe passage to Italy for the rest of the Trojans. His victim proves to be Palinurus, the helmsman of Aeneas' flagship, whose fate is humorously prefigured by an espisode in the boat race (104–603 n.), a famous instance of how comedy in the *Aeneid* repeatedly gives way to tragedy.

Another powerful critical approach involves the perception of parallels between the heroic rituals depicted in book 5 and historical Roman institutions. For the ancient Roman reader, Aeneas' commemoration of his father must have recalled aspects of the Parentalia festival (59 n.). The games themselves resemble events staged by Augustus to entertain the urban populace while advertising his own power and authority (Feldherr (1995) 248). In particular, the Troy game was revived by Augustus as a deliberate link with Rome's (and his family's) Trojan origins (545–603 n.). Finally, the entire spectacle of book 5 takes place against the backdrop of Mt. Eryx (see p. 15), from which the cult of Venus Erycina was imported to Rome during the third cen-

---

45 This was seen clearly by Servius (*ad Aen.* 4.1), who declares that *Aen.* 4 in its entirety is taken from *Arg.* 3, meaning that Aeneas plays the role of Apollonius' Jason and Dido that of his Medea.

tury BCE at a time when the Aeneas legend was becoming a significant part of Roman national identity (1–103 n., 759–61 n.). Together with other etymological details, such as the names of several contestants in the games who are identified as the ancestors of different Roman *gentes* (114–23 n., 117 n., 121 n., 123 n., 569–70 n.), these motifs reinforce the theme of making a society cohesive by celebrating shared ancestral institutions, whether real or fictive.

The structure of book 5 is beautifully worked out, but seldom commented upon. The book is bracketed by a pair of deaths (those of Dido and Palinurus), the circumstances and significance of which remain mysterious to the Trojans, and by a pair of sea voyages (from Africa to Sicily and then from Sicily to Italy). The lengthy central episode (104–761, 658 lines) takes place on a single day. The briefer episodes that surround it (1–103, 762–871) are similar in length (103 and 110 lines) and are separated from the events of the central episode by an interval of nine days in each case (64, 762). In counterpoint to this impressively balanced structure, a studied asymmetry pervades the episodes that take place on the day of the games (104–761 n.). The book is a masterpiece of narrative composition, so effective and seemingly natural in its rhetorical and emotional effect that the artistic means by which it achieves its goals can easily go unnoticed.

Bibliography. On book 5 in relation to the poem as a whole: Swallow (1952–1953), Galinsky (1968); to Homer: Heinze (1914) 145–70 = (1993) 121–41, Otis (1964) 41–61, Cairns (1989) 215–48; to Apollonius: Nelis (2001) 186–226; to the theme of sacrifice: Putnam (1965) 64–104; to that of spectacle: Feldherr (1995, 2002).

Mount Eryx, in the province of Trapani (Drepanum), Sicily

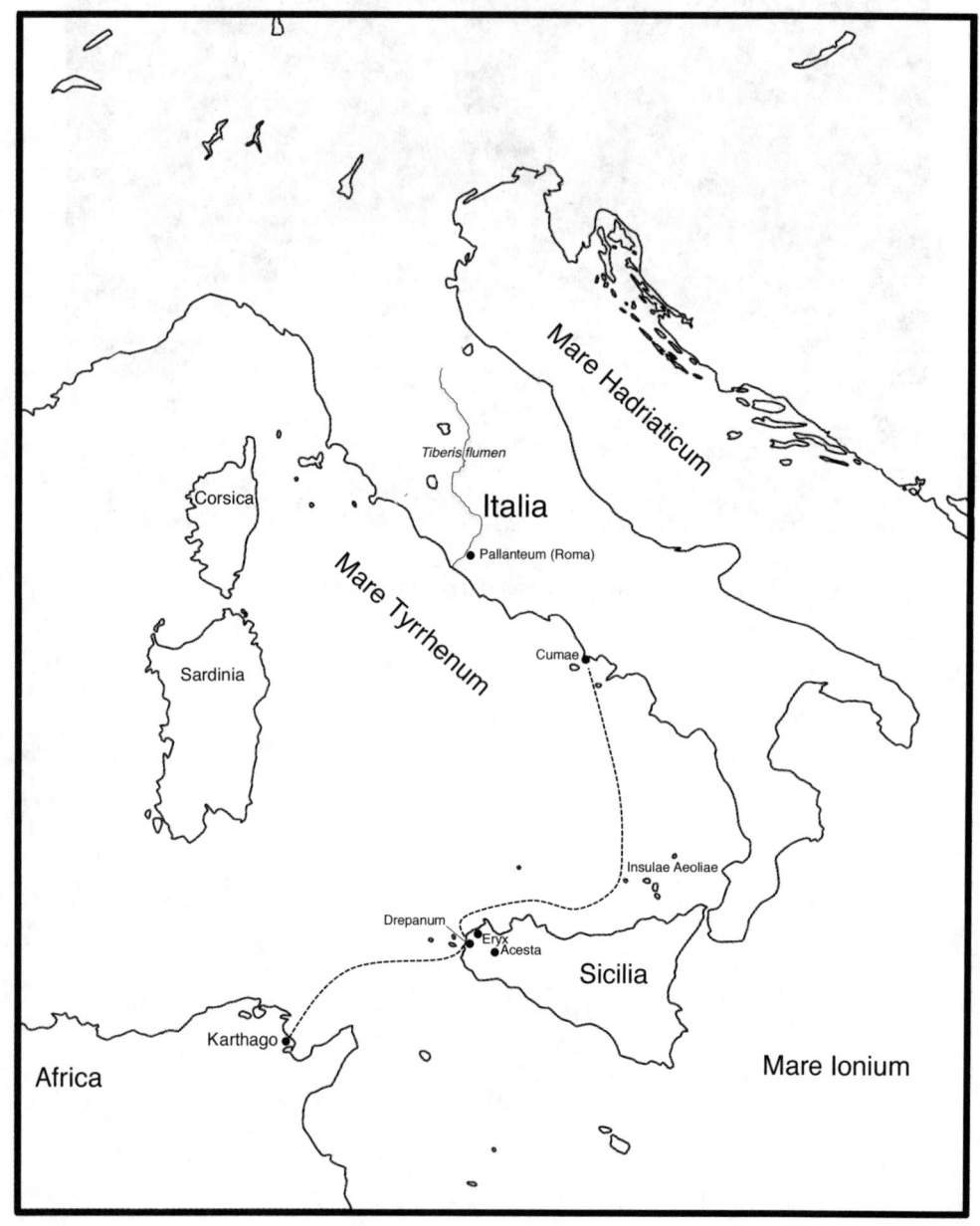

Aeneas' voyage from Carthage to Cumae

Liber Quintus

Please note: When reference is made to a passage from *Aeneid* 5, the line number alone is given, without the book number (e.g. "cf. 110"), along with reference to the note on that passage, if relevant (e.g. "cf. 110 n."). When reference is made to another book of the *Aeneid*, the number of that book is given as well (e.g. "cf. 1.203"). Reference to notes in other commentaries is made by using the name of the commentator (details on which editions are cited can be found in the bibliography). References to *Allen and Greenough's New Latin Grammar* (see Mahoney (2001) in "Works Cited") are provided by section number (e.g. AG §471c). An asterisk marks terms that are defined in Appendix B. An inverted breve under a vowel (i̯ or u̯) indicates that the vowel is being treated as a consonant for the sake of the meter. A small circle under a vowel (ḁ) indicates an elision* or prodelision.

1–103: The Trojans Return to Sicily on the Anniversary of Anchises' Death

Even as Aeneas turns his thoughts and emotions away from Dido and towards Anchises, he seems not to have come fully to terms with the loss of either one of them or with the mantle of leadership that he himself must at last assume. From the time that he left Troy to his first arrival in Sicily (book 3), Aeneas looked to Anchises as his guide and interpreter of the gods' will — even though Anchises was often mistaken about what fate had in store. After his father's death, Aeneas immediately "lost his way" (thanks to Juno's meddling) and was driven by storm from Sicily not to Italy, but to Carthage, where he became the lover of Queen Dido, herself an exile and the founder of a city — a leader of the very sort that he himself must become. But Aeneas' affair with her was Dido's undoing. However aware or unaware Aeneas may be of this fact, he seems to view his return to Sicily as an opportunity to go back to a point before his ill-fated Carthaginian sojourn, as if he could just erase an entire year of his life, forgetting about past feminine entanglements and resolving to avoid them in the future. The return to Sicily thus symbolizes an effort to begin anew, a theme appropriate to the first book of the middle third of the poem (books 5–8).

Aeneas evidently regards Sicily as a paternal space because Anchises died and was buried there (26–31). But the very landscape of Sicily is dominated by reminders that it is Aeneas' mother, and not his father, who has always been and who remains his most efficacious guide and protector. When foul weather from the west drives the Trojan fleet towards Sicily, there are indications that Venus is the cause (19 n.). The Trojan settlement in Sicily where the main action of the book takes place is adjacent to Mt. Eryx, in antiquity the site of an important Venus cult.

The mountain takes its name from a hero who was Venus's son by the Argonaut Butes — and thus, like Cupid, Aeneas' maternal half-brother (24, 412; cf. 1.667). Thus it is Venus who watches over Aeneas and the Trojans more effectively than father Anchises ever did or could do now; and the reader is aware, even if father Aeneas is not, that he would have been lost without his divine mother.

Bibliography. On Sicily and the formation of the Trojan legend see Galinsky (1969), Gruen (1992) 6–51, Casali (2010) 37–51.

> INTEREA medium Aeneas iam classe tenebat
> certus iter fluctusque atros Aquilone secabat
> moenia respiciens, quae iam infelicis Elissae

1–41, The Voyage from Carthage to Sicily

1-7. The Trojans, departing from Carthage, see the blaze from Dido's pyre and brood over its meaning.

1. **Interea:** as the first word of a new book, this unassuming adverb connects the continuing narrative with the events that immediately precede it. At the same time, it unobtrusively marks the beginning of the middle third of the poem: cf. the following note.

1-2. **medium ... iter:** an adjective-noun phrase frames the first complete thought: having cast off and got clear of the harbor, Aeneas is now heading into the *medium iter*, the main part of the crossing between departure and arrival. In a larger sense, he is at the "midpoint" of his journey to Italy: his journey is no longer to the west but, as he rounds Cape Drepanum, the westernmost tip of Sicily (and the turning point of Aeneas' voyage: see Nelis (2001) 215–21), back east to Italy. The phrase has metapoetic relevance to the structure of the *Aeneid* as well: books 1–4 contain the Trojans' stay in Carthage, books 9–12 their war against Turnus. Here we begin the middle third of the poem according to this triadic structure. Middle positions are emphasized repeatedly in this book: cf. 109–10 n., 113 n., 160 n., 288 n., 290 n., 304 n., 835–8 n. **Aeneas:** visually, the word stands in the very center of line 1, iconically representing the idea that Aeneas is now in the very middle of his journey. **tenebat:** an inceptive imperfect (AG §471c), indicating that Aeneas was just starting the middle section of his voyage (8 n.; cf. 159 n., 721, 853 n.).

2. **certus:** "unwavering," in contrast to his previous indecisiveness; Aeneas leaves Carthage behind with a new sense of resolve, which will, however, be sorely tested in this book. **Aquilone:** a stormy wind that blows from the northeast, the very direction in which the Trojans must sail to reach Italy. When they first left Carthage (4.562), Zephyrus was blowing favorably from the west; now it is as if the elements were conspiring to prevent them from going farther (19–20 n., 22–3 n., 32–3 n.).

3. **respiciens:** in spite of his resolve to move on and complete his mission, Aeneas continues to look back to the past — often, as here, with only partial or even faulty comprehension. **infelicis:** Dido's perpetual epithet* (1.749, 4.596, 6.456). **Elissae:** there is an ancient tradition that this was Dido's original name, and that she began to be called Dido, which is Punic for *virago*, "heroic woman" (Hexter (1992) 348–50), only after she committed suicide rather than betray the memory of her husband Sychaeus by marrying an African prince (Servius auctus *ad* 1.340; Vergil acknowledges part of this tradition in the prayer of Iarbas, 4.198–218). In the *Aeneid*, her name is always Dido except, as here, in oblique cases, where he prefers the grammatically straightforward *Elissa* (other writers vary between the Greek genitive *Didūs* and the Latin *Didonis*, and similarly between the accusatives *Dido* and *Didonem*, etc.).

conlucent flammis. quae tantum accenderit ignem
causa latet; duri magno sed amore dolores   5
polluto, notumque furens quid femina possit,
triste per augurium Teucrorum pectora ducunt.
ut pelagus tenuere rates nec iam amplius ulla

---

4. **quae ... latet (5):** *quae causa* is the subject of *accenderit*, which is perfect subjunctive in an indirect question depending on the impersonal *latet*, "it is unclear...."

5. **magno ... amore ... polluto (6):** ablative of cause (AG §404) depending on *duri ... dolores*. This arresting phrase is capable of different interpretations: did Dido defile her own love for Sychaeus (cf. 4.552), or did Aeneas defile her love for himself? *Polluo* is a striking word emphasized by enjambment*. Elsewhere Vergil uses it literally (3.234) or in reference to a religious transgression (3.61, 7.467). Here it introduces an important theme that derives from Vergil's imitation of Apollonius (see the introductory note to this book; cf. Nelis (2001) 190–8). **sed:** Vergil and other poets frequently postpone the conjunctions and pronouns that signal the beginning of a new clause as an artful variation on normal word order and sometimes to emphasize a more colorful word (such as *magno* here) that appears before it. So in the poem's very first line, the narrator announces that he will sing about the man *Troiae qui primus ab oris ... venit*, with *qui* "postponed" (cf. *quid* 6, *quoniam* 22, *cum* 84, *quo* 117, 121, *quam* 119, *unde* 123, *ut* 178, 329, 388, 667, *quos* 190, *at* 264, *quem* 274, *quibus* 303, *quam* 312, *sed* (again) 320, *et* 325, 344, 667, 764, *qui* 355, 370, 439, 544, 713, *quam* 563, *quo* 599, *quod* 651, *quae* 675, *donec* 698, *quem* 814).

6. **notum ... possit:** *notum* is the neuter participle used as a substantive, "a known thing" and so "a piece of knowledge" (cf. 7.8 *perlitatum*, 7.22 *temptatum*); but the word retains its verbal capacity to introduce the indirect question *quid ... possit*; construe as "the knowledge (of) what a mad woman might do." **furens quid:** for the word order cf. *sed* 5 n. *Quid* is cognate accusative with *possit* (AG §390c). **femina:** in ordinary Latin "woman" is *mulier*, but the more dignified genres of poetry prefer *femina*, "lady."

7. **augurium:** a word with strong religious overtones. It introduces the theme of interpretation, especially of the gods' will, which recurs throughout this book (and indeed the poem). **pectora:** "minds" (by metonymy*), because it was believed that the heart was the seat of intelligence as well as emotion.

8-34. *A storm threatens and the helmsman advises Aeneas to make for shelter. Aeneas agrees, and the fleet lands on Sicily near the tomb of Anchises.*

8-11. A nearly verbatim repetition in epic style of 3.192–5, modeled on the similar repetition of Hom. *Od.* 12.403–6 and 14.301–4. Aeneas' crossing to western Sicily is correlated with Odysseus' approach to Scylla and Charybdis, which ancient geographers placed in the Straits of Messina between eastern Sicily and Italy.

8. **ut:** ≈ *cum*, introducing a temporal clause (AG §543). **tenuere:** = *tenuerunt*; the variant ending was attractive to poets both as an archaism,* which lends dignity, and also because it offers different metrical possibilities than the usual form (-*rĕ* instead of -*rŭnt*). Note the tense (and cf. *tenebat* 1 n.): the Trojans are now well on their way and beyond sight of land.

occurrit tellus, maria undique et undique caelum,
olli caeruleus supra caput astitit imber   10
noctem hiememque ferens et inhorruit unda tenebris.
ipse gubernator puppi Palinurus ab alta:
"heu quianam tanti cinxerunt aethera nimbi?"

---

9. **occurrit tellus:** understand *oculis* (dative), "no land met their eyes," i.e. "they saw no land." *Tellus,* ≈ *terra,* but is elevated in tone by its religious associations: Earth was worshipped in Rome as Tellus since at least the third century BCE and perhaps much earlier. See Richardson (1992) 378 s.v. Tellus, Aedes. **maria ... caelum:** ≈ 3.193, *caelum undique et undique pontus.*

10. **olli ... quianam (13):** cited by Quintilian (8.3.24) as archaisms* for *illi* and *cur,* respectively. *Olli* occurs fairly frequently as either the masc. dative sing. (here, 284, 358) or nom. plur. (197, 580), but *quianam* occurs only once again in the entire poem (10.6).

11. **inhorruit unda tenĕbris:** = 3.195, where Conington-Nettleship (1858–83) note, "The picture seems to be of the surface of the water roughened or curled partly by the wind, partly by the darkness, which would change its outline to the eye." *Tenebris* then is formally an ablative of cause (AG §404), while the logic whereby darkness "causes" choppy seas is entirely poetic. The natural pronunciation is *tĕnĕbrīs* (2.92, 6.734), but here the mute + liquid consonant cluster *-br-* is treated as "making position," artificially lengthening, and so shifting the word accent* to, the second syllable: see Appendix A, n. 7, Allen (1989) 89–90).

12. Here, as often in signaling the beginning or end of a speech, Vergil omits the actual verb of speaking (e.g. *ait, dixit*), which is easily understood by the reader and would become tedious if regularly expressed. **Palinurus:** previously (3.202) the helmsman was unable to find his way in bad weather; now he successfully charts a course for Sicily. After years of wandering, the Trojans are better able to fend for themselves than they once were (22–3 n.). In book 5 Palinurus appears only in this initial episode and in the last (827–71), where the roles of helmsman and hero are brought dramatically together (868 n.).

13. **quianam:** 10 n. **cinxerunt aethera nimbi:** clouds within the heavier lower atmosphere (*aër* 19–20 n.) are said to have formed a "belt" (*cinxerunt*) below the bright upper air or *aether.* This image differs from English usage, in which a belt normally encircles something from without rather than from within. *Aethera,* the masculine accusative singular of the third declension in Greek, was the preferred form in classical Latin, as well; cf. 140 and *aëra* 839 n.

> quidve, pater Neptune, paras?" sic deinde locutus
> colligere arma iubet validisque incumbere remis, 15
> obliquatque sinus in ventum ac talia fatur:

---

14. **quidve, pater Neptune, paras?:** Palinurus' question foreshadows the end of the book, where Neptune demands the helmsman's life as compensation for Aeneas' safe passage to Italy (800–15 n., 827–71 n.). **pater:** frequently used for any god (cf. the more elevated *genitor,* also used of Neptune at 817, 1.155), but also the first occurrence in this book of an important thematic word. **sic deinde locutus:** = 400; 7.135 *sic deinde effatus* (but contrast 303 n.). Deponent verbs offer the possibility of using a perfect active participle, which Latin otherwise lacks: construe as "having spoken (or) after speaking (and not just 'speaking') thus." In prose *deinde* would follow the participle, the force of which it sums up (2.391 *sic fatus deinde . . . induitur*), but Virgil often places *deinde* in unexpected positions (e.g. 1.195, 3.609) precisely to avoid a prosaic tone. Note too that he always scans *deĭndĕ* as a trochee*, combining the first and second syllables (*de* + *in*) by synizesis*.

15. **colligere arma:** the meaning is uncertain. If it refers to gathering loose equipment that would become dangerous in a storm, it means roughly "to batten down the hatches." Servius however explains it as meaning *vela contrahere* "to shorten sail" so as to maintain better control of the ship in high winds. **arma:** not "weapons" here but "equipment" more generally, an archaic* usage that Vergil may have revived (see Mynors (1990) on *Geo.* 1.160), though perhaps it never lost currency in spoken Latin. **iubet:** there is no need to supply a subject accusative (such as *eos* or *viros*) for *colligere* if the main verb is construed not as "he orders (them to . . .)" but "he gives the order (to . . .)." **validis . . . remis:** perhaps an instance of enallage* or transferred epithet*. If the oars are strong, so too must be those who handle them.

16. **obliquat:** "sets slantwise," one of several verbs occurring first in Vergil that are formed from adjectives (here from *obliquus*) or nouns. The maneuver described is "tacking": by setting the sail so that the wind strikes it at an angle, it becomes possible to move against the wind on a zig-zag pattern. Because ancient ships lacked a keel deep enough to provide balance and leverage against a crosswind, the maneuvre was more difficult than it would be for modern ships and so was more of a coping mechanism than something that could be maintained over the long haul. **sinūs:** fourth declension accusative plural; a poetic synonym of *vela,* "sails"; literally the "folds" or "billows" of the sailcloth.

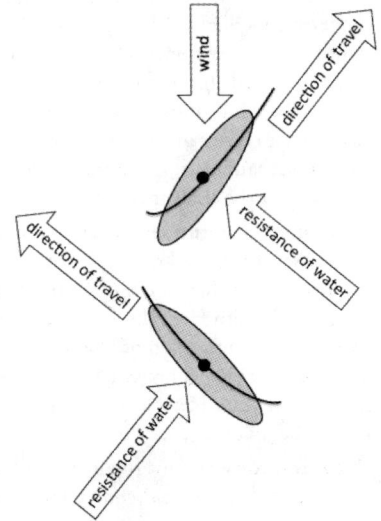

Figure 1: diagram of tacking procedure

"magnanime Aenea, non, si mihi Iuppiter auctor
spondeat, hoc sperem Italiam contingere caelo.
mutati transversa fremunt et vespere ab atro
consurgunt venti, atque in nubem cogitur aër.   20
nec nos obniti contra nec tendere tantum

17-18. **auctor | spondeat:** both words are formal in tone. *Spondeo* is regularly used of entering into a contractual agreement. *Auctor* has significance in both the legal ("security" or "guarantor") and the parliamentary ("supporter" or "proposer" of a motion) spheres.

18. **sperem . . . contingere:** *spero* normally takes a subject accusative plus future infinitive. The construction with the present infinitive alone is an archaism* that remained common in poetry. **hoc . . . caelo:** ablative of manner (AG §412) denoting attendant circumstance (because Palinurus himself is not responsible for the conditions). **Italiam:** the natural quantity of the initial vowel is short, but Vergil and other poets regularly treat it as long (cf. 629, 730; cf. *rēliquias* 47, 787), because a four-syllable word that starts with three shorts cannot fit into dactylic verse. The adjective *Ítalus*, with only three syllables, is easier to manage, and Vergil normally leaves its first syllable short (82, 117, 565, 703), but he occasionally lengthens it, as well (e.g. *Ítala regna* 3.185).

19-20. **mutati . . . venti:** passive forms of *muto* and other words meaning "to change" or "to turn" (e.g. *verto*) often have intransitive or reflexive force, just as in English one says that the winds *have changed* (not *have been changed*). **transversa fremunt:** *fremunt*, "they roar," can be understood as *fremitum faciunt*, "they make a roar." Although *fremitus* is masculine and singular, an unexpressed "cognate accusative" (AG § 390b) of this sort can be modified by a neuter accusative adjective in the singular ("to (make a) roar *across* (our path))" or in the plural, like *transversa* here (to do so repeatedly). Such phrases are best rendered adverbially, "they keep roaring *across* (our path)." **vespere ab atro | consurgunt venti:** *vesper* by metonymy* means "the west" (where the "evening star" sets), forcing the Trojans towards the east (cf. 1 n.). But literally Vesper is the evening star, i.e. the planet Venus. The winds thus blow again (2 n.) from the goddess' precinct, urging the Trojans eastwards to Sicily in an expression of divine will. It is dark in the west because the Trojans set sail before dawn (4.584-8), and also because of the storm; but this darkness may suggest the trials that still await the Trojans as well as their ignorance of those trials.

in nubem cogitur äēr: according to ancient science, weather occurs in the lower atmosphere or *aër*, below the bright, fiery *aether* (13 n.), and clouds are merely *aër* in condensed form (Cic. *Nat. D.* 2.101). Some of Homer's ancient critics connected *aër* allegorically with Hera (because the Greek words, ἀήρ and Ἥρα, sound similar). Vergil, aware of this conception of Homer's gods, applies it to his own. Thus in book 1, Juno (the Roman Hera) conjures a storm to prevent Aeneas from reaching Italy, driving him to Africa instead. Here, as Aeneas retraces his steps, when his route is again blocked by storm, the divine agency behind it is not made explicit (but see above).

21-2. **contra:** construe adverbially ("in the opposite direction") with both *obniti* and *tendere* (the so-called *apo koinou** construction). **tantum:** adverbial accusative (*OLD* s.v. *tantum* B7) = *satis* (i.e. *quantum opus est*), modifying *sufficimus* (22) "we are not strong *enough.*" **sufficimus:** not previously found with the complementary infinitive, but poetry in general uses the infinitive more freely than does classical prose.

sufficimus. superat quoniam Fortuna, sequamur,
quoque vocat vertamus iter. nec litora longe
fida reor fraterna Erycis portusque Sicanos,
si modo rite memor servata remetior astra." 25
tum pius Aeneas: "equidem sic poscere ventos
iamdudum et frustra cerno te tendere contra.
flecte viam velis. an sit mihi gratior ulla,

22-3. Palinurus interprets the storm as a sign of divine will that the Trojans put in at Drepanum. His correct inference shows that Aeneas and his people have made progress in understanding what fate requires of them. **superat . . . vocat:** *Fortuna* is the subject of both verbs. **vertamus iter:** the phrasing emphasizes the idea that the Trojans have reached the turning point of their journey (Nelis (2001) 215–21). For the word order *superat quoniam* cf. 5 n.

23-4. **nec litora longe | fida reor fraterna Erycis:** understand *esse* (as in *longe . . . erit* 12.52); Vergil freely omits most forms of the verb "to be" (but cf. 192 n.). "The brotherly shores of Eryx" by enallage* for "the shores of your brother Eryx" (cf. 630). The figure endows the shores themselves with brotherly feelings (the "pathetic fallacy"). The genealogical element is important: Eryx, like Cupid (1.667), is the half-brother of Aeneas (*germanus* 412) because he is also the son of Venus (by the Argonaut Butes according to Servius *ad loc.* (cf. Nelis (2001) 13–14, 205–9), who notes that others say the father was Neptune (on which see Leigh (2010))). These "brotherly shores" are therefore — and more importantly, if we judge by how much Venus does to support Aeneas' mission — maternal ones as well. But here as for the most part elsewhere in book 5, Venus' influence is implied rather than made explicit. (For the main exception see 779–826 n.) **portusque:** fourth declension accusative plural. **Sicanos:** "Sicilian" (by metonymy*). The Sicani were the oldest named inhabitants of Sicily (Thuc. 6.2.2).

25. **si modo:** "if only," a common phrase. The adverb *modō* was originally *modŏ*, ablative of *modus*, but in classical Latin is distinct from it (cf. 599 n.). **servata:** *servo* (*OLD* s.v. 2) is used regularly of "observing" the stars.

26-31. Aeneas has anticipated Palinurus in divining the will of the gods. By battling the winds, the helmsman had been misreading or resisting signs from above; Aeneas understands and accepts the signs and welcomes the opportunity to visit the site of his father's tomb. Vergil, like most Romans, drew freely on the views of different philosophical schools. Here both Aeneas and Palinurus exemplify in different ways an attitude recommended by the Stoics and best expressed about a century after the *Aeneid* was written by the Neronian courtier and Stoic philosopher Seneca the Younger in a famous *sententia*: "fate leads the willing man, and drags the unwilling" (*Ep.* 107.11). Aeneas prospers not by realizing his personal desires (here, to reach Italy as soon as possible), but by recognizing what higher powers require of him (a temporary return to Sicily) and making that his goal. On Stoicism in Vergil cf. Bowra (1933–34).

26. **tum pius Aeneas:** understand *dixit* (cf. 12 n.).

27. **iamdudum:** construe with both *cerno* and *poscere* (26). **tendere contra:** cf. *contra . . . tendere* 21. Aeneas speaks directly to Palinurus' concerns. Again *contra* is adverbial (cf. 21–2 n.).

> quove magis fessas optem demittere navis,
> quam quae Dardanium tellus mihi servat Acesten   30
> et patris Anchisae gremio complectitur ossa?"
> haec ubi dicta, petunt portus et vela secundi
> intendunt Zephyri; fertur cita gurgite classis,
> et tandem laeti notae advertuntur harenae.
>   At procul ex celso miratus vertice montis   35
> adventum sociasque rates occurrit Acestes,

---

29. **quove:** the relative adverb *quo* "to which" (not the pronoun). **magis . . . optem:** periphrasis* for *malim* (= *magis velim*) "prefer." According to Austin (1955) on 4.24 *optem* is a "potential subjunctive of assertion, like *velim,* but a much stronger word, for *optare* marks an ambition or an ideal"; cf. AG §447. **optem demittere:** *optem* + infinitive is common in poetry (2.635; cf. 21–2 n.), but not in prose. **demittere:** "to bring to harbor" (*OLD* s.v. 4d). Latin (and Greek) conceive of both land and sea as sloping down to meet one another, so that going from land or sea to the shore is imagined as moving downhill.

30. **Acestēn:** The form is a Greek accusative, τὸν Ἀκέστην from ὁ Ἀκέστης.

31. **patris Anchisae:** for the death of Anchises see 3.710. **gremio complectitur ossa:** the metaphor* of earth "embracing" the bones of the dead is conventional in Latin as it is in English. Here *gremio* intensifies the metaphor and personifies the land, so that we may catch a hint of something more: the land belongs to Venus, and Anchises is her former consort. Now she embraces the hero in death as she once did in love.

32. **haec ubi dicta:** = 315; understand *sunt* or perhaps *dedit,* since *haec ubi dicta dedit* occurs 8x in the *Aeneid.*

32-3. **secundi . . . Zephyri:** when the Trojans were still hoping to sail directly to Italy, they were hindered by "gales from the dark west" (19). Now that they have changed course for Sicily, the westerly gales have become "favorable Zephyrs." Zephyrus is the Greek name for the Latin Favonus, the wind associated with the coming of spring (Nisbet-Hubbard (1970) on Hor. *Carm.* 1.4.1) and with the goddess Venus as well. **cita:** predicate adjective grammatically modifying *classis,* but logically expressing the fleet's rapid progress, as if it were an adverb (*cite*) modifying *fertur* (AG §290).

34. **laeti:** predicate adjective modifying the understood subject, with adverbial force (cf. *cita* 32–3 n.). **advertuntur:** cf. 19–20 n. **harenae:** dative of end of motion with the compound verb *advertuntur* (AG §428h), a poetic construction that seeps into prose after Vergil's time.

35-41. Acestes hurries to meet the Trojans and welcomes their return with a feast.

36. **adventum sociasque rates:** an instance of hendiadys*, to be construed *apo koinou* ("in common") as the object of both the participle *miratus* ("he wondered at *the arrival of friendly ships*") and the finite verb *occurrit* ("and went to meet *them*").

horridus in iaculis et pelle Libystidis ursae,
Troia Criniso conceptum flumine mater
quem genuit. veterum non immemor ille parentum
gratatur reduces et gaza laetus agresti   40

---

37. **horridus in:** construe with both *iaculis* and *pelle*. **et pelle Libystidis ursae:** = 8.368. *Libystidis ursae* probably refers to the Atlas bear (*Ursus arctos crowtheri*, also known as Shimera), a subspecies of the Brown bear once found in North Africa from Morocco to Libya, but probably extinct since the nineteenth century. It is mentioned by Greek writers as early as Herodotus (4.191) and was known in Rome from its appearances in *venationes* (*ursos Numidicos*, Plin. *Nat. Hist.* 8.131; but Pliny does not regard them as native to Africa, cf. 8.228). **Libystidis:** "Libyan," a Greek form (properly τῆς Λιβυστίδος, feminine genitive singular from ἡ Λιβυστίς), here given the equivalent Latin ending (*-is* for the Greek -ος). The word must have sounded exotic: Vergil uses it only twice in the *Aeneid* (against thirteen occurrences of the more straightforward Latin word, *Libycus -a -um*), here and at 8.368 when Aeneas reaches the future site of Rome. Libya in the *Aeneid* is generally synonymous with Carthage according to the ancient Greek usage by which all of Africa was called Libya, even though by Virgil's time Libya was a well-defined area that did not include Carthage (*OCD* s.v. *Libya*). Exoticizing reference to Punic influence throughout the western Mediterranean in the heroic period may remind the reader that Carthage was to remain Rome's rival for centuries after the events depicted in the poem. Such a reminder has special point in an episode set in the vicinity of Mt. Eryx, possession of which was specifically contested between the Romans and the Carthaginians during the First and Second Punic Wars (Traill (2001)). On the other hand, *Libystis* appears only in scenes where Aeneas is warmly welcomed, here by Acestes and subsequently by Evander, as indeed he had been welcomed by Dido.
38. A silver line*. **Trŏĭă:** trisyllabic, from the adjective *Trŏĭus* (not the noun *Trŏ̄ĭă:* cf. 61 n.). **mater:** Servius (on 1.550) relates the story of the Trojan woman Egesta who, banished by Laomedon, bore Acestes to the Sicilian river god Crinisus.
39. **veterum non immemor . . . parentum:** this phrase sums up one of the major themes of the book, and indeed of the poem. Acestes remembers the ancestry that he shares with Aeneas and extends him hospitality; Aeneas remembers his father, who had shared and relieved the hero's burdens throughout most of his wanderings (3.709); the reader will recognize throughout the book details that recall the antiquity of the Roman people and their ancestral connections to Troy. **ille:** Acestes. This is the resumptive use of the demonstrative pronoun, an instance of pleonasm*; cf. 186, 334, 457. **non immemor:** litotes* for emphasis ("ever mindful" rather than merely "not forgetful").
40. **gratatur reduces:** supply *esse* (cf. 23–4 n.). Acestes congratulates the Trojans for being *reduces,* returned to his town in safety. The accusative + infinitive construction with *gratari* (archaic* for *gratulari*) appears here for the first time. **gaza:** a loan-word from Persian (Servius on 1.119). Its exotic color suggests the opulence that Romans associated with the great kingdoms of of the east. It occurs only three times in the poem (cf. 2.763), always with reference to Troy, here emphasizing Acestes' Trojan ancestry. **agresti:** in combination with *gaza* almost an instance of oxymoron*, possibly connoting the uncouth and unkempt, but also bearing more positive associations with simplicity, frugality, and honesty.

excipit, ac fessos opibus solatur amicis.
    Postera cum primo stellas Oriente fugarat
clara dies, socios in coetum litore ab omni
advocat Aeneas tumulique ex aggere fatur:
"Dardanidae magni, genus alto a sanguine divum,   45
annuus exactis completur mensibus orbis,
ex quo reliquias divinique ossa parentis
condidimus terra maestasque sacravimus aras.
iamque dies, nisi fallor, adest, quem semper acerbum,
semper honoratum (sic di voluistis) habebo.   50

42-103: The Anniversary of Anchises' Death

42-71. Aeneas assembles the Trojans for a sacrificial banquet in remembrance of Anchises, and announces athletic contests on the ninth day thereafter.

42. **primo ... Oriente:** ablative of time, "at the first (appearance of the) rising (sun)" (cf. 3.588). **fugarat:** = *fugaverat* by syncope.*

45. **Dardanidae:** from *Dardanides, -ae*, m., "descendants of Dardanus," son of Jupiter by Electra, daughter of Atlas (8.134–7); a patronymic* or name derived from that of one's father or a more distant male ancestor. Such words are native to Greek and are a particular feature of epic language. Though Vergil uses them freely throughout the *Aeneid*, in this book they reinforce the important theme of paternity. **divum:** = *divorum*, as again at 56; Vergil uses this archaic* form mainly with certain ethnic names and other nouns that denote a significant class or category, all masculine and most of the second declension (but see 622 n.).

46. A silver line*.

47. **ex quo:** = *ex quo tempore*, "from what time" or "from the time when," i.e. "since." **rēliquias:** cf. *Ītaliam* 18 n. **divini ... parentis:** Servius (on line 45) sees an allusion here to Augustus' relationship with his divine parent, Divus Iulius.

49. **iamque:** one of Vergil's favorite transitional words, occurring nine times in this book alone, all but once (225 n.) at the start of a line, but carefully varied by combination with other words; cf. 159–60 n. **dies ... adest:** on anniversaries in Roman culture and as a theme in the *Aeneid* see Feeney (2007) 148–66. Imposing order and regularity on the reckoning of time was an important part of Augustus' cultural program, and Aeneas' observance of this anniversary may be a graceful acknowledgement on Vergil's part of the Princeps' contributions in this area.

50. **(sic di voluistis):** a brief, parenthetical apostrophe*. **habebo:** like English "hold" in the sense of "regard," with *acerbum* (49) and *honoratum* as predicate accusative modifiers of *quem <diem>* (AG §391–3).

hunc ego Gaetulis agerem si Syrtibus exsul,
Argolicove mari deprensus et urbe Mycenae,
annua vota tamen sollemnisque ordine pompas
exsequerer strueremque suis altaria donis.
nunc ultro ad cineres ipsius et ossa parentis   55
haud equidem sine mente, reor, sine numine divum
adsumus et portus delati intramus amicos.

51-4. Aeneas would celebrate the anniversary of Anchises' death even under the most adverse circumstances, such as captivity in Greece or exile in Africa. The historical enmity between Romans and Africans began with the Punic Wars and continued (thanks to such foes as Jugurtha, Cleopatra, and others) down to Vergil's lifetime (1.12–33, 4.621–9). But by pairing Africa and Greece, home of the Trojan's traditional enemies, Vergil projects this historical situation back into the heroic period. Aeneas has never been taken prisoner by the Greeks, but he has of course spent a year of his exile in Africa.

51. **Gaetulis . . . Syrtibus:** the Trojans themselves have run afoul of the Syrtes (1.111); but Aeneas' words here recall those of Anna to Dido (4.40–1) where she mentions both the Syrtes and the hostile Gaetuli (as well as the Numidians) as dangers that surround the new Carthaginian settlement in Africa. Does this similarity suggest that Aeneas has adopted a Carthaginian perspective? Or does he use *Gaetuli* by synecdoche* for Africans generally, avoiding explicit reference to his onetime friends, now enemies, the Carthaginians? **agerem:** governing *hunc* (*diem*), "*spend* this (day).*"

52. **deprensus:** "caught" or "captured" by the Greeks (hence the emphasis placed on *Argolico* and *Mycenae*, which refer to the kingdoms of the Greek leaders Agamemnon and Menelaus), balancing the sense of *exsul* in the preceding line (an exile in Africa, a prisoner in Greece). **urbe Mycenae:** genitive of apposition (AG §282, 343d; like the English idiom, "city *of* New York"). The simple appositive (*urbe Mycenā*) would be more common in Latin, but here Vergil uses the rarer construction (cf. 1.247, 565; 3.293). The singular *Mycena, -ae* is also much rarer than the plural *Mycenae, -arum*. The construction is not confined to cities (cf. 288–9 n., 340 n.).

53-4. **vota . . . pompas | exsequerer:** zeugma*; *vota exsequi,* "to fulfill vows," but cf. *pompas exsequi,* "to conduct a funeral procession." **suis:** in place of *propriis,* "due" or "appropriate," with reference to *altaria* (AG §301c). **altaria:** according to Servius altars belonging to the gods of the upper world (*di superi*), not those used in cults of heroes or the dead (*di inferi*). Its occurrence here perhaps suggests that Anchises has achieved some exceptional status beyond what is normally associated with ancestor worship.

55. **ultro:** "beyond expectation," used of acts and situations that go beyond (cf. *ultra*) what is normal or usual. Aeneas finds it remarkable that he has returned to the site of Anchises' tomb on the anniversary of his death; cf. 446. **ipsīus:** the usual pronunciation, with long penultimate syllable (cf. 410). But Vergil does not hesitate to treat the syllable as short when the meter requires (cf. 535).

56. **haud . . . :** litotes*. On Aeneas' divination of the gods' will, see 26–31 n. **divum:** cf. 45 n.

57. **delati:** cf. *demittere* (29 n.).

ergo agite et laetum cuncti celebremus honorem:
poscamus ventos, atque haec me sacra quotannis
urbe velit posita templis sibi ferre dicatis.   60
bina boum vobis Troia generatus Acestes
dat numero capita in navis; adhibete penatis
et patrios epulis et quos colit hospes Acestes.
praeterea, si nona diem mortalibus almum
Aurora extulerit radiisque retexerit orbem,   65
prima citae Teucris ponam certamina classis;

---

58. **honorem:** "ritual" (*OLD* s.v. *honor* 2b); cf. 94, 601.

59. **poscamus ventos:** *poscere* takes two accusatives, of the person asked and of the thing requested (AG §396). *Ventos* is the latter; for the former, understand *Anchisen* (and cf. 60 n.). **haec . . . sacra quotannis:** Aeneas' actions anticipate the Parentalia festival, held annually at Rome in honor of the dead and described by Ovid (*Fast.* 2.543) as instituted by Aeneas in honor of Anchises. Cf. 49 n., 64–5 n.

60. **velit:** understand *Anchises* as subject.

61-2. **bina boum . . . capita:** "head of cattle by twos," a grandiloquent way of saying "two oxen apiece," though *bina,* the distributive form of *duo,* is used properly here, since pairs of cattle are being distributed to each ship; similarly 306, 557, *ternos* 247, *seni* 561; cf. 85 n. *Numero* (ablative of specification, AG §418), "in all" (*OLD* 1 b). **Troia:** two syllables, from the noun *Trŏjă* (not the adjective *Trŏĭŭs:* cf. 38 n.), and pronounced "Trō-ya" (not "Troy-a"; cf. Allen (1978) 38–9; ablative of source (AG §403.2a) with *generatus.* **in:** "among," as regularly with distributive expressions (*OLD* A.4). **adhibete penatis:** the gods thus "summoned" were traditionally believed actually to attend and partake of the feast (Hor. *Carm.* 4.5.31).

64-5. **si . . . extulerit:** not "if" but "when"; conditional clauses are idiomatic in such expressions (Cat. 14.17 *nam, si luxerit, ad librariorum | curram scrinia.* **nona:** Roman funeral observances lasted nine days (Porphyrion on Hor. *Epod.* 17.48). Since the Trojans' return from Carthage to Sicily takes place in winter (4.309), Vergil may conceive of Aeneas' foundational celebration as taking place during the nine-day period from February 13–21, the date of the Parentalia in both the Numan and Julian calendars. This festival was celebrated mainly within the family, but its last day, the Feralia, was celebrated publicly, and this detail too corresponds to Aeneas' decision to celebrate Anchises' memory publicly nine days after his announcement. **extulerit . . . orbem:** cf. 4.119 *extulerit Titan radiisque retexerit orbem.*

66-9. Aeneas specifies five events, of which four are found in the narrative of the games (104–544): a boat race (*classis* 66: 114–285), a footrace (*pedum cursu* 67: 286–361), archery (*sagittis* 68: 485–544), and boxing (*caestu* 69: 362–484). The order of events follows that of Aeneas' announcement here, except that the archery and boxing contests are reversed. The javelin throw (*iaculo* 68) does not occur in *Aen.* 5 (but cf. 534 n.).

quique pedum cursu valet, et qui viribus audax
aut iaculo incedit melior levibusque sagittis,
seu crudo fidit pugnam committere caestu,
cuncti adsint meritaeque exspectent praemia palmae.   70
ore favete omnes et cingite tempora ramis."
　　Sic fatus velat materna tempora myrto.
hoc Helymus facit, hoc aevi maturus Acestes,
hoc puer Ascanius, sequitur quos cetera pubes.

67-8. **viribus . . . iaculo . . . sagittis:** ablatives of specification (AG §418, though *viribus*, depending on *audax*, has perhaps some causal force; *iaculo* and *sagittis*, depending on *melior*, are more straightforward). *Vis* (sing.) means, simply, "violence," while *vires* (plur.) has the more benign sense of "strength" or "physical prowess," but the relationship between the two concepts, and further puns involving *vir*, *virtus*, and similar words, recur throughout the book. **incedit:** Servius (on 1.46) glosses this verb as a synonym of *ambulare*, but with the added idea of a certain dignity, which is specified by the predicate adjectives *audax* and *melior*: each contestant "presents himself (*incedit*) with boldness (*audax*) because of his (prowess at) javelin or archery"; cf. 553.

69. **seu:** (following *aut*) "or if," implying doubt whether any one will have the courage to undertake this dangerous contest. **fidit:** practically = *audet*, with the complementary infinitive *committere:* construe "has (enough) confidence (in himself) to . . . ." For the *caestus* itself see 401–5 with notes.

70. **cuncti:** nearly synonymous with *omnes*, but with reference to the collectivity rather than to the individuals that compose it. Aeneas' words thus imply more than just a prize for everyone who takes part in the games (though he is very liberal in dispensing such prizes: cf. 305 n.). In a larger sense, if one bears in mind that the games represent the Trojans' struggle to reach Italy, Aeneas' words allude to the one great prize that awaits them all. In this sense, it is significant that the women, who do not take part in the games, will not partake of this prize (cf. 613–15 n., 654 n., 678–9 n., 767–9 n.)

71. **ore favete:** any ill-omened words would spoil the performance of a sacred ritual. It was therefore customary to ask observers "to show favor with their speech" (*os* "mouth," but by metonymy* "speech"), i.e. to utter none but favorable words; and as the safest way to do this was to say nothing, the phrase usually means "be silent" (Hor. *Carm.* 3.1.2 *favete linguis* (with Nisbet-Rudd (2004) *ad loc.*); Prop. 4.6.1 *sacra facit vates, sint ora faventia sacris*).

72-103. *Aeneas offers sacrifice at his father's tomb. A snake appears, tastes the offerings, and disappears. Aeneas declares it the tutelary deity of the spot, or the attendant spirit of Anchises, and renews the sacrifice, which is followed by a feast.*

72. **materna:** because myrtle is sacred to Venus (see Thomas (1988) on *Geo.* 1.28).

73. **Helymus:** evidently a companion of Aeneas, whose name recalls that of the Elymi, one of the peoples who occupied the region around Mt. Eryx; cf. 300 n. **aevi:** genitive of specification (AG §394d; 2.638 n.).

ille e concilio multis cum milibus ibat 75
ad tumulum magna medius comitante caterva.
hic duo rite mero libans carchesia Baccho
fundit humi, duo lacte novo, duo sanguine sacro,
purpureosque iacit flores ac talia fatur:
"salve, sancte parens, iterum salvete, recepti 80
nequiquam cineres animaeque umbraeque paternae.
non licuit finis Italos fataliaque arva
nec tecum Ausonium, quicumque est, quaerere Thybrim."
dixerat haec, adytis cum lubricus anguis ab imis

---

75. **ille:** Aeneas. As often, the demonstrative pronoun signals a change of subject (AG §297a–b); cf. 90, 169, 336, 394, 439, 444, 482, 510, 609, 676.

77-8. **duo . . . duo . . . duo:** the repetition connotes the care and solemnity with which the ceremony is conducted. **mero . . . Baccho:** syntactically between the ablative of description (AG §415), in which the ablative phrase directly modifies a noun, and the ablative of means (AG §409a), since *carchesia* here means not just "cups" but "cupfuls of" or "cups filled with." On offerings to the dead see 3.62–8, 3.300–5. *Baccho* stands by metonymy* for *vino*. **carchesia:** tankards somewhat narrowing in the middle with two handles reaching to the foot.

80. **salve . . . :** the ritual greeting of the deceased (cf. 2.644, 3.67–8, 6.231 and 506, 9.483–4, 11.97–8; Hom. *Il.* 23.179, Catullus 101.10). **iterum:** in reference to the *salve* that was uttered at Anchises' actual funeral, which is now repeated.

80-1. **recepti | nequiquam cineres:** *recepti* is nominative modifying the proleptic* *cineres* ("ashes saved in vain" from the destruction of Troy), not genitive ("ashes of him who was saved . . . "): so Servius, who nevertheless finds the expression strained. **animae . . . umbrae:** the plural is often used of a single apparition (*umbris* 4.571).

82. **Ĭtalos:** cf. *Ĭtalia* 18 n.

83. **quicumque est:** in ironic contrast with its later fame. Note that everything about the promised land is still quite strange to Aeneas.

84. **dixerat haec, adytis cum . . . :** the main clause is completely colorless, the point of the sentence being contained in a *cum* clause. This is a standard means of adding variety to a narration and throwing emphasis on what is important (cf. AG §546a on *cum inversum*). Moreover, *cum* is postponed from its expected initial position in the clause that it introduces (cf. 5 n.), throwing emphasis on the more interesting word *adytis,* which suggests both the retreat of a serpent to an inaccessible place and, especially, the shrine of a divinity, ἄδυτον ("unentered") being the Greek name for that part of a temple that could be visited only by priests. The serpent represents the spirit of the dead, which was regarded as inhabiting (or visiting, 98 n.) the tomb, and which by partaking of the offerings indicates his happy acceptance of them.

septem ingens gyros, septena volumina traxit 85
amplexus placide tumulum lapsusque per aras,
caeruleae cui terga notae maculosus et auro
squamam incendebat fulgor, ceu nubibus arcus
mille iacit varios adverso sole colores.
obstipuit visu Aeneas. ille agmine longo 90
tandem inter pateras et levia pocula serpens
libavitque dapes rursusque innoxius imo
successit tumulo et depasta altaria liquit.
hoc magis inceptos genitori instaurat honores,
incertus geniumne loci famulumne parentis 95
esse putet; caedit binas de more bidentis
totque sues, totidem nigrantis terga iuvencos,

---

85. **septem ... septena:** in poetry the distributive is often used as a synonym of or replacement for cardinal numbers for the sake of *variatio*;* cf. AG §137d. **gyros:** the circuits round the altar. **volumina:** the undulations of the serpent's body. **traxit:** governs both *gyros* and *volumina* but in slightly different senses (zeugma*); the snake "drew a circle" in the dust and "drew the coilings" of its body along as it moved.

87-8. **notae ... incendebat fulgor:** both nouns form the compound subject of *incendebat*, which agrees in number (and in sense) with the nearer of them.

89. **mille ... colores:** cf. 4.701 *mille trahens varios adverso sole colores.*

90. **ille:** the snake, here pointedly juxtaposed with the previous subject, Aeneas; cf. 39 n. **agmine:** *agmen* consists of the verbal stem *ago* + the nominal suffix *-men*, so that its basic meaning is "a driving" or "a going"; cf. *OLD* s.v. 1b and 211 n. The familiar military sense of *agmen* as "an army on the march, a column" (*OLD* s.v. 5; cf. 580 n.) and related military uses (804–5 n.) are specific and narrower aplications of the general idea.

92. **dapes:** a ritual feast, in contrast to *cena,* the more general word for "dinner."

94. **instaurat:** "the technical term for repeating a religious ceremony invalidated by some error or omission in the first performance (Liv. 5.52). Vergil uses it for 'renew,' especially of something solemn or religious" (Perkell on 3.62; cf. *OLD* s.v. 1b, "to renew, after an interval"). Here there is no implication that Anchises' burial rites had been literally flawed in any way, but the idea of formal repetition of these rites may be connected to the theme of pollution and expiation (see introductory note, 1–103 n., 5 n.). **honores:** cf. 58 n.

95. **genium ... :** the tutelary deity of places or persons was represented under the form of a serpent; the same was true of the *famulus* that was thought to attend demigods and heroes.

96-7. **binas:** cf. 61–2 n. **bidentis ... sues ... iuvencos:** the technical name for this sacrifice was *suovetaurilia.* **nigrantis terga iuvencos:** = 6.243; *nigrantis,* the present active participle of *nigro,* "to be black," a poetic equivalent of *nigros.* The dark black hue that it denotes is often associated with death and the underworld (*OLD* s.v. *niger* 7); cf. 736, 6.153. *Terga* is accusative of specification (AG §397b; cf. 135 n.), denoting, as often, the part of the body affected; although here the part probably stands for the whole, an instance of synecdoche*.

vinaque fundebat pateris animamque vocabat
Anchisae magni manisque Acheronte remissos.
nec non et socii, quae cuique est copia, laeti   100
dona ferunt, onerant aras mactantque iuvencos;
ordine aëna locant alii fusique per herbam
subiciunt veribus prunas et viscera torrent.

98. **vinaque:** perhaps "measures of wine," but possibly just "wine," i.e. a true "poetic plural," equivalent to the singular; in Vergil *vinum* is always plural in the nominative and accusative, singular in the other cases (Williams (1960) *ad loc.*). The device presumably originated as a way of using words that were metrically inadmissable except in the plural, and was then extended to other words. **animamque . . . :** cf. *Il.* 23.219. Just as the gods are summoned to a feast (62), so the dead are summoned to come and enjoy the offerings made to them.

100. **nec non et:** "and also, to be sure"; the double negative = a strong affirmative (an instance of litotes*). **quae cuique est copia, laeti:** all were happy to contribute, each in proportion to his means. On distributive pronouns in relative clauses see AG §313a.

104–761: The Day of the Games

At 658 lines, this is by far the longest of the book's three sections, but like the other two it takes place on a single day, which is separated from each of the others by a nine-day interval (64, 104–5, 762). While it is the centerpiece of a highly symmetrical book (see introductory note), its internal structure is enlivened by a studied asymmetry. The games (104–603, see n.) occupy three quarters of the space alloted to the day on which they occur (499 lines out of 658), while the day's second major occurrence, the burning of the ships (604–761, see n.), takes up only one quarter (157 lines). Within the games themselves, by the principle of *variatio*, longer episodes alternate with shorter ones (Heinze (1993) 123). After brief preliminaries (104–13, 10 lines), the first event (boat race) occupies 172 lines, the second (foot race) 76, the third (boxing) 123, and the fourth (archery) 60. The fifth and final, non-competitive event, the Troia, signals the closure of the contests by re-establishing a sense of symmetry, being almost exactly as long as (58 lines) as the previous event.

104–603: The Games

This episode is modeled on several previous epic accounts of athletic contests. Most obvious is book 23 of the *Iliad*, which describes the funeral games celebrated by Achilles in honor of Patroclus. This is the most extensive "intrusion" of Iliadic material into the Odyssean *Aeneid*. This incursion is made all the more striking by the fact that Vergil "moves" only the games to this part of the poem; Patroclus' actual burial — which gruesomely includes human sacrifice — does not figure in the memorial rites for Anchises in book 5, but rather becomes the model for Pallas' funeral in book 11, a book that not only occurs in the "Iliadic" half of the poem but one that, like *Iliad* 23, stands in the next-to-last position. But the "intrusion" of this Iliadic episode here is "justified" by the fact that the *Odyssey* too contains athletic contests, which are held at the court of Alcinous, king of the Phaeacians: details from this episode are woven into Vergil's games which, like those in the *Odyssey*, occur just before the narration of the central episode of both poems, the hero's visit to the world of the dead (Cairns (1989) 178–79). Similarly, Nelis (2001) 8–21) shows that the games in book 4 of Apollonius of Rhodes' *Argonautica* — themselves a skillful imitation of the games episodes in both of Homer's epics — are scarcely less important to Vergil than are Homer's, not least because they call the reader's attention to the importance of the Sicilian episode in Vergil's Argonautic program (Nelis (2001) 186–226).

Vergil's skill in refashioning his sources is especially evident in this episode. Where Homer relates a long series of increasingly shorter episodes, Vergil selects just four, and alternates longer (boat race, boxing) with shorter (foot race, archery) contests. To these he adds a fifth, non-competitive event, the Troia, that has no Homeric or Apollonian counterpart. Where the earlier contests develop in a relatively straightforward way, Vergil's are full of unexpected twists; and instead of presenting the individual contests mainly as discrete episodes, Vergil relates them closely and in a variety of ways to major themes and turns of plot elsewhere in the *Aeneid*.

In some respects, however, the purpose of the games in Homer, Apollonius, and Vergil is very similar. In *Iliad* 23, Achilles has abandoned his allies over a personal vendetta with Agamemnon, and has returned to battle only to pursue a new vendetta with Hector. By presiding over the burial of his beloved friend Patroclus and holding games in his honor, Achilles begins to see himself once again as a member of the warrior society that he had left in the first book of the poem. Apollonius' games, as Nelis stresses, follow the death of Medea's brother Apsyrtus, and thus perform an expiatory function. Aeneas, left without guidance upon his father's death, becomes involved with Dido, temporarily loses sight of his goal, and tragically (if inadvertently) causes her death as well. Because Aeneas' return to Sicily immediately follows Dido's suicide, these games, as Nelis (2001) 190-8 shows, perform some of the expiatory function of those in Apollonius. At the same time, they allow Aeneas, as he honors his deceased father, to establish himself as a leader in his own right and thus to assume his proper place among his people, much as Homer's games do for Achilles.

From another point of view, Vergil's games can be seen as a microcosm of the Trojans' experience in the poem as a whole: after a sea voyage ($\approx$ boat race) they will face a series of trials on land; and the land events (foot race, boxing, archery, Troia) come increasingly to resemble the arts of war. Notable too is the emphasis throughout the games on sacrifice, a dominant theme of the book and of the poem (Putnam (1965)). As the games progress, the motif of sacrifice becomes more literal and, in places, involves explicit refererence to human sacrifice. In the boat race Gyas pitches his helmsman overboard in a comical anticipation of the sacrifice of Palinurus; with a long lead in the foot race Nisus slips in some sacrificial blood, but turns his misfortune to the advantage of Euryalus, thus "sacrificing" himself for his friend (and anticipating the devotion that he shows in deadlier circumstances in book 9); Entellus with a mighty blow of his fist literally sacrifices a steer, his prize as victor in the boxing match, calling it a more appropriate victim than the opponent whom he nearly killed in the ring; and the object of the archery contest is to shoot and kill a dove tethered to a ship's mast.

Bibliography: with a focus on intertextual relations to Homer, Apollonius, and others: Heinze (1914) 145-70 = (1993) 121-41, Otis (1964) 41-61, Knauer (1964a and b), Glazewski (1972-73), Rose (1982-83), Poliakoff (1985), Cairns (1989) 215-48, Nelis (2001) 186-226, Leigh (2010); with a focus on political and historical elements: Briggs (1975), Feldherr (1995, 2002), Traill (2001), McGowan (2002).

Exspectata dies aderat nonamque serena
Auroram Phaethontis equi iam luce vehebant, 105
famaque finitimos et clari nomen Acestae
excierat: laeto complerant litora coetu
visuri Aeneadas, pars et certare parati.
munera principio ante oculos circoque locantur
in medio, sacri tripodes viridesque coronae 110
et palmae pretium victoribus, armaque et ostro
perfusae vestes, argenti aurique talenta;

Preliminaries (104–13). The Trojans and their Sicilian hosts gather on the appointed day, and prizes are displayed.

105. **Phaëthontis:** the sun itself, as in Homer, and not the son of Helios and Clymene (Ovid, *Met.* 1.747–2.332). The spelling reflects the Greek Φαέθων, in which αε is not a diphthong.

106. **nomen:** "race" or "nation" (*OLD* s.v. 19); so *nomen Latinum*, "Latin people."

108. **visuri:** future active participle expressing purpose (AG §499.2). **pars et:** as a collective noun, *pars* can take modifiers that do not agree with it in either gender or number (AG §286b; cf. 280a, 317d). *Pars . . . pars* is a very common way of saying "some do this, while others do that" (e.g. 1.423–5). Vergil occasionally omits the first *pars* (557–8, 660–1). Here the addition of *et* gives the expression a slightly different force from the usual: the Sicilians all come to see the games, *and some also* to compete.

109. **munera:** "prizes." *Munus* means both "a service rendered," whether obligatory or not, and "a present," whether given freely and spontaneously or in recognition of some service or achievement. In this book it usually has the latter sense (247, 282, 348, 354, 361, 532, 537), but cf. 337 n., 652 n., 846 n.

109-10. **circo . . . in medio:** as Feldherr (1995) 246 notes, the phrase is "slightly incongruous since the spectators have already gathered on the shore," but at the same time it "serves to recast the boatrace about to commence as a circus spectacle by superimposing the physical structure of the circus over the space of the competition." Cf. 288–9 n. On *medio* cf. 1–2 n. **sacri tripodes:** called *sacri* because they were commonly used as votive offerings, tripods were also regular prizes in Greek games (Hom. *Il.* 23.259, Hor. *Carm.* 4.8.3).

111. **palmae pretium victoribus:** the palm is a symbol of victory (Nisbet-Hubbard (1970) on Hor. *Carm.* 1.1.5).

112. **talenta:** both *talenta* and *talentum* are supported by the manuscripts; the plural is preferable, because a talent is generally a weight of some particular substance (cf. *argenti . . . magnum talentum* 248), not several substances mixed together. Thus Aeneas offers (presumably) one talent each of gold and silver. Cf. 11.333 *auri eborisque talenta*. The talent was a widespread ancient measure (by weight) of precious substances; it varied over time and from place to place. Even in antiquity Homeric scholars debated the actual value of talents given as prizes in the funeral games of Patroclus, and ancient scholars of Vergil commented on this passage in exactly the same way. In Vergil's mind, the fact that the talent was recognized as a Homeric measure was probably much more important than its exact value.

et tuba commissos medio canit aggere ludos.
Prima pares ineunt gravibus certamina remis
quattuor ex omni delectae classe carinae. 115

---

113. **commissos . . . ludos:** "the opening of the games," an instance of the *ab urbe condita* construction (AG §497); cf. the common phrase *committere proelium*, "to join battle." The games of the *Iliad* are a temporary diversion from the war; those of the *Aeneid* give the reader a foretaste of the conflict that is to come. **medio:** placed iconically in the middle of the line (cf. 1–2 n.). **aggere:** the herald stands on an elevated spot, perhaps the same one used earlier by Aeneas (44).

First Event: The Boat Race (114–285)

    This event — the first and longest of the four — is modeled on the chariot race — the first and longest of Homer's events (*Il.* 23.262–650)—with many additional contributions from Apollonius (*Arg.* 1.364–5; 2.345–8, 588–90, 932–5; 4.1541–5, etc.; Nelis (2001) 209–21.

114-23. The captains Mnestheus, Gyas, Sergestus, and Cloanthus enter the race. All but Gyas are to become the eponymous ancestors of specific Roman gentes.

    Greek intellectuals linked the foundation of Rome to heroes of the Trojan War as early as the fifth century, and the idea had gained currency at Rome by the third century. Not long before Vergil began the *Aeneid*, the senator and scholar M. Terentius Varro wrote a book *De familiis Troianis* to record and perhaps sort out the competing traditions, but apart from a few citations it does not survive. The families singled out here are curious choices, since they are decidedly not among the most important or the most admirable in Roman history. The names of the ships — Pristis, Chimaera, Centaurus, and Scylla — are surprising as well, in that they refer to monsters of a type that mythology usually represents as enemies of civilization (cf. *Pristim* 116 n.). All the captains appear elsewhere in the poem. In book 1, Aeneas mourns the loss of Gyas and Cloanthus in the storm (222) but then unexpectedly finds them as well as Sergius at Dido's court (510, 612). Mnestheus first appears in book 4 when Aeneas bids him and Sergestus (along with Serestus) to prepare to leave Carthage (288 ≈ 12.561), but he becomes the most prominent of the four captains in book 9, where he assumes the role of Ascanius' chief advisor in Aeneas' absence, and he is mentioned more frequently than any of the other captains in book 12, where Gyas and Sergestus are also mentioned. Of the four contestants, only Cloanthus, after he is declared the victor (245), disappears from the narrative.

114. **pares:** "well-matched."

velocem Mnestheus agit acri remige Pristim,
mox Italus Mnestheus, genus a quo nomine Memmi,
ingentemque Gyas ingenti mole Chimaeram,
urbis opus, triplici pubes quam Dardana versu
impellunt, terno consurgunt ordine remi;   120

---

116. **Mnestheus:** pronounced as two long syllables. As in all Greek names ending in *-eus*, *eu* represents the Greek diphthong ευ. **remige:** "oarsmen," collective singular (like *milite*, "troops," 2.495: AG §317d n. 2) of the ablative of means. **Pristim:** the name for a class of warship (Liv. 35.26.1 and 44.28.1, Polyb. 16.2.9), which Vergil may have used to strengthen the connection between the heroic past and his own day. But its basic meaning, "sea-monster" (Perkell on 3.427), is paralleled by the names of the three other ships (Chimaera 118, Centaur and Scylla 122). These monstrous elements, which are in general associated with Aeneas' enemies (Hardie (1986)), remind the reader that the boatrace is an allegory that possesses moral and ethical, political, historical, and cosmic dimensions; and not only the pious victor (who disappears from the narrative as soon as his victory is announced), but the unruly behavior of Gyas (whose own name recalls the rebellious Giants of Greek myth: cf. Harrison on 10.318) and Sergestus (the ancestor of a historical revolutionary: cf. 121 n.) remind the reader of all the forces that come into play in the process of nation-building.

117. **Ítalus:** cf. *Italiam* (18 n.). **Mnestheus . . . Memmi:** a fanciful etymology*. The Memmii were not known as an especially ancient or important *gens,* although they were active in politics from the time of the Jugurthine War (112–104 BCE) until the end of the Republic. One of them, C. Memmius, was praetor in 58, and the following year as propraetor and governor of Bithynia he had Catullus (together with Catullus' friend and fellow poet C. Helvius Cinna) on his staff; see poems 10.7, 30; 25.7; 28.9; 31.5. Memmius is also the addressee of Lucretius' *De rerum natura* (see 1.26, 42, 411, *et passim*). **genus a quo:** for the word order cf. *sed* 5 n. The verb of this relative clause is an understood *est* (cf. 23–4 n.); in prose one would say *ortum est*.

118. **ingentemque . . . ingenti mole Chimaeram:** emphatic repetition in the epic style (Hom. *Il.* 16.776); cf. 10.842 = 12.640; cf. 447 *gravis graviterque*. For the entire expression cf. Lucretius 4.902 *trudit agens magnam magno molimine navem*. **ingenti mole:** ablative of quality (AG §415) or description.

119. **urbis opus:** "as big as a city." A similar phrase in Cicero suggests the colossal size of a ship (*Verr.* 5.4.89 *navis . . . urbis instar*), but here the comparison between ship and city-state suggests the destiny that awaits this crew. **triplici . . . versu:** the oarsmen are arranged one above the other in three banks. The detail is anachronistic, since triremes were invented in about 700 BCE, after the end of the heroic age (Thuc. 1.13). **triplici pubes quam:** for the word order cf. *sed* 5 n.

120. **terno:** cf. 85 n. **consurgunt:** Vergil encourages the mind's eye to move from the lowest bank of oars to the middle one to the highest as they "rise" one above the other, thus emphasizing the enormous size of the ship.

Sergestusque, domus tenet a quo Sergia nomen,
Centauro invehitur magna, Scyllaque Cloanthus
caerulea, genus unde tibi, Romane Cluenti.
    Est procul in pelago saxum spumantia contra
litora, quod tumidis summersum tunditur olim   125
fluctibus hiberni condunt ubi sidera Cauri;
tranquillo silet immotaque attollitur unda
campus et apricis statio gratissima mergis.
hic viridem Aeneas frondenti ex ilice metam

---

121. **domus ... a quo:** cf. *genus a quo* 117 n. **Sergia:** feminine modifying *domus*. This family's best-known member was the revolutionary L. Sergius Catilina, whose attempted *coup d'état* Cicero successfully opposed in 63 BCE. Vergil envisions Catilina as being punished in the underworld at 8.668.

122. **magna:** feminine as if in agreement with the common noun *navis* (which Vergil does not use here) instead of with the (masculine) name of the ship, *Centaurus* (which he does). **Cloanthus:** like *Sergestus* (121) subject of *invehitur* (122).

123. **genus unde tibi:** cf. *genus a quo* 117 n. **Cluenti:** the best-known Cluentius was a defendant whom Cicero got acquitted of a murder charge: cf. *pro Cluentio*.

124-50. *The course is out to sea, around a rock, and home. They draw lots for places, and after a pause of breathless excitement the signal is given and they dash away amid the cheers of the onlookers.*

125. **tumidis ... tranquillo** (127): successive clauses marked by contrasting initial words. **olim:** "from time to time" (*OLD* s.v. 4).

126. **Cauri:** northwesterly storm winds (Pliny, *Nat. Hist.* 18.338), perhaps bringing the showers for which Aeneas will soon pray (685–98).

127. **tranquillo:** neuter adjective used idiomatically as a one-word ablative absolute, "in fine weather" (AG §419.b.3).

128. **apricis:** properly of places, here (by enallage*) of those who enjoy such places.

129. **metam:** the turning post, just as in the Circus Maximus. Otis (1964) 52 notes that by calling attention to the *meta,* the midpoint of the race, in this initial description of the course, Vergil proleptically* focuses the reader's attention on the place where the action of the race decisively (and literally) turns. Feldherr (1995) 246 adds that in so doing, "Vergil presents his audience with a view of the course in its entirety which replicates the perspective of a spectator in the elevated stands of the circus." Cf. 109–10 n., 288–9 n.

    If the boat race does in some sense stand for the sea voyages that have dominated Aeneas' life since the fall of Troy, then this *meta* may have significance for his wanderings as well. In purely geographical terms, the games are set at virtually the westernmost point in those wanderings. Once Aeneas rounds this point of Sicily, he turns back towards the east and towards Italy. Socially and psychologically as well it is here that Aeneas begins to reverse the failures in leadership and, to some extent, in character that have plagued him up to this point. It must also be relevant that Vergil has placed these games near the midpoint of his narrative.

constituit signum nautis pater, unde reverti 130
scirent et longos ubi circumflectere cursus.
tum loca sorte legunt ipsique in puppibus auro
ductores longe effulgent ostroque decori;
cetera populea velatur fronde iuventus
nudatosque umeros oleo perfusa nitescit. 135
considunt transtris, intentaque bracchia remis;
intenti exspectant signum, exsultantiaque haurit

---

130. **pater:** in apposition to Aeneas and given adverbial force by the word-order (cf. *heros* 1.196, *dea* 1.412, etc.). Aeneas acts with a father's care for his people. This is the first time in book 5 that Aeneas is called *pater* (cf. 348, 358, 424, 461, 545, 700, 827, 867). **unde:** equivalent to *ut inde* introducing a relative clause of purpose (AG §531.2).

132. **sorte:** from *sors,* a "token" or "lot," here a literal ablative of means (AG §409). The lots are used to determine each contestant's starting position, which could be decisive, since those with an inside track had a shorter path to the turning post. For a description of the full procedure of using lots cf. 490–1 n.

133. **ductores:** "captains," not "helmsmen" (which is *rector* (161) or *magister* (176)).

134. A silver line*. **populea:** the poplar was sacred to Hercules, hero of athletes.

135. **umeros:** "retained" accusative of specification, so called because it is imagined as if the direct object of an active sentence (e.g. *perfudit umeros,* "he oiled his shoulders") had been "retained" after the verb was changed to the passive voice (e.g. *perfusus est umeros,* "he was oiled (about his) shoulders." It is common in poetry, as here, with the perfect passive participle (*perfusa;* but cf. 97 n.). The construction exists in early Latin, but is more common in Greek, so that it is sometimes called a "Greek accustive," and Vergil uses it freely in imitation of his Greek models (cf. AG §397b–c).

136-50. Vergil's always careful management of verb tenses (Mack (1977)) is particularly noticeable in these lines. A series of present-tense verbs (*considunt* 136, *exspectant* and *haurit* 137) describe conditions that persist up to the start of the race. These are suddenly followed by simple perfects that describe the starting signal (*dedit sonitum* 139) and the boats leaping forward (*prosiluere* 140; cf. 243 *condidit*). The narration then switches back to the present tense (*ferit* 140, *spumant* 141, *infindunt* and *dehiscit* 142) for vividness. The simile* repeats and intensifies the pattern: a pair of simple perfects (*corripuere* 145, *concussere* 147) precede and share subjects with a pair of presents (*ruunt* 145, *pendent* 147), thus connoting a single, abrupt action followed by sustained effort. The string of present tenses that closes out the passage (*consonat* and *uolutant* 149, *resultant* 150) draws the reader back from the heat of action to the calmer and more distant perspective of the audience.

136-7. **intentaque ... intenti:** construe both participles as predicate adjectives (AG §495), *intenta* following an understood *sunt* (cf. 23–4 n.) and *intenti* modifying the understood subject of *exspectant* (137). The repetition involves a type of zeugma* – *intenta* is used literally ("and their arms are *stretched out on* the oars"), while *intenti* is metaphorical* and is best rendered adverbially ("they *anxiously* await the signal," cf. *cita* 32–3 n.). **haurit:** as if the tension literally "drained" blood from the heart.

corda pavor pulsans laudumque arrecta cupido.
inde ubi clara dedit sonitum tuba, finibus omnes,
haud mora, prosiluere suis; ferit aethera clamor   140
nauticus, adductis spumant freta versa lacertis.
infindunt pariter sulcos, totumque dehiscit
convulsum remis rostrisque tridentibus aequor.
non tam praecipites biiugo certamine campum
corripuere ruuntque effusi carcere currus,   145
nec sic immissis aurigae undantia lora
concussere iugis pronique in verbera pendent.

---

138. **pavor:** "excitement" rather than "fear."
139. **dedit sonitum tuba:** Latin poetry uses *dare* in various phrases that are equivalent to some other verb alone (e.g. *insonuere tubae,* Lucan 1.578). Although English has some similar expressions (e.g. "to give a shout" ≈ "to shout"), it is often more idiomatic to use a verb different from "to give," as in "to make a sound."
140. **prosiluere:** perfect indicative of *prosileo* (= *prosiluerunt,* cf. 8 n.). **aethera:** accusative (cf. 13 n.).
141. **nauticus:** adjective instead of the genitive *nautarum* (as 3.128). **versa:** from *verto* "turn" not *verro* "sweep." Although the metaphor* of rowing as sweeping is common in Vergil (3.208 = 4.583; 3.290 = 5.778; 6.320), that of sailing as plowing is further developed in this passage (142 *infindunt . . . sulcos* "they split furrows"; 143 *convulsum . . . aequor* "the plowed-up plain"), and *verto* is frequently used of "turning" or "plowing" fields (e.g. *Geo.* 1.1–2).
144-7. A famous simile* with a long pedigree. Homer compares ships to chariots at *Od.* 13.81–5, a sign that this episode owes something to the games of the Phaeacians; but the general shape of this contest along with many details derive (as ancient critics realized: see Servius *ad loc.*) from the chariot race of *Il.* 23 (114–285 n.), and a simile comparing ships with chariots seems to invite the reader to compare the Vergilian passage with its model (cf. 157–8 n.). If so, then Vergil's claim that these (enormous: 118–19 n.) ships are faster than Homeric chariots is hyperbolic* and signals an element of competition (*aemulatio*) in Vergil's imitation (*imitatio*) of Homer (Nugent (1992)).
144-5. **campum | corripuere:** the phrase suggests immense speed: the chariots are said to "grab up the field" as they move quickly over it; cf. 316 n. *corripuere* is the perfect indicative of *corripio* (= *corripuerunt,* cf. 8 n.).
146. **immissis:** the regular word for running at full gallop, here modifying *iugis* 147, but normally used (as at 662) of the reins that are "let go" so as not to restrain the horses.
147. **concussere:** perfect indicative of *concutio* (= *concusserunt,* cf. 8 n.). **iugis:** "pairs" of horses, as elsewhere of oxen. **in verbera pendent:** literally, "lean into their blows": the drivers hang over the backs of their horses as they lash them on to greater speed.

tum plausu fremituque virum studiisque faventum
consonat omne nemus, vocemque inclusa volutant
litora, pulsati colles clamore resultant. 150
    Effugit ante alios primisque elabitur undis
turbam inter fremitumque Gyas; quem deinde Cloanthus
consequitur, melior remis, sed pondere pinus
tarda tenet. post hos aequo discrimine Pristis
Centaurusque locum tendunt superare priorem; 155
et nunc Pristis habet, nunc victam praeterit ingens
Centaurus, nunc una ambae iunctisque feruntur
frontibus et longa sulcant vada salsa carina.

---

148. **virum:** = *virorum* (cf. 45 n.). **studiis:** the plural of an abstract noun denotes "instances" or "displays of" that quality; hence *studia*, "cheers" (AG §100c). **faventum:** Latin generally prefers substantive participles even where synonymous nouns are available (e.g. *amans* instead of *amator* for "lover"). Thus here *faventes* (rather than *fautores*), "partisans."

150. **colles . . . resultant:** the hills "leap back" or "echo." The metaphor* derives from the more explicitly "scientific" explanation given at *Geo.* 4.49–50, where it is said that an echo "leaps back" (*resultat*) after striking against a stony surface.

151-82. *The race. Gyas gets off first, Cloanthus next, with the other two behind and almost even. As they come to the turning-point, Menoetes, Gyas' helmsman, swings far to the right. Cloanthus makes a narrower turn and takes the lead. Gyas angrily pitches Menoetes overboard, delighting the spectators.*

151. **primisque:** the waves before Gyas are the "first" over which any boat passes.

152. **deinde:** cf. 14 n.

153-4. **pondere pinus | tarda tenet:** the repetition of initial consonants (alliteration*) seems to suggest Cloanthus' difficulty in moving his ship along. **aequo discrimine:** ablative of manner (AG §412). The Pristis and the Centaurus are "at the same distance" behind Cloanthus, even with one another.

155. **tendunt superare:** here *tendunt* takes a complementary infinitive as if it were a verb of desire (AG §457a); cf. *certant inludere* 2.64. **superare:** usually means to overcome or defeat someone in a contest (184 *Gyan superare*), not to "win" or "secure" a prize or, as here, a position. **priorem:** not "first" (which would be *primum*), but "prior" with respect to one another—the Pristis and the Centaurus are vying for clear possession of third place.

156. **habet:** understand *locum priorem* from 155.

157-8. **iunctisque . . . frontibus:** the ships start off evenly, their prows side by side, not literally "joined," though this expression could be another sly reminder that Vergil's model is a chariot race (cf. 144–7 n.).

iamque propinquabant scopulo metamque tenebant
cum princeps medioque Gyas in gurgite victor   160
rectorem navis compellat voce Menoeten:
"quo tantum mihi dexter abis? huc derige gressum;
litus ama et laeva stringat sine palmula cautes;
altum alii teneant." dixit; sed caeca Menoetes
saxa timens proram pelagi detorquet ad undas.   165
"quo diversus abis?" iterum "pete saxa, Menoete!"
cum clamore Gyas revocabat, et ecce Cloanthum
respicit instantem tergo et propiora tenentem.
ille inter navemque Gyae scopulosque sonantis

159-60. **iamque . . . cum:** a more elaborate example of the *cum inversum* construction than the previous one (cf. 84 n.). Here the main clause (*iamque . . . tenebant*) contains the circumstantial information that would normally be found in a subordinate clause, and the *cum* clause supplies the essential points that actually drive the story forward. As often in Vergil, *cum inversum* is anticipated and balanced by *iamque* at the beginning of the main clause: "*already* were they approaching . . . *when* . . . "); cf. 693 n.

159. **metamque tenebant:** cf. *mediumque tenebat* 1. Similar phrasing reinforces the logical link between the turning post of the boatrace and the midpoint of Aeneas' voyage. *Tenebant* is an inceptive imperfect (cf. 1 n. *tenebant*): translate "they were beginning to have" or "they almost had the turning post."

160. **medio . . . in gurgite:** construe closely with *victor*, "victorious (i.e. leading) at the half-way mark" (*metam* 159). Gyas at the midpoint of the race is in a position like that of Aeneas as he rounds the westernmost tip of Sicily en route to Italy (1–2 n.). Like Aeneas he will be severely tested at this crucial point; like Aeneas he will lose his helmsman and will have to steer the ship himself (176 n., 868 n.).

162. **mihi:** ethic dative (AG §380) indicating strong personal interest; equivalent to a parenthetical "tell me."

163. **ama:** "hug" i.e. "stay close to" (*OLD* s.v. 4b); cf. Hor. *Carm*. 1.25.3 *amatque ianua limen*. **stringat sine:** the imperative *sine* (from *sino;* not the preposition *sine*) in parataxis* with the jussive subjunctive is redundant and colloquial.

166. **quo . . . Menoete:** the short, unadorned sentences reflect Gyas' growing agitation and disbelief at the conservative course that Menoetes is steering. **Menoetē:** vocative of the Greek first declension, ὦ Μενοίτη.

167-8. **revocabat . . . respicit:** on the different tenses see 136–50 n.

168. **propiora:** = *propiora loca* ("holding (those places that are) closer (to the rock)").

169. **ille:** Cloanthus; cf. 75 n.

radit iter laevum interior subitoque priorem 170
praeterit et metis tenet aequora tuta relictis.
tum vero exarsit iuveni dolor ossibus ingens
nec lacrimis caruere genae, segnemque Menoeten
oblitus decorisque sui sociumque salutis
in mare praecipitem puppi deturbat ab alta; 175
ipse gubernaclo rector subit, ipse magister
hortaturque viros clavumque ad litora torquet.
at gravis ut fundo vix tandem redditus imo est
iam senior madidaque fluens in veste Menoetes
summa petit scopuli siccaque in rupe resedit. 180

---

170. **radit iter laevum interior:** "scrapes his path inside and to the left (of Gyas)." For *radit iter*, cf. 3.700, 7.10 (but contrast 217). *Laevum* and *interior* are both predicate adjectives, best construed adverbially (cf. *cita* 32–3 n.), the former modifying *iter,* the latter *ille* (169), subject of *radit.*

171. **metis:** obviously a "poetic plural" (see 98 n.), since there is only one *meta.*

172. **dolor:** "indignation" (*OLD* s.v. 3). **ossibus:** 1.660 n.

173. **nec lacrimis caruere genae:** modeled on Hom. *Il.* 23.385, where Diomedes weeps at losing his whip in the race; but in general, "tears were consistent with heroic character" (Ganiban on 1.459). *Caruere* is the perfect indicative of *careo* (= *caruerunt,* cf. 8 n.).

174. **decoris:** "dignity." Servius comments that to lose one's temper is disgraceful, particularly for one in command. **socium:** = *sociorum,* cf. 45 n.

175. **deturbat:** "pitches," a vivid and rather blunt word (cf. Plautus, *Mercator* 116 *deturbare in viam* "to kick out into the street"). It appears again at 6.412, 10.555.

176. **ipse . . . ipse:** the repetition emphasizes the extraordinary (and, as it turns out, ill-considered) nature of Gyas' actions (see below). **rector . . . magister:** predicate nominatives denoting two normally separate jobs that Gyas tries to perform at once: "he takes his place at the tiller *as steersman* (following the copulative verb *subit* (AG §284)) and (continuing in his previous role) urges his men *as captain* . . . ." By taking Menoetes' place here Gyas anticipates Aeneas when he takes Palinurus' place at the end of the book (868 n.).

177. **clavumque ad litora torquet:** "steers shorewards." Strictly speaking, the pilot would move the *clavus* ("tiller") *opposite* to the direction he wants to go; cf. (more straightforwardly) *proram pelagi detorquet ad undas* (165).

178. **gravis:** glossed by *iam . . . veste* (179). **ut:** for the word order cf. *sed* 5 n.

180. **summa:** = *summa loca* (cf. 168 n.).

illum et labentem Teucri et risere natantem
et salsos rident revomentem pectore fluctus.
   Hic laeta extremis spes est accensa duobus,
Sergesto Mnestheique, Gyan superare morantem.
Sergestus capit ante locum scopuloque propinquat,   185
nec tota tamen ille prior praeeunte carina;
parte prior, partim rostro premit aemula Pristis.
at media socios incedens nave per ipsos
hortatur Mnestheus: "nunc, nunc insurgite remis,

181-2. Multiple repetitions (of the main verb *risere . . . rident*; of the present participle in *labentem, natantem, revomentem*; and of *et . . . et . . . et*) imitate the repeated outbursts of laughter. Page's rendering captures the spirit beautifully: "They laughed at him tumbling and laughed at him swimming, and now they laugh at him belching up the brine." *Risere* is the perfect indicative of *rideo* (= *riserunt*, cf. 8 n.).

183-226. Sergestus and Mnestheus try to catch Gyas. Sergestus, having a slight lead, runs onto the rock. Mnestheus passes him, overtakes Gyas, and gains on the leader Cloanthus. Cloanthus, by making a vow to the sea-gods, just manages to come in first.

183-4. **spes . . . superare:** infinitive instead of the genitive of the gerund (AG §501) after the noun *spes* by analogy with the verb *spero, sperare*. **Mnesthei:** a Greek form, masculine dative singular, τῷ Μνησθεῖ from ὁ Μνησθεύς. Note that *ei* is a diphthong standing for the Greek ει, which forms a single long syllable (cf. *Mnestheus* 116 n.).

186. **ille:** the subject is still Sergestus; cf 39 n. **praĕĕunte:** Vergil shortens the diphthong *ae* before a vowel only here and at 7.524.

189-97. Mnestheus' speech to his crew is very loosely modeled on that of Antilochus to his horses at *Iliad* 23.402–16. But while Antilochus threatens his horses if they do not perform well, Mnestheus gallantly inspires his men to perform almost beyond their natural abilities by recalling their resiliance in past trials and by setting them the realistic challenge not of placing first, but of overtaking their immediate predecessors and not finishing last.

Hectorei socii, Troiae quos sorte suprema   190
delegi comites; nunc illas promite viris,
nunc animos, quibus in Gaetulis Syrtibus usi
Ionioque mari Maleaeque sequacibus undis.
non iam prima peto Mnestheus neque vincere certo
(quamquam o!—sed superent quibus hoc, Neptune, dedisti),
extremos pudeat rediisse: hoc vincite, cives,   196

---

190. **Hectŏrĕī socii:** Mnestheus urges his men to be worthy of their former champion. The Greek name combines with the Latin adjectival suffix *-e-* and regular first- and second-declension endings (*-us, -a, -um*) to produce a modifier that is functionally equivalent to the genitive of possession *Hectoris*. The suffix remains a separate (short, unaccented*) syllable (in contrast to the declension of purely Greek names: cf. *Menestheus* 116 n., *Menesthei* 183–4 n.). **Troiae quos:** for the word order cf. *sed* 5 n.; for the pronunciation of *Troiae*, cf. 61 n. **sorte suprema:** a dense expression. First, it is syntactically ambivalent between the simple ablative of time ("on Troy's final night") and of attendant circumstance (cf. 18 n.), as if that final night had been analogous to a lottery (the literal meaning of *sors*: cf. 132 n.) that would throw together groups of survivors whose future actions would determine what fate had in store for the remnants of Troy. Second, the image of a lottery is conflated with the idea that Mnestheus *chose* these men in particular to be his companions. Both points of view are characteristic of the poem as a whole: the formation of his band was due to chance, but now they must themselves strive to achieve the best possible outcome, as if their fate were in their own hands. And in the event their efforts are rewarded by *casus* (201), "chance."

191. **illas:** antecedent of *quibus* (192), and very emphatic. Mnestheus exhorts his men to show no ordinary courage, but to draw upon the heroism that got them through their greatest trials.

192. **usi:** = *usi estis* (cf. 23–4 n.). Forms of *sum* are only rarely omitted in the first (cf. 414 n.) or (as here) second persons, generally (as in both passages) when deponent verbs are involved; cf. 789 n.

193. **sequacibus:** "pursuing," as if the notoriously dangerous seas off Cape Maleas would not let a ship get away unharmed.

194. **prima:** = *prima loca* (cf. 168 n. and, for the "poetic plural," 98 n.). **Mnestheus:** added pleonastically* at the end with proud resignation – "No longer do I, Mnestheus, seek the first place." On the pronunciation and scansion cf. 116 n. **vincere certo:** cf. 155 n.

195. **quamquam o! – sed:** by breaking off his thought (aposiopesis*; see Ganiban on 1.135) Mnestheus emphasizes what he does not say and thus kindles the idea of victory in his men's minds.

196. **hoc:** cognate accusative (AG §390c) depending on *vincite* – "win *this* (victory)," i.e. avoid the stigma of finishing last. As often *hoc* points back to something just mentioned (AG §297a), namely *extremos rediisse*. **cives:** reminds the men and the reader that something more than sport is involved in these games (cf. 119 n., 202 n.).

et prohibete nefas." olli certamine summo
procumbunt: vastis tremit ictibus aerea puppis
subtrahiturque solum, tum creber anhelitus artus
aridaque ora quatit, sudor fluit undique rivis.   200
attulit ipse viris optatum casus honorem.
namque furens animi dum proram ad saxa suburget
interior spatioque subit Sergestus iniquo,
infelix saxis in procurrentibus haesit.
concussae cautes et acuto in murice remi   205
obnixi crepuere inlisaque prora pependit.
consurgunt nautae et magno clamore morantur
ferratasque trudes et acuta cuspide contos
expediunt fractosque legunt in gurgite remos.
at laetus Mnestheus successuque acrior ipso   210
agmine remorum celeri ventisque vocatis
prona petit maria et pelago decurrit aperto.
qualis spelunca subito commota columba,
cui domus et dulces latebroso in pumice nidi,

---

197. **nefas:** finishing last would be "the unspeakable" (in English we might have said "the unthinkable"); but the word is very strong for the context, more appalling than mere "disgrace" (*dedecus*) and with religious overtones. **olli:** = *illi*, here masc. nom. plur. (cf. 10 n.).

199. **subtrahiturque:** "is taken away," "disappears" – they move so swiftly that the ocean itself seems to rush to get behind them. **solum:** the water's surface is called "the ground," a reminiscence of the simile* in which these ships were compared to chariots and also of Vergil's Homeric model, the chariot race (141 n., 144–7 n.).

200. **rivis:** ablative of manner (AG §412b n.): the sweat flowed off him "in streams" (i.e. as heavily as streams do).

202. **furens:** Sergestus exhibits the recklessness that would make his descendant a revolutionary (121 n.). **animi:** locative depending on *furens* (AG §358).

203. **iniquo:** "insufficient."

205. **murice:** a rock-ridge that is jagged like the shell of the *murex*.

206. **crepuere:** perfect indicative of *crepo* (= *crepuerunt*, cf. 8 n.).

211. **agmine:** not the "line" of oars (so *OLD* s.v. 3) but their "movement" or "drive" (cf. *OLD* s.v. 1b); cf. 90 n.

212. **prona:** "shoreward" as opposed to *in altum*, "out to the (high) sea," but perhaps with the additional suggestion that the course was easy, with wind and tide in their favor.

213-17. The simile* is modeled on Ap. Rhod. *Arg.* 2.933–5 (Nelis (2001) 214).

214. **cui:** dative of possession (AG §373) with an understood verb *sunt* (cf. 23–4 n.).

fertur in arva volans plausumque exterrita pennis 215
dat tecto ingentem, mox aëre lapsa quieto
radit iter liquidum celeris neque commovet alas:
sic Mnestheus, sic ipsa fuga secat ultima Pristis
aequora, sic illam fert impetus ipse volantem.
et primum in scopulo luctantem deserit alto 220
Sergestum brevibusque vadis frustraque vocantem
auxilia et fractis discentem currere remis.
inde Gyan ipsamque ingenti mole Chimaeram
consequitur; cedit, quoniam spoliata magistro est.
    Solus iamque ipso superest in fine Cloanthus: 225
quem petit et summis adnixus viribus urget.
tum vero ingeminat clamor cunctique sequentem
instigant studiis, resonatque fragoribus aether.
hi proprium decus et partum indignantur honorem
ni teneant, vitamque volunt pro laude pacisci; 230
hos successus alit: possunt, quia posse videntur.
et fors aequatis cepissent praemia rostris,

215-16. **plausum ... dat:** = *plaudit* (cf. 139 n.).

218-19. **ultima ... aequora:** "the final leg." **impetus:** "momentum" in both a physical and a psychological sense.

221. **brevibus ... vadis:** "shallows" (so *brevia* alone: cf. Ganiban on 1.111).

224. **cedit:** the subject is *Chimaera* (understood).

225. **Solus iamque:** *iamque* usually comes as the first word in a line (49 n.), but here it is postponed (5 n.) to emphasize *solus*.

227-43. The contest for second place.

227. **ingeminat:** intransitive, "doubles (itself)."

228. **instigant studiis:** *instigo* is from the same root as *stimulus* (= *sti(g)mulus*) "goad." The repetition of *st* in the two words represents the metaphorical* goading that the spectators repeatedly apply to the crews. On the plural *studiis* cf. 148 n.

229. **hi ... hos (231):** *hic* is often repeated in contrasts (*OLD* s.v. 13) – thus *hi* refers to Cloanthus' crew, *hos* to that of Mnestheus. **proprium ... partum:** i.e. in anticipation. Cloanthus' crew regard the victory as already theirs, already won.

231. **possunt, quia posse videntur:** *possunt* and *posse* are used absolutely (i.e. without a complement), "they can"; with *videntur* understand *sibi*, "they seem to themselves to ... ," "they think that they ... ." (*OLD* s.v. *uideo* 21). A famous *sententia*; cf. Livy 22.3.4 *dum se putant vincere, vicere.*

232. **fors:** "perhaps": not in fact an adverb (so *OLD* s.v. *fors*²) but an idiomatic use of the noun related to expressions like *forsan, forsitan, fortasse.*

ni palmas ponto tendens utrasque Cloanthus
fudissetque preces divosque in vota vocasset:
"di, quibus imperium est pelagi, quorum aequora curro,   235
vobis laetus ego hoc candentem in litore taurum
constituam ante aras voti reus, extaque salsos
proiciam in fluctus et vina liquentia fundam."
dixit, eumque imis sub fluctibus audiit omnis
Nereidum Phorcique chorus Panopeaque virgo,   240
et pater ipse manu magna Portunus euntem
impulit: illa noto citius volucrique sagitta
ad terram fugit et portu se condidit alto.

---

233. **palmas ... utrasque:** the plural of *uterque* frequently means "both" (*OLD* s.v. 3b). **ponto:** dative of end of motion (cf. 34 n.), here with an uncompounded verb.

234. **in vota vocasset:** ≈ 514; Cloanthus summons the gods "into (witness of) his vows."

235. **aequora:** cognate accusative with *currunt* (AG §390; cf. 1.524).

236. **laetus:** ≈ *libens* (cf. 3.438).

237. **voti reus:** "condemned (to payment) of my vow." A vow (*votum*) is a promise to do something for the gods if they first do something for you; when they have done their part you become *reus* (or, in prose, *damnatus*) *voti* (genitive of the charge or penalty, AG §352a) until the vow is fulfilled.

237-8. **extaque ... fundam:** ≈ 775-6.

238. **proiciam:** the verb means, simply, "to throw" or even "to fling" and is often used in contexts where the action implies contempt. At the same time, it is evidently the correct word to denote the offering of a sacrifice to a sea god by throwing it into the water (so Servius; cf. Varro, *R.R.* 1.29.3). **vina:** perhaps "libations of wine," but cf. *vinaque* 98 n. **liquentia:** from *liqueo;* elsewhere Vergil has *liquentia* from the deponent *liquor*.

240. **Panopeaque virgo:** = 825. Panope appears in Homer's catalogue of Nereids (*Il.* 18.45). Cf. *Panopesque* 300 n.

241. **manu magna:** a typically epic phrase (*Il.* 15.694; Ennius, *Ann.* fr. 581 in Skutsch (1985), fr. 541 in Warmington (1935-40); cf. 487 *ingenti manu*). Gods and heroes are conceived as being larger than mere mortals. Ap. Rhod. 2.598-600 (Nelis (2001) 223-6). **Portunus:** the Roman god of harbors (< *portus*), identified with the Greek Palaemon (823).

242. A fully dactylic line imitating the speed of the ship's movement after the push, which is emphasized by the diaeresis* after *impulit*. **illa:** Cloanthus' ship; cf. 75 n.

243. **condidit:** the perfect connotes rapidity (136-50) – the boat shoots forward and, almost before you can see it, has taken its berth in the harbor.

Tum satus Anchisa cunctis ex more vocatis
victorem magna praeconis voce Cloanthum 245
declarat viridique advelat tempora lauro,
muneraque in navis ternos optare iuvencos
vinaque et argenti magnum dat ferre talentum.
ipsis praecipuos ductoribus addit honores:
victori chlamydem auratam, quam plurima circum 250
purpura Maeandro duplici Meliboea cucurrit,

---

244. **Tum sătus Anchisa:** = 424. The adjective *sătus*, though often (as here) used substantively as a poetic synonym of *filius*, was originally the perf. part. of *sero* ("to sow"); it thus takes the ablative of source (*Anchisā*, AG §403.2a) rather than the genitive of possession.

244-67. Aeneas distributes rewards to all the crews and special prizes to the captains – a robe embroidered with the story of Ganymede, a suit of armor, and a pair of vases and silver cups.

246. **declarat:** = *declaverat* by syncope.*

247-8. **muneraque:** cf. 109 n. **ternos:** cf. 61–2 n. **optare . . . ferre:** Vergil commonly uses the infinitive of purpose after the verb *do* (AG §460a). The syntax varies, however, in different passages. Here it is possible to detect the influence of a Greek phrase (δῶκε δ' ἄγειν, Hom. *Il.* 23.512) that is found in the model for this entire scene. **vina:** perhaps "casks of wine," but cf. *vinaque* 98 n.; at any rate, not different "wines" (i.e. kinds of wine) as in English.

250-7. An ecphrasis* of the winner's prize, a cloak on which is embroidered an image of the abduction of Ganymede. The passage was imitated by Statius (*Theb.* 1.548–51) and Valerius Flaccus (*Arg.* 2.409–17). The significance of the image described is debated: does it depict abduction as an emblem of human loss and divine caprice (Putnam (1998) 55–74) or apotheosis as an emblem of Cloanthus' victory and of ultimate Trojan success (Hardie (2002))?

250-1. **chlamydem:** the *chlamys* was a Greek cloak of which the Romans rather disapproved (Cicero, *Rab. Post.* 27, Val. Max. 3.6.2–3). Putnam (1998) 222 n.14 lists several ominous *chlamydes* in the *Aeneid*. At the same time this garment's colors (gold and purple) are those of the *vestis triumphalis* in historical times, and its border resembles that of a senator's toga (see below). Vergil thus projects contemporary customs back into the heroic period, simultaneously using exoticism to suggest chronological distance. **auratam:** in Vergil's day an especially luxurious garment might be made of fabric interwoven with gold threads. **circum:** i.e. around the edge of the garment, as a border. **plurima . . . purpura:** connotes both the richness of the hue and breadth of the stripes. In historical times a toga with a broad purple border denoted senatorial rank, while a narrow stripe signaled membership in the equestrian order. **Maeandro:** a river in Asia Minor famous for its twists and turns. Its name became a common noun for any sort of winding road, whether literal or metaphorical*, including both the rhetorical and, as here, graphic varieties. The name is also, of course, the source of the English derivative "meander." **Meliboea:** Meliboea in Thessaly was an important source of exotic purple dye (Lucr. *DRN* 2.500). *Meliboeus* is an adjectival form (cf. Harrison on 10.156 *Aeneia puppis*).

intextusque puer frondosa regius Ida
velocis iaculo cervos cursuque fatigat
acer, anhelanti similis, quem praepes ab Ida
sublimem pedibus rapuit Iovis armiger uncis: 255
longaevi palmas nequiquam ad sidera tendunt
custodes, saevitque canum latratus in auras.
at qui deinde locum tenuit virtute secundum,
levibus huic hamis consertam auroque trilicem
loricam, quam Demoleo detraxerat ipse 260
victor apud rapidum Simoenta sub Ilio alto,
donat habere, viro decus et tutamen in armis.
vix illam famuli Phegeus Sagarisque ferebant

---

252. **puer ... regius:** i.e. Ganymede (cf. 1.28); the same phrase denotes Ascanius at 1.677–8. Ganymede is apparently represented twice on the *chlamys*, first hunting, then being carried away, a common means of telling a story in the visual arts.

254. **praepes:** a technical term from augury meaning "a bird of good omen." According to Aulus Gellius (*NA* 7.6), Vergil was criticized by Julius Hyginus, the first director of Augustus' Palatine Library, for using the word in a non-augural context. But Vergil often draws on specialized diction, especially from the religious sphere, as a means of achieving a suitably elevated style. For an argument that augury is in fact thematically relevant to the passage see Hardie (2002) 345–6.

255. **sublimem:** proleptic*. **armiger:** because he carries the thunder-bolt (Hor. *Carm*. 4.4.1 *ministrum fulminis alitem*) – so, "bearer of weapons," not of body-armor.

256. **sidera:** perhaps a reference to the identification of Ganymede with the constellation Aquarius (Eratosthenes, *Catasterismi* 26, Hyginus 2.29, Ovid, *Fast.* 2.145).

257. **in auras:** "to the sky." The dogs are depicted as gazing upwards and barking at the disappearing eagle.

258. **deinde:** cf. 14 n.

259-60. **lēvibus:** "smooth" (not *lĕvibus* "light"). **auroque trilicem | loricam:** ≈ 3.467. "*lorica* is the common word for 'cuirass' in Latin, supposedly derived from its original material of leather (*lora*, 'thongs', cf. Varro *L.L.* 5.116); those of the *Aeneid* seem to reflect the Roman armor of Vergil's day in being largely of chain-mail" (Harrison on 10.485).

261-2. **Iliŏ alto:** no elision*, but hiatus* with correption,* in imitation of Homer's metrical practice. **viro:** not just "man" but, as often, "hero"; a poetic use of the dative of purpose, depending on *decus*, "an adornment (fit) for a hero" (cf. AG §382.2).

263. **illam:** emphasizes the heroic size and weight of that particular breastplate, a relic of the Trojan War; cf. 404–5, 410–11. The idea is Homeric, and the line as a whole is modeled on *Il.* 5.303 where Diomedes alone hefts a stone "such as no pair of men could lift, such as men are today." **Phegeus Sagarisque:** both will be killed by Turnus (9.575, 765). A second Phegeus appears at 12.371. There is a Trojan Phegeus at *Il.* 5.9. The name is disyllabic (cf. *Mnestheus* 116 n.).

multiplicem conixi umeris; indutus at olim
Demoleos cursu palantis Troas agebat.   265
tertia dona facit geminos ex aere lebetas
cymbiaque argento perfecta atque aspera signis.
iamque adeo donati omnes opibusque superbi
puniceis ibant evincti tempora taenis,
cum saevo e scopulo multa vix arte revulsus   270
amissis remis atque ordine debilis uno
inrisam sine honore ratem Sergestus agebat.
qualis saepe viae deprensus in aggere serpens,

---

264. **indutus at:** for the word order cf. *sed* 5 n.

266. **geminos ex aere lebetas:** "twin caldrons (made) of bronze." The adjective *aereus* ("brazen") becomes a cretic in the form required (*āĕrĕōs*, masculine accusative plural) and so will not fit into a hexameter line. The adverbial expression *ex aere* ("(made) of bronze") is so closely held in between *geminos* and *lebetas* that it can take the place of an attributive adjective. Such phrases are common in Latin poetry, which imitates Greek word order in this respect. **lebetas:** a Greek form, τοὺς λέβητας, masculine accusative plural from ὁ λέβης.

267. **cymbia:** the κυμβίον was a type of Greek drinking cup. **argento perfecta atque aspera signis:** the elegant word-order of this phrase (chiasmus*) connotes the fine craftsmanship of the cups themselves. **aspera signis:** i.e. embossed with so many "figures" (*signis*, ablative of specification, AG §418) that they are "rough" (*aspera*) to the touch.

268-85. *Sergestus, with oars broken but using his sails, manages to get home and receives a consolation prize.*

268-70. **iamque adeo . . . cum:** see 49 n., 159–60 n. "Vergil frequently places *adeo* second in a clause to strengthen the preceding word. Here it emphasizes the transition in the narrative, which is marked by *iamque*, as being an important one" (Ganiban on 2.567; cf. 864–7 n.).

268. **donati:** "having been gifted," i.e. "having received their prizes" (cf. 305 n.). **opibus:** ablative of cause (AG §404) with *superbi*.

269. **taenis:** a rare contraction (AG §603c) for *taeniis*.

271. **ordine debilis uno:** "maimed on one side," lit. "(rendered) hard to handle (*debilis* = *dehabilis*) with respect to one row" (ablative of specification, AG §418) of oars, i.e. the ones on the portside, which broke against the rocks, 202–9.

273-81. With its portside oars broken and useless the ship can only wriggle along like a crippled serpent. On the simile* see Swallow (1952–53) and Rose (1982–83).

273. **qualis saepe:** a compressed form of *qualis, ut saepe fit*. Here, paradoxically, the strange idea that the image of a crippled snake is something that one sees "often" emphasizes the strangeness and peculiarity of the crippled ship's effort to drag itself to port. **aggere:** Roman roads were raised above ground level and banked with a rampart.

aerea quem obliquum rota transiit aut gravis ictu
seminecem liquit saxo lacerumque viator;   275
nequiquam longos fugiens dat corpore tortus
parte ferox ardensque oculis et sibila colla
arduus attollens; pars vulnere clauda retentat
nexantem nodis seque in sua membra plicantem:
tali remigio navis se tarda movebat;   280
vela facit tamen et velis subit ostia plenis.
Sergestum Aeneas promisso munere donat
servatam ob navem laetus sociosque reductos.
olli serva datur operum haud ignara Minervae,
Cressa genus, Pholoe, geminique sub ubere nati.   285
  Hoc pius Aeneas misso certamine tendit

---

274. **aerea quem:** for the word order cf. *sed* 5 n. **gravis ictu:** a kind of enallage*, equivalent in meaning to *gravi ictu*: the *viator* (275) has been "*heavy in beating* (ablative of specification, AG §418) the snake, i.e. he has dealt the snake *a heavy blow,* and has left him half dead; cf. *gravis . . . dictis* 387 n.

275. **saxo:** ablative of means, to be taken closely with *lacerumque.*

276. **dat . . . tortus:** ≈ *se torquet* (or, in prose, *se flectit*), "it writhes" (cf. 139 n.).

277. **sibilă colla:** a "poetic plural" (cf. *vinaque* 98 n.) that fits this metrical position where the equivalent singular (*sībĭlŭm cōllŭm*) would not.

278. **arduus:** predicate adjective, grammatically modifying the subject but logically referring neither to it nor (adverbially: cf. *cita* 32–3 n.) to the participle *attollens* (or any finite verb: cf. 480 n.), but to the direct object *colla:* "raising his slithery neck up high"; cf. 567.

278-9. Note the multiple instances of alliteration* (*ar*duus *a*ttollens, *p*ars . . . *p*licantem, *n*exantem *n*odis, *s*e . . . *s*ua) and rhyme (nex*antem* . . . plic*antem*), all suggesting the snake's repeated struggles.

282. **promisso munere:** everyone was to have some reward (70, 305; cf. 109 n.).

284. **olli:** = *illi* (cf. 10 n.). **datūr:** the final syllable is short by nature and would normally remain short before a vowel, but it is treated as long in arsis* (see Appendix A). **operum . . . Minervae:** *operum* is objective genitive depending on *ignara*. The "works of Minerva" are weaving and spinning.

285. **nati:** a poetic equivalent of *filii* (see 383 n.).

Second Event: The Foot Race (286–361)

Vergil's second event (of four) is modeled on Homer's fourth (of eight), which is also a foot race (*Il.* 23.740–97).

286-314. Aeneas goes to a grassy spot shaped like a circus and offers prizes for a foot-race, which many competitors enter.

286. **Hoc . . . misso certamine:** "this (i.e. the previous) contest having been dismissed." *Misso* is a poetic* variation on the compound (*dimisso*) that one would expect in prose. *Certamine* stands by metonymy* for the contestants.

gramineum in campum, quem collibus undique curvis
cingebant silvae, mediaque in valle theatri
circus erat; quo se multis cum milibus heros
consessu medium tulit exstructoque resedit.   290
hic, qui forte velint rapido contendere cursu,
invitat pretiis animos, et praemia ponit.
undique conveniunt Teucri mixtique Sicani,
Nisus et Euryalus primi,
Euryalus forma insignis viridique iuventa,   295

---

288. **media ... in valle:** not (as often) "in middle of the valley" but "in the valley that lay in the midst (of these surrounding hills)"; cf. 1–2 n.

288-9. **theatri | circus:** *theatri* is genitive of apposition (cf. 52 n.). The phrase indicates an oblong course surrounded by slopes on which the spectators could sit and which made it into a natural theater — like the valley of the Circus Maximus in Rome; cf. the natural *scaena* in the Libyan harbor (1.164). On the theatrical aspect of the games and its relation to the theme of sacrifice see Feldherr (1995).

289. **quo:** the adverb, "where," best translated here as a connective relative (AG §308f), "and there," "and to this place . . . ."

290. **consessu:** "the (seated) crowd" (cf. 340); ablative of specification (AG §418) with *medium*. Aeneas chose a place where he would be "central with respect to the crowd," i.e. in the middle of the crowd; cf. 1–2 n. **exstructo:** perfect passive participle of *exstruo*, used absolutely as a noun only here, in the ablative of place where, perhaps of a platform built for Aeneas, or else simply of an elevated position within the valley that formed the circus.

291. **hic:** the adverb, "here." **velint:** subjunctive in a conditional relative clause (AG §519) because Aeneas does not invite "those who do wish" but "any who may wish" (486).

293. **mixtique Sicani:** "Sicanians mixed in (among the Trojans)." Grammatically, *mixti* modifies *Sicani* alone, but logically it applies to both the crowd of Trojans and Sicilians together. The intermingling of the spectators and contestants presumably anticipates the foundation of Segesta as a Trojan setlement in Sicily (709–18, 749–61).

294. **Nisus et Euryalus primi:** ≈ 9.467, also a half-line, i.e. one that was left unfinished at the time of Vergil's death. Donatus, in his *Life of Vergil*, says that on his deathbed Vergil asked that the *Aeneid* be burned, but he ultimately left it in the hands of Varius and Tucca to edit without adding anything that Vergil would not have added, leaving any incomplete verses just as they found them. There are roughly 58 such verses in the entire poem (the number is disputed because some original "half-lines" may have been completed by scribes). For more on half-lines, see O'Hara (2010).

First to enter the race, Nisus and Euryalus will be at the center of a controversy over who finishes first. Their sporting adventures here prefigure their military exploits later in the poem (9.176–502). For the *eu* diphthong in Euryalus' name cf. *Mnestheus* 116 n.

295. **formā:** ablative of specification (AG §418) with *insignis*.

Nisus amore pio pueri; quos deinde secutus
regius egregia Priami de stirpe Diores;
hunc Salius simul et Patron, quorum alter Acarnan,
alter ab Arcadio Tegeaeae sanguine gentis:
tum duo Trinacrii iuvenes, Helymus Panopesque,   300
adsueti silvis, comites senioris Acestae;
multi praeterea, quos fama obscura recondit.
Aeneas quibus in mediis sic deinde locutus:
"accipite haec animis laetasque advertite mentes.

---

296. **amore pio:** Vergil presents Nisus' love for Euryalus in idealized "platonic" terms of admiration for his character rather than physical attraction. **pueri:** objective genitive (AG §348) with *amore*. **quos:** connective relative (AG §308f); translate "and them" (not "whom"). **deinde:** cf. 14 n. **secutus:** = *secutus est* (cf. 23–4 n.).

297. **Diores:** in Homer the name belongs not to a son of Priam but to a Greek captain (*Il.* 2.622) felled by Peirus the Thracian (*Il.* 4.517) and survived by his son Automedon (*Il.* 17.429, 474). Vergil's character will, together with his brother Amycus, become a victim of Turnus (12.509–12).

298. **hunc:** Diores (297), direct object of *secutus* <*est*> (296). **Salius ... Patron:** a pair of Greeks who evidently joined Aeneas when he visited Helenus at Buthrotum in book 3.

298-9. **alter ... alter:** "(the) one (was) ... (and) the other (was)," with understood *erat*. One would expect the order to follow that of the names given in 298, but in earlier versions of the Aeneas legend Salius is an Arcadian who eventually founded the *Salii,* a college of dancing priests in the Roman state religion (a story told by Servius *ad* 8.285 and attributed to Varro by Isidore, *Orig.* 18.50), while Patron was an Acarnanian sent by Helenus to accompany Aeneas (Dion. Hal. 1.51).

299. **Arcadio Tegeaeae sanguine gentis:** understand *est* (cf. 23–4 n.). Note the artful word order, on the one hand parallel (adjective, adjective, noun, noun) and on the other interlocking (ablative, genitive, ablative, genitive), the latter figure an instance of chiasmus.*

300. **tum duo Trinacrii iuvenes, Helymus Panopesque:** the Sicilian Helymus shares a name with one of Aeneas' Trojan companions (73 n.), which probably means that he is to be regarded as the eponymous ancestor of the Elymi, a Sicilian people who inhabited the vicinity of Mt. Eryx and were thought by some to be descended from the Trojans (Thuc. 6.2.3, Dion. Hal. *Ant. Rom.* 1.47, 1.52; cf. 24 n.). In Homer Panopeus is the father of Epeius (victor in the boxing match at *Il.* 23.665) and the eponymous hero of a town in Phocis (*Il.* 2.520, 17.307; *Od.* 11.581). *Panopes* therefore is a heroic name associated with athleticism and foundation legend. Cf. 240 and 825 *Panopaeaque virgo.*

301. **silvis:** dative with the compound *adsueti* (301; cf. AG §370, 383–4).

303. **Aeneas quibus in mediis:** for the word order cf. *sed* 5 n. Take *quibus* as a connective relative (AG §308f), "and in their (not 'whose') midst." Here the contrast is between Aeneas as patron of the event and all the contestants. On *mediis* see 1–2 n. **sic deinde locutus:** = 14 (cf. n.); *locutus* = *locutus* <*est*> (cf. 23–4 n.).

nemo ex hoc numero mihi non donatus abibit.   305
Gnosia bina dabo levato lucida ferro
spicula caelatamque argento ferre bipennem;
omnibus hic erit unus honos. tres praemia primi
accipient flavaque caput nectentur oliva.
primus equum phaleris insignem victor habeto;   310
alter Amazoniam pharetram plenamque sagittis
Threiciis, lato quam circum amplectitur auro
balteus et tereti subnectit fibula gemma;

---

305. **mihi non donatus:** the negative goes very closely with the participle (on which cf. 268 n.). *Mihi* is dative of agent (AG §374–5) governed by (*non*) *donatus*, "ungifted by me," "without a gift from me"; but, as Williams (1960) well observes *ad loc.*, "the dative of agent . . . is very often in some other kind of dative relationship to the sentence" and that "here *mihi* is as much ethic ("I will see to it") as agent with *donatus*." For the ethic or ethical dative cf. AG §380.

306. **bina:** cf. 61–2 n. **dabo:** understand a dative of indirect object such as *cuique*, "to each (contestant)." **levato . . . ferro:** ablative of description (AG §415a) modifying *spicula* and referring to the iron tips, which balanced the long wooden shafts of the spear for easier handling and more effective throwing.

307. **spicula:** "arrows" by synecdoche*. **caelatam . . . argento:** "embossed with silver," probably on the handle; *argento* is ablative of material with no preposition, as often in poetry (AG §403.2, n. 1). **ferre:** after *dabo* (247–8 n.).

308. **unus:** "alike" or "common" to all (cf. 616 *una*). **praemia:** here "special prizes" opposed to those that all will receive (cf. 305 n.).

309. **flava . . . oliva:** Latin color terms generally have to do with saturation and intensity rather than exact hue. *Flavus* is used of gold, blond hair, a lion's coat, and the Tiber, things that are yellow but tending towards tan or even, as here, olive. **caput:** a "retained" accusative of specification (cf. 135 n.) with *nectentur*, "they shall have their head(s) crowned."

310. **insignem:** cf. 295 n. **habeto:** future imperative. Such forms were not in common use, but were familiar from archaic*, and particularly legal and religious, texts; here they lend a formal tone to Aeneas' proclamation.

311. **alter:** "second" (*OLD* s.v. *alter*[1] 3d).

311-12. **Amazoniam pharetram plenamque sagittis | Threïciis:** the enclitic *-que* grammatically links the two adjectives ("a quiver (that was) Amazonian *and* full of Thracian arrows"), but the two exotic ethnic names form the logical pair. The Amazons and Thracians were allies of the Trojans against the Greeks (1.490–1, 3.13–14) as well as famous for their archery. Note that *phărĕtram* here receives its natural pronunciation, as also at 558; but cf. 501 n.

312-13. **lato quam:** for the word order cf. *sed* 5 n. *Quam* is the direct object of *amplectitur* and *subnectit*; its antecedent is *pharetram* (311). **lato . . . auro . . . tereti . . . gemma:** ablative of material (cf. 302 n.) modifying *balteus*. **circum:** adverbial, modifying *amplectitur*. **tereti . . . gemma:** ablative of material modifying *fibula*.

tertius Argolica hac galea contentus abito."
Haec ubi dicta, locum capiunt signoque repente   315
corripiunt spatia audito limenque relinquunt,
effusi nimbo similes. simul ultima signant,
primus abit longeque ante omnia corpora Nisus

---

314. **abito:** cf. *habeto* 310 n.

315. **Haec ubi dicta:** cf. 32 n.

315-39. Nisus takes a long lead followed by Salius and Euryalus, then by Helymus with Diores close behind. As Nisus nears the goal he falls, but manages to trip Salius so that Euryalus comes in first.

316. **corripiunt spatia:** for the metaphor* cf. 144–5 n. *Spatia* properly means "laps" (*Geo.* 1.513), but here (and 325) it is either the two "legs" (out and back) of a one-lap race or else simply the areas traversed by the contestants over the entire course. **limen:** "starting line," an easily understood, but not very common metaphor*.

317. **effusi nimbo similes:** *nimbo* is dative with *similis* (AG §384), but the runners are like a cloud in their "bursting" or, more literally, "being poured out" from the starting line, which makes them more like the raindrops that burst from a cloud, as in *effusus nubibus imber* (*Geo.* 4.312), than like the cloud itself. Vergil presumably remembered the earlier passage and varied it to produce a more striking expression. **simul ultima signant,:** punctuation is debated among editors. Those who take *simul ultima signant* as the conclusion of the sentence that precedes it translate "and they all together mark (with their eyes) the far end of the course" (*ultima=ultima loca*; cf. 168 n.), which is an unusual meaning of *signare*. Those who take the phrase as the beginning of a new sentence treat *simul* as *simul ac* or *simul atque*, "as soon as they mark (with their feet) the far end of the course. . . ." This use of *simul* is not uncommon, and the result is a livelier and more pointed narration: instead of standing and looking at the far end of the course, the runners have reached it as soon as it is mentioned. In addition, beginning a new sentence with *simul* avoids bringing the narrative to a momentary halt at the end of the line.

318-26. These lines are beautifully effective in suggesting the relative speed of the various contestants. Williams (1960) well notes the identical pattern of dactyl-spondee-spondee-dactyl in the first four feet of 318, 319, and 320, and the presence of single words of dactylic shape filling the fourth foot of each line (318 *omnia,* 319 *fulminis,* 320 *proximus*). All of this produces a vivid impression of rapid movement. In the first two of these lines, which describe the lead runner, Nisus, the impression of speed is heightened by the presence of fifth-foot dactyls as well (318 *corpora,* 319 *ocior*). But the following line, which describes the second-place runner, Salius, ends unexpectedly with the ponderous, slow-footed, four-syllable word *intervallo*. This is a quite rare device that Vergil generally reserves for some particular effect; here he drives home the great difference in speed between the runners in first and second place. By contrast, a different mixture of dactyls and spondees coupled with the repetition *calcemque . . . calce* in 324 suggest how very closely the fifth-place runner, Diores, is following Helymus, the runner ahead of him: and the three long syllables of

emicat et ventis et fulminis ocior alis;
proximus huic, longo sed proximus intervallo,   320
insequitur Salius; spatio post deinde relicto
tertius Euryalus;
Euryalumque Helymus sequitur; quo deinde sub ipso
ecce volat calcemque terit iam calce Diores

---

incumbens that open the following line may suggest the sound of Diores' approaching footsteps to Helymus as he tries to maintain his slim lead. Finally, the two short, unaccented* syllables of *prior* (326) suggest the margin by which Diores might have slipped ahead (*elapsus* 326) of Helymus, if the course had been just a bit longer.

It is remarkable that in the middle of this virtuoso display we find one of those most visible tokens of the poem's unfinished state, a half-line (322). Williams (1960) again notes that the name of Euryalus, "one of the most tenderly drawn characters in Virgil," occurs in three unfinished lines (289, 322, 9.467), "almost as though Virgil found it hard to get the words he wanted for Euryalus."

318. **corpora:** synecdoche* for *viri*, emphasizing physical beauty over other qualities (but cf. 344 and 729 n.).

319. **fulminis . . . alis:** "the wings of lightning," i.e. "the winged lightning."

320. **proximus:** "next," but (contrary to what English derivatives like "proximity" would suggest) without implying closeness. *Secundus*, on the other hand (again, unlike "second"), does imply closeness: thus Horace (*Carm.* 1.12.19) says that there is nothing "second" (*secundum*) to Jupiter, but Pallas is "next" in honor (*proximos occupavit honores*). **longo sed:** for the word order cf. *sed* 5 n. **intērvāllō:** on the effect of this impressive spondaic* line, see 318–26 n.

321-3. **deinde . . . deinde:** cf. 14 n.

322. **tertius Euryalus:** understand *insequitur* from the previous line or, simply, *est* (cf. 23-4 n.).

323. **quo:** connective relative, to be translated "and . . . him" rather than "whom." **sub:** not "under" but "behind" (*OLD* 7); cf. *subsequor*, "to follow close behind," and English "subsequent." Although both Helymus and Diores are running as fast as they can, the ablative with *sub* (which denotes place where, not motion towards) suggests that they are in a fixed position relative to one another; cf. 327 n. **ipso:** intensive pronoun, grammatically modifying *quo*, but the emphasis that it contributes to the Latin sentence is best reflected in idiomatic English by an adverb modifying a different word (here *sub*): not "and behind him himself" but "and right behind him"; cf. 332 n.

324. **calcem . . . terit . . . calce:** *calcem terere* is idiomatic Latin for "to tread on (someone's) heel(s)" (i.e. to follow very closely). The repetition *calcem . . . calce*, as in similar phrases (see 429 n., 10.361), is to emphasize just how close the contestants are. The line is modeled on a passage from the funeral games of Patroclus (*Il.* 23.763–4).

incumbens umero, spatia et si plura supersint   325
transeat elapsus prior ambiguumque relinquat.
iamque fere spatio extremo fessique sub ipsam
finem adventabant, levi cum sanguine Nisus
labitur infelix, caesis ut forte iuvencis
fusus humum viridisque super madefecerat herbas.   330

325-6. **spatia et:** for the word order cf. *sed* 5 n. **supersint | transeat . . . relinquat:** logically, the conditional clause introduced by *si* (325) is contrary to fact ("if more laps (had) *remained*," which was not the case, " . . . he would (have) . . . "); and this normally calls for the imperfect or pluperfect subjunctive (in primary or secondary sequence, respectively, AG §517). Instead, Vergil uses the present subjunctive, representing the situation from Diores' point of view as a future less vivid condition ("if more laps *should* remain," as if somehow this might be the case, "he *would* . . ."), with the race still undecided and victory still within his grasp; cf. 1.58, 6.292-4, 11.912-14. **prior:** predicate adjective following *elapsus*, "having slipped 'ahead.'"

327-38. In Homer's footrace Athena causes Ajax to slip in some dung so that Odysseus is able to win (*Il.* 23.771-86). The low comedy of the Homeric episode (noted with disapproval by ancient commentators) is transformed here in two ways. First, Vergil maintains epic decorum by having Nisus slip not in dung but in blood. Second, he links the episode to one of the central themes of the book and of the poem by specifying that this blood is the result of sacrifice (*caesis* 329, *sacro* 333). When Nisus then trips Salius so that his beloved Euryalus may win the race, the reader is thus invited to reinterpret his accidental fall and unsportsmanlike act as a "sacrifice" on behalf of his friend, one that anticipates his more tragic sacrifice at 9.384-445.

327-8. **iamque fere . . . cum:** see 159-60 n. *Fere* with temporal adverbs makes the indication of time only approximate (Perkell on 3.135; cf. 835-8 n.). **spatio extremo:** not "at the last course" but "at the end of the course." "Superlatives (and more rarely Comparatives) denoting order and succession . . . usually designate not *what object,* but *what part of it,* is meant" (AG §293). **sub ipsam | finem:** again *sub* expresses closeness (cf. 323 n.), but here with the accusative it means that the runner (in this case, Nisus) is moving towards his goal, getting closer and closer. Note that *finem* here is feminine (cf. 384, 2.554, 3.145, 12.793), not masculine (as in 82, 225, 630, and regularly elsewhere).

328. **lēvi:** from *lēvis* ("smooth" and so "slippery"), not *lĕvis* ("lightweight"). **cum:** the conjunction ("when"),

329. **caesis . . . iuvencis:** ablative absolute with causal force (AG §420.2): the slaughtering explains why the pool of blood was there. **caesis ut:** for the word order cf. *sed* 5 n. Commentators differ on whether *ut* here means "as" or "where" (*OLD* s.v. 24 a–b).

330. **fusus:** understand *sanguis* (from *sanguine* 328). **super:** adverbial, modifying *fusus*, "on top of" (*OLD* s.v. *super*² 2); the compound verb *superfundo* ("to pour on or over") is mainly prosaic.

hic iuvenis iam victor ovans vestigia presso
haud tenuit titubata solo, sed pronus in ipso
concidit immundoque fimo sacroque cruore.
non tamen Euryali, non ille oblitus amorum:
nam sese opposuit Salio per lubrica surgens,   335
ille autem spissa iacuit revolutus harena:
emicat Euryalus et munere victor amici
prima tenet, plausuque volat fremituque secundo.
post Helymus subit et nunc tertia palma Diores.

331-2. **hic:** the adverb ("here"), not the pronoun ("this"). **presso ... solo:** ablative absolute with concessive force (AG §420.3); although he tried to plant his feet as firmly as possible, they tottered (*titubata*) and he could not hold (*haud tenuit*) his balance. **titubata:** = *quae titubaverunt,* as if deponent; cf. 4.38 *placito,* 6.746 *concretam.*

332. **ipso:** cf. 323 n. Here the intensive pronoun modifies *fimo* and *cruore* (333), but in idiomatic English is best rendered adverbially instead of adjectivally ("*right* in the ..." instead of "in the *very* ...").

334. **non ... non:** the repetition creates a parallel that is best conveyed in English by repeating the verb *oblitus* (= *oblitus est:* cf. 23–4 n.). **Euryali ... amorum:** genitives with a verb of forgetting (AG §350b). Though one is singular and one plural, the words are not only grammatically parallel, but also synonymous, the plural of *amor* being a colloquial expression for one's "beloved." **ille:** the pleonastic* use of the pronoun (see 39 n.) emphasizes Nisus' devotion: *others* in this situation might think only of themselves, but *not he.*

335. **Salio:** dative of indirect object with *sese opposuit.* **lubrica:** = *lubrica loca* (cf. 168 n.).

336. **ille:** Salius; see 75 n. **spissa ... harena:** the image of "hard-packed sand" is at odds with the *gramineum campum* previously mentiond as the venue of the race (287), and is perhaps meant to suggest the arena (the derivative of *harena, -ae,* "sand") as it was in Vergil's day. **iacuit revolutus:** the combination of perfect participle plus finite verb expresses the sequence of action: "after being spun down, he lay there ...."

337. **Euryalūs:** cf. *datūr* 284 n. **munere ... amici:** ablative of cause + genitive (by analogy with *causā, gratiā,* etc.), "by the grace of (or) thanks to his friend" (*OLD* s.v. *munus* 6b).

338. **prima:** cf. 194 n. **plausu ... fremituque secundo:** ablative of attendant circumstance (cf. 18 n.).

339. **post:** adverbial. **subit:** cf. *sub* 323 n., 327–8 n. The verb means "to come next, succeed (in position or order)" and "to come in as a substitute or replacement" (*OLD* s.v. *subeo* 8 and 9b), and both meanings seem relevant here; cf. 346. Two closely related meanings, "to grow up (so as to fill a vacant space)" and "to succeed to the place of" (9a and c), are more broadly relevant to one of the larger themes of this book (cf. introductory note). **tertia palma:** predicate nominative. A double metonymy* is involved: Diores comes in third *place,* which is called third *prize;* and in *winning* third prize, he is said *to be* it. Vergil says the same thing in the same words, but more straightforwardly, at 344–5. **Diores:** construe as subject of *subit,* parallel to *Helymus,* or of an understood *est* (cf. 23–4 n.).

hic totum caveae consessum ingentis et ora 340
prima patrum magnis Salius clamoribus implet,
ereptumque dolo reddi sibi poscit honorem.
tutatur favor Euryalum lacrimaeque decorae,
gratior et pulchro veniens in corpore virtus.
adiuvat et magna proclamat voce Diores, 345

340-61. Salius appeals the decision in favor of Euryalus. Aeneas disallows the objection, but presents Salius with a lion's skin and Nisus with a shield.

The argument over prizes is modeled on the aftermath of Homer's chariot race (*Il.* 23.539–653). But in Homer, when Menelaus accuses Antilochus of having won only by performing a risky and unfair maneuver, Antilochus conciliates Menelaus by conceding his prize to him. In contrast, Nisus not only fails to acknowledge the justice of Salius' complaint against him, but in fact demands a prize for himself, though he did not even finish the race. Similarly, all of Vergil's contestants make claims which they stubbornly refuse to yield, leaving them for Aeneas to settle. This he does, like Achilles in the Homeric episode, by lavishly awarding extra prizes, and his amusement (*risit* 358) at the situation that Nisus has created keeps the tone light and cheerful.

340. **caveae consessum:** *cavea* means the part of a theater where the spectators sit, and *consessus* (from *con* + *sedeo,* "a (place for) sitting together") is also used of spectacles. So the words are nearly synonymous, and *caveae* is a genitive of apposition (cf. 52 n.). Vergil uses this phrase again (8.636), as Lucretius had done previously (4.78).

340-1. **ora prima patrum:** a projection into the heroic past of a contemporary custom by which special seats in the front tiers of the circus were reserved for members of the Senate (Livy 1.35.8). On *prima* cf. *extremo* 327–8 n. **clamoribus implet:** Salius fills the *ora patrum* (literally the "mouths of the fathers," but by synecdoche* their "faces," conventionally with reference to seeing, not speaking) with his loud complaints; an instance of synaesthesia (confusion of two different senses), perhaps evocative of the complete ruckus that Salius is making.

342. **reddi . . . poscit:** a poetic construction; in prose *posco* requires *ut* + subjunctive.

343. **lacrimaeque decorae:** the Greeks and Romans regarded tears as consistent with heroic character; cf. 771 and see Ganiban on 1.459. Euryalus's tears are becoming in two senses – although they register his feelings, they do so without the clamor raised by Salius, and (as Servius comments) they enhance his natural beauty.

344. A silver line*. **gratior et:** for the word order cf. *sed* 5 n. **veniens:** "when it presents itself" or "appears" (*OLD* s.v. *venio* 7); cf. 373, 400, *Geo.* 1.29 *an deus immensi venias maris.*

345. **adiuvat et . . . proclamat:** to understand *Euryalum* as direct object of *adiuvat* is easy ("he helps (Euryalus) and proclaims . . .), but rather flat; alternatively, the two verbs can be construed as a kind of hendiadys*, with one of them rendered adverbially: "he helpfully proclaims (or) helps by proclaiming . . . ."

qui subiit palmae frustraque ad praemia venit
ultima, si primi Salio reddantur honores.
tum pater Aeneas "vestra" inquit "munera vobis
certa manent, pueri et palmam movet ordine nemo;
me liceat casus miserari insontis amici."   350
sic fatus tergum Gaetuli immane leonis
dat Salio villis onerosum atque unguibus aureis.
hic Nisus "si tanta" inquit "sunt praemia victis,
et te lapsorum miseret, quae munera Niso
digna dabis, primam merui qui laude coronam   355
ni me, quae Salium, fortuna inimica tulisset?"

346-7. **subiit palmae ... ad praemia venit:** two synonymous expressions, varied by diction and syntax and graced by chiastic word order (verb-noun, noun-verb). *Palmae* is dative with *subiit* (cf. 34 n., AG §370); for a different construction cf. 339 n. *Praemia* (*ultima*), "(last) prize," is a "poetic plural" (98 n.). **venit ... si ... reddantur:** a mixed conditional sentence. Diores "*has* come in third to no purpose (a simple past apodosis), *should* the first prize be given to Salius (a future less vivid protasis)." Different manuscripts give *redduntur*, which produces a future more vivid protasis, and *redduntur*, a simple present protasis: both readings, as well as *reddantur* which is preferred here, may be correct and all three give equally good sense.

348. **munera:** cf. 109 n.

349. **pueri et palmam:** if followed by an additional comma, *pueri* could easily be understood as a vocative addressing all the prize winners (cf. *vestra* 348), but most editors print *pueri et ...*, taking the word as a genitive of possession depending on *palmam* and indicating Euryalus. On the word order *pueri et* cf. 5 n.

350. **casūs:** accusative plural. Although similar verbs (*misereor, miseresco*) usually govern the genitive (AG §354a), with *miseror* the accustive is more common; cf. *miseret* 354. For the "poetic plural" cf. *vinaque* 98 n.

350. **me:** construe as subject accusative of *miserari*, not with *liceat*, which requires the dative (AG §565 n. 2).

352. **onerosum:** modifies *tergum* 351. **āurēis:** two long syllables. *Au* is regularly a diphthong in Latin; *ei* is usually not (cf. *Hectŏrēī* 190 n.), but here it is here scanned as a single long syllable by synizesis* (cf. *deinde* 14 n).

353. **victis:** dative of indirect object with *sunt* (AG §366a, "if there are such great prizes for the defeated"), not dative of possession. ("if the defeated have such great prizes").

354. **quae:** interrogative. **munera:** cf. 109 n.

354. **te lapsorum miseret:** the impersonal *miseret*, like the personal *misereor*, takes a genitive of the cause of feeling and an accusative of the person affected (AG §354a–b); cf. Aeneas' *casus miserari* (350 n.), to which Nisus pointedly alludes, as if to say, "if 'pity for the fallen' is your motto, what will you do for me?"

355-6. **primam merui qui:** for the word order cf. *sed* 5 n. **tulisset:** not a true mixed condition, but an ellipsis* – Nisus maintains that he earned (*merui*) first prize *and would have received it* if bad luck had not taken it away (uncompounded form *tulisset* for the compound *abstulisset*).

et simul his dictis faciem ostentabat et udo
turpia membra fimo. risit pater optimus olli
et clipeum efferri iussit, Didymaonis artis,
Neptuni sacro Danais de poste refixum.   360
hoc iuvenem egregium praestanti munere donat.
    Post, ubi confecti cursus et dona peregit:
"nunc, si cui virtus animusque in pectore praesens,
adsit et evinctis attollat bracchia palmis."
sic ait, et geminum pugnae proponit honorem,   365

---

357. **simul his dictis:** though usually an adverb, *simul* is sometimes used as a preposition governing the ablative (*OLD* s.v. 12): "together with these words . . . " or, more loosely, "as soon as he said this . . . ."

358. **olli:** = *illi* (cf. 10 n.).

359. **Didymaonis:** otherwise unknown. **artis:** accusative in apposition to *clipeum*; a "poetic plural" (cf. *vinaque* 98 n.).

360. **Danais:** dative of agent. It was apparently debated in antiquity how Aeneas would have obtained a shield taken by the Greeks from a (presumably Trojan) temple. Servius mentions a tradition that it came into Helenus' hands—perhaps along with Pyrrhus' kingdom?—and that he gave it to Aeneas. Page argues strenuously instead that it was some Greek soldier who removed from a Greek temple a shield previously dedicated to Neptune, used it in battle, and lost it to Aeneas or to another Trojan. It may be that Vergil deliberately planted the seeds of such *quaestiones* in the hope of provoking a critical discussion of the *Aeneid* similar to the one that had by his time long surrounded the *Iliad* and the *Odyssey*.

Third Event: The Boxing Match (362–484)

The third event is the most complex of all in terms of sources. Its basic structure derives from the second event in *Iliad* 23, but crucial details come from other epic bouts between Odysseus and Irus (*Od.* 18) and Polydeuces and Amycus (Ap. Rhod. *Arg.* 2.1–97, Theoc. *Id.* 22). For a detailed analysis of how these sources are combined see Nelis (2001) 8–21.

Apart from epic predecessors, McGowan (2002) finds within this episode elements of political allegory recalling an episode from the First Punic War.

362-86. Aeneas offers prizes for both winner and loser. Dares stands forward and, seeing no challengers, demands the winner's prize.

362. **Post:** adverbial, instead of the prosaic *postea*. **confecti:** = *confecti sunt:* cf. 23–4 n.

363. **si cui virtus . . . :** understand *est* (or, in view of the compound subject, *sunt*) with *cui* (= *alicui* following *si*) as dative of posession (AG §373). Conditional clauses containing an indefinite pronoun that refers to the subject of the main clause are often best translated by using an English indefinite pronoun without "if," perhaps defined by a relative clause: so here, "Let whoever (or) anyone who has courage . . . come forward (*adsit* 364) . . . ."

364. **evinctis . . . bracchia palmis:** the ancient boxing glove (*caestus*) consisted of leather thongs, studded with lead, which were bound round the hand and arm (cf. 401–5).

victori velatum auro vittisque iuvencum,
ensem atque insignem galeam solacia victo.
nec mora; continuo vastis cum viribus effert
ora Dares magnoque virum se murmure tollit,
solus qui Paridem solitus contendere contra,   370
idemque ad tumulum quo maximus occubat Hector
victorem Buten immani corpore, qui se
Bebrycia veniens Amyci de gente ferebat,
perculit et fulva moribundum extendit harena.
talis prima Dares caput altum in proelia tollit,   375
ostenditque umeros latos alternaque iactat
bracchia protendens et verberat ictibus auras.
quaeritur huic alius; nec quisquam ex agmine tanto

---

366. **velatum auro vittisque:** the horns of a sacrificial beast were gilded and decked with garlands.

369. **Dares:** on the etymology* of the name (from Gk. δείρω, "to flay") and its dramatic significance see McGowan (2002). **magno . . . virum . . . murmure:** the phrase recalls the storm scene of book 1 (cf. 55, 124) and so suggests Dares' destructive power. *Magno . . . murmure* is ablative of attendant circumstance (cf. 18 n.); *virum* (= *virorum;* cf. 45 n.) is subjective genitive (AG §343 n. 1).

370. **solus qui:** for the word order cf. *sed* 5 n. **Paridem:** in Homer Paris is unwarlike and effeminate (cf. 4.215), but a favorite of Aphrodite (Venus), whose presence in this book is subdued, but pervasive (Farrell (1997)). His boxing prowess evidently figured in the epic cycle (Hyg. *Fab.* 91, 273). **solitus:** = *solitus est* (cf. 23–4 n.).

372-3. **victorem . . . ferebat:** Dares had defeated a certain Butes (not the father of Eryx, 24 n.; but this recurrence of the name is intriguing) at the funeral games of Hector. If Vergil is alluding to an earlier literary treatment of these games, that source is lost to us. If we had it, both Butes' identity and the syntax and full meaning of the sentence might be clearer. The word order suggests that *victorem* and *immani corpore* are to be taken closely with *Buten* (as appositive and ablative of quality (AG §415) – "Butes the (previously) victorious (though not in his contest with Dares), of enormous physique" – and that *se ferebat* ("he flaunted himself as" or "he boasted that he") calls for an infinitive of indirect discourse (easily supplied as an understood *esse*; cf. 23–4 n.) followed by the prepositional phrase *Bebrycia . . . Amyci de gente*. *Veniens* is a circumstantial participle: Butes made his boast "as he arrived (on the scene)," perhaps as an univited participant in Hector's funeral games.

Amycus, king of the Bebryces and a legendary boxer and braggart, was killed in a contest with Polydeuces (Ap. Rhod. 2.1–97, Theoc. *Id.* 22). Butes, Amycus' descendant, was also a great boxer (*victorem* 372) and braggart who met a similar fate against Dares. Dares' own boastfulness follows a pattern that predicts the outcome of this contest.

372. **Būtēn:** a Greek form, τὸν Βούτην (masculine accusative singular) from ὁ Βούτης.

audet adire virum manibusque inducere caestus.
ergo alacris cunctosque putans excedere palma 380
Aeneae stetit ante pedes, nec plura moratus
tum laeva taurum cornu tenet atque ita fatur:
"nate dea, si nemo audet se credere pugnae,
quae finis standi? quo me decet usque teneri?
ducere dona iube." cuncti simul ore fremebant 385
Dardanidae reddique viro promissa iubebant.
    Hic gravis Entellum dictis castigat Acestes,
proximus ut viridante toro consederat herbae:
"Entelle, heroum quondam fortissime frustra,
tantane tam patiens nullo certamine tolli 390
dona sines? ubi nunc nobis deus ille (magister
nequiquam memoratus) Eryx? ubi fama per omnem
Trinacriam et spolia illa tuis pendentia tectis?"
ille sub haec: "non laudis amor nec gloria cessit

---

383. **nate dea:** "(you who are) goddess-born," a common way of addressing Aeneas (= 474, 709); *nate* is the vocative of *nātus*, a more dignified synonym of *filius* in prose and poetry since archaic* times. Here as often it is an adjective used as a substantive, but it originated as the perf. part. of *nascor* ("to be born"), and so can govern the ablative of source (*deā*: cf. 244 n. on the metrically useful variant *sătus*) as well as the genitive of possession (592 n.).

384. **quo . . . usque:** tmesis*.

385. **ducere dona iube:** supply *me* as subject accusative.

386. **Dardanidae:** cf. 45 n.

387-425. Acestes goads Entellus, an old fighter once taught by the hero Eryx, into accepting the challenge.

387. **gravis . . . dictis:** a kind of enallage*, equivalent in meaning to *gravibus dictis*; cf. *gravis ictu* 274 n.

388. **proximus ut:** for the word order cf. *sed* 5 n. **toro:** the patch of ground on which Acestes lies is metaphorically* a "couch"; cf. Johnston on 6.674.

391. **ubi:** construe with understood *est* (cf. 23-4 n.). **nobis:** ethic dative (AG §380). **deus:** a common form of hyperbolic* praise for exceptional individuals (*OLD* s.v. *deus* 2a, *Ecl.* 5.64). **ille:** "usually following its noun," as here, to denote "what is famous or well known" (AG §297b).

392. **nequiquam:** Entellus' reverence for Eryx would be pointless if he refused to fight. **ubi:** construe with understood *sunt* (cf. 23-4 n.).

393. **illa:** see 391 n.

394. **ille:** Entellus; see 75 n. **sub haec:** "thereupon," lit. "immediately after these things"; in prose *sub haec dicta, sub mentionem, sub hanc vocem*.

pulsa metu; sed enim gelidus tardante senecta   395
sanguis hebet, frigentque effetae in corpore vires.
si mihi quae quondam fuerat quaque improbus iste
exsultat fidens, si nunc foret illa iuventas,
haud equidem pretio inductus pulchroque iuvenco
venissem, nec dona moror." sic deinde locutus   400
in medium geminos immani pondere caestus
proiecit, quibus acer Eryx in proelia suetus
ferre manum duroque intendere bracchia tergo.
obstipuere animi: tantorum ingentia septem
terga boum plumbo insuto ferroque rigebant.   405

---

395. **sed enim:** "'but indeed,' an archaic* combination of which Vergil was fond (Quintilian 9.3.14)" (Ganiban on 1.19). Here understand, "but (there is no use in my competing,) for . . . ."

396. **hebet:** a bold metaphor*; literally "to be blunt" or "dull," as a weapon.

397-8. **quae . . . illa:** the relative clause precedes its antecedent; more straightforwardly, the sentence would run *si nunc mihi foret illa iuventas, quae quondam fuerat*. . . . The inversion creates anticipation and greatly emphasizes *illa iuventas*.

397. **fuerat:** for the pluperfect see Fordyce on 8.358 and on Cat. 10.28, 64.158. **quaque:** ablative of cause with *exsultat* 398 (AG § 404a). **improbus:** i.e. Dares: construe as substantive, "boor." **iste:** used to express contempt, as often (but not invariably).

398. **fidens:** predicate modifier of *improbus* 397; construe adverbially after *exsultat*, "(so) confident(ly)," "with (such self-)assurance" (cf. *cita* 32–3 n.).

400. **nec . . . moror:** "I do not care about" (*OLD* s.v. *moror* 4); cf. 2.287. **sic deinde locutus:** = 14 (cf. n.); *locutus* = *locutus <est>* (cf. 23–4 n.).

402-3. **suetus | ferre manum:** poetic license permits the use of simplex verbs (like *suetus* (= *suetus erat*; cf. cf. 23–4 n.) and *ferre*) instead of the more prosaic compounds (*consuetus* and *conferre*), as if one were to say in English "customed" instead of "accustomed." *Conferre manum* is a military phrase, "to fight hand-to-hand," but a boxing match is hand-to-hand combat in a very literal sense. Vergil often refreshes the meaning of a common phrase in this way.

403. **intendere bracchia tergo:** *intendere bracchia* normally means "to stretch (or extend) one's arms." But with the ablative, the verb changes its force, as Entellus' arms are not stretched but "covered" or "wrapped" with leather thongs. See *OLD* s.v. *intendo* 6, 3b, and cf. 829, O'Hara on 4.506.

404-5. Vergil's source is Homer's description of Ajax's seven-layered shield (*Il.* 7.222), itself already hyperbolic*; to describe a pair of gloves in such terms is considerably more so. The size and weight of Entellus' gloves mark them as heroic relics of a bygone age; cf. 263, 410–11.

404. **obstipuere:** perfect indicative of *opstipesco* (= *obstipuerunt*, cf. 8 n.).

ante omnis stupet ipse Dares longeque recusat,
magnanimusque Anchisiades et pondus et ipsa
huc illuc vinclorum immensa volumina versat.
tum senior talis referebat pectore voces:
"quid, si quis caestus ipsius et Herculis arma   410
vidisset tristemque hoc ipso in litore pugnam?
haec germanus Eryx quondam tuus arma gerebat
(sanguine cernis adhuc sparsoque infecta cerebro),
his magnum Alciden contra stetit, his ego suetus,
dum melior viris sanguis dabat, aemula necdum   415
temporibus geminis canebat sparsa senectus.
sed si nostra Dares haec Troïus arma recusat
idque pio sedet Aeneae, probat auctor Acestes,
aequemus pugnas. Erycis tibi terga remitto
(solve metus), et tu Troianos exue caestus."   420

---

406. **longeque recusat:** an elliptical phrase well glossed by Williams (1960) as *longe refugit recusans certamen*.

408. **huc illuc:** "this way and that," an extremely common phrase; cf. 701 and 430–1 n.

410-11. The thought is from the conversation of the Argonauts among themselves following the boxing match between Polydeuces and Amycus at Ap. Rhod. 2.145–6, "Consider what they would have accomplished with their cowardly deeds | if ever a god had brought Heracles here." But Heracles had been a crewmate of the Argonauts; in the *Aeneid*, only Entellus here and Evander in book 8 are old enough to remember him.

410. **ipsíus:** cf. 55 n.

411. **tristem:** because Hercules killed Eryx in that bout.

412. **germanus Eryx . . . tuus:** cf. 23–4 n.

413. **cernis:** understand *ea* (from *arma* 412) as direct object (rather than subject accusative) and construe the participle *infecta* as predicate modifier (rather than perfect passive infinitive with understood *esse:* cf. 23–4 n.): "you see them stained . . . ." (not "you see that they have been stained . . . ."). **cerébro:** cf. 480 n., *tenebris* 11 n.

414. **suetus:** = (*con*)*suetus* (cf. 402–3 n.) *sum* (cf. 192 n.).

415. **aemula:** age is proverbially "jealous" (*OLD* s.v. *aemulus*[1] 2) because it robs us of our former powers (cf. Hor. *Carm.* 1.11.7 *invida aetas*).

416. **sparsa senectus:** old age in the form of whitening hair is "sprinkled" over Entellus' head.

417. **Trŏĭŭs:** cf. 38 n.

418. **sedet:** "is settled" (*OLD* s.v. *sedeo* 11a). **Aeneae:** dative of reference (AG §378).

420. **Trōĭănōs:** cf. *Troia* 61 n. **exue caestus:** here *exuo*, as usual, takes as its object the garment that is removed (but cf. 422–3 n.).

haec fatus duplicem ex umeris reiecit amictum
et magnos membrorum artus, magna ossa lacertosque
exuit atque ingens media consistit harena.
tum satus Anchisa caestus pater extulit aequos
et paribus palmas amborum innexuit armis.   425
constitit in digitos extemplo arrectus uterque
bracchiaque ad superas interritus extulit auras.
abduxere retro longe capita ardua ab ictu
immiscentque manus manibus pugnamque lacessunt,
ille pedum melior motu fretusque iuventa,   430
hic membris et mole valens; sed tarda trementi
genua labant, vastos quatit aeger anhelitus artus.

---

421. **duplicem ... amictum:** modeled on Amycus' cloak in Ap. Rhod. *Arg.* 2.32; cf. Hom. *Il.* 3.125; *Od.* 13.224, 19.225.

422-3. Alliteration,* the slow movement enforced by the double caesura*, and a hypermetric* elision* suggest Entellus' great bulk. **magna ... exuit:** here (contrast 420 n.) *exuo* takes as its object the limbs that are stripped of their covering.

424. **tum sătus Anchisa:** cf. 244 n.

426-60. *As the bout begins Dares shows his agility while the older Entellus stands on the defensive. When Entellus attempts a knockdown blow he misses, loses his balance, and falls. Embarrassed, he rises in fury and attacks Dares with a tempest of blows.*

426-7. These lines closely paraphrase Ap. Rhod. *Arg.* 2.67–9, the beginning of the boxing match between Polydeuces and Amycus (cf. 410–11 n.), thus signaling the start of a more extended allusion (426–60 ≈ *Arg.* 2.67–97). For details see Nelis (2001) 16–18.

428. **abduxere:** perfect indicative of *abduco* (= *abduxerunt*, cf. 8 n.).

429. **pugnamque lacessunt:** normally the object of *lacesso* is one's opponent, not the fight itself.

430-1. **ille ... hic:** "this one ... that one" (*OLD* s.v. *hic*[1] 11; cf. 408 n., 441 n.) or "the former ... the latter" (*OLD* s.v. *ille* 16, AG §297a–b), Dares and Entellus, respectively, reflecting the order in which they first entered the narrative.

430. **motu:** "nimbleness" (cf. 442 *adsultibus*).

432. **gĕnŭă labant:** = 12.905 (in a simile* that anticipates the death of Turnus). *Gĕnŭă* by nature consists of three short syllables, so that it cannot occur in dactylic verse unless the final -*a* is elided (cf. *gĕnŭă ăegră trăhēntĕm* | 468) or the medial vowel *u* is treated as a consonant (*u̯* = *v*, pronounced as English *w*) so that it has no syllabic value of its own but combines with the preceding *n* to make the first syllable long by position (cf. 589 n.).

multa viri nequiquam inter se vulnera iactant,
multa cavo lateri ingeminant et pectore vastos
dant sonitus, erratque auris et tempora circum   435
crebra manus, duro crepitant sub vulnere malae.
stat gravis Entellus nisuque immotus eodem
corpore tela modo atque oculis vigilantibus exit.
ille, velut celsam oppugnat qui molibus urbem
aut montana sedet circum castella sub armis,   440
nunc hos, nunc illos aditus, omnemque pererrat
arte locum et variis adsultibus inritus urget.
ostendit dextram insurgens Entellus et alte

433-8. Some of the blows delivered miss, some hit; the latter are distinguished both by where they strike and by the sounds that they produce – they either echo feebly about the hollow ribs, or make a good thud (*vastos sonitus*) on the solid chest. **vulnera . . . tela:** both words stand for *ictus*, "blows"; a good illustration of the difference between metonymy* and metaphor*. Wounds are the product of blows, and so are logically associated; thus to call blows wounds involves an anticipatory change of name (metonymy). But there is no necessary connection between blows and weapons: to make such a link involves a movement from one field, sport, to another, war (metaphor). In this case, however, the two fields involved are not very distant, and the metaphor supports the idea that these games are a kind of preparation for the battles that the Trojans will face in Italy.

435. **dant sonitus:** ≈ *sonant* (cf. 139 n.).

438. **corpore:** "by (moving) just (*modŏ*; cf. 25 n.) his body," evidently a boxing idiom in Latin (*OLD* s.v. *corpus* 7a) with no precise English equivalent, although modern boxers too are trained to turn and twist in various ways so as to lessen the force of blows that they cannot entirely avoid; cf. 445 n. **tela . . . exit:** "he escaped the blows"; though usually intransitive, *exeo* can be transitive and so take a direct object (*OLD* s.v. 13b), as is common for compounds of intransitive verbs (cf. Ganiban on 2.542).

439. **ille:** Dares; cf. 75 n. **celsam . . . qui:** for the word order cf. *sed* 5 n. **molibus:** commentators are divided as to whether this word means "bulwarks" (Page, ablative of specification (AG §418) with *celsam* referring to the walls and towers of the besieged town) or "siege engines" (Conington-Nettleship (1858–83), ablative of means with *oppugnat*). In either case, "Such hyperbole* is used especially of important heroes of great awesomeness. Thus the endurance of the mighty boxer Entellus . . . is equated with that of a city or a fortress" (Hardie (1987) 286).

440. **sedet:** "encamps," a continuation of the siege metaphor* (439 n.).

441. **nunc hos, nunc illos:** cf. 430–1 n.

extulit: ille ictum venientem a vertice velox
praevidit celerique elapsus corpore cessit;   445
Entellus viris in ventum effudit et ultro
ipse gravis graviterque ad terram pondere vasto
concidit, ut quondam cava concidit aut Erymantho
aut Ida in magna radicibus eruta pinus.
consurgunt studiis Teucri et Trinacria pubes;   450
it clamor caelo primusque accurrit Acestes
aequaevumque ab humo miserans attollit amicum.
at non tardatus casu neque territus heros
acrior ad pugnam redit ac vim suscitat ira;
tum pudor incendit viris et conscia virtus,   455

---

444. **ille:** Dares; cf. 75 n. **a vertice:** prosaically, this phrase means "straight down," just as *in* (or *ad*) *verticem* means "straight up" (*OLD* s.v. *uertex* 3d); hence English "vertical." But *vertex* itself means "the highest point (of the sky), zenith" (*OLD* s.v. 3c); cf. 1.114, where a wave that has risen "up to the stars" (102–3) comes crashing down *a vertice* (114) to overwhelm the ship of Orontes. Here Entellus' attempted blow similarly falls *a vertice*, introducing a cosmic frame of reference that continues and amplifies Vergil's hyperbolic* treatment of this contest (cf. 439 n.).

445. **celeri . . . corpore:** probably related to the idiom discussed in 438 n., but more readily intelligible as an ablative of cause: Dares avoided Entellus' attacks thanks to his "swift(ness of) body."

446. **ultro:** the very force of Entellus' attempted blow causes him to fall, untouched by Dares.

447. **gravis graviterque:** cf. 118 n.

448-9. Homer reserves the image of a felled tree for the death of men in battle (e.g. *Il.* 5.560, with the commentary of Kirk (1990) *ad loc.*). **Erymantho:** 6.623 n.

450. **studiis:** one-word ablative of manner (AG §412b, note), lit. "with (shows of) eagerness" (cf. 148 n.); virtually equivalent to the adverb *studiose*, "eagerly" (cf. Ganiban on 1.105). **Trinācria:** elsewhere (e.g. 300) *Trinăcria*. For the artificial lengthing cf. *tenebris* 11 n.

451. **caelo:** dative of end of motion (cf. 34), here with an uncompounded verb (cf. 233 n.).

454. **vim suscitat irā:** similar clausulae at 10.263 *spes suscitat iras* and especially 12.108 (Aeneas) *se suscitat irā*. As in the latter example the ablative is instrumental and so, as often in the case of immaterial "instruments" (AG §408), can be construed as expressing means (the hero "sets violence in motion by means of his anger") or manner (the hero "angrily sets violence in motion"). This is the first of just three occurrences of singular *vis* or *vi* (sing.) in this book (as against fourteen of the plur. *vires:* on the difference see 67–8 n.), each of which marks an instance of violence that exceeds what the situation strictly requires: cf. 641 n., 855 n.

455. **tum:** different commentators construe the adverb either in the ordinary temporal sense, "then" or as "moreover," "in addition" (*OLD* s.v. 8).

praecipitemque Daren ardens agit aequore toto
nunc dextra ingeminans ictus, nunc ille sinistra.
nec mora nec requies: quam multa grandine nimbi
culminibus crepitant, sic densis ictibus heros
creber utraque manu pulsat versatque Dareta. 460
    Tum pater Aeneas procedere longius iras
et saevire animis Entellum haud passus acerbis,
sed finem imposuit pugnae fessumque Dareta
eripuit mulcens dictis ac talia fatur:
"infelix, quae tanta animum dementia cepit? 465
non viris alias conversaque numina sentis?
cede deo." dixitque et proelia voce diremit.
ast illum fidi aequales genua aegra trahentem
iactantemque utroque caput crassumque cruorem
ore eiectantem mixtosque in sanguine dentes 470
ducunt ad navis; galeamque ensemque vocati
accipiunt, palmam Entello taurumque relinquunt.

---

457. **ille:** Entellus; see 39 n.

458-60. **quam . . . Dareta:** Nelis (2001) 467 suggests a connection with Ap. *Arg.* 2.1083–89. Alliteration* in *culminibus crepitant,* the sibilants in *densis ictibus heros,* the weak caesuras* in 460, and assonance* in the frequentative verbs *pulsat versatque* (AG §263.2), all represent the ceaselessness of Entellus' blows. **Darēta:** Greek accusative, τὸν Δάρητα from ὁ Δάρης. **versat:** lit. "keeps turning," i.e. knocking from side to side.

461-84. *Aeneas stops the fight. The reeling Dares is led away while Entellus, to show his strength, kills with a single blow the bullock he received as a prize and then declares his determination never to fight again.*

466. **non:** = *nonne,* which is very rare in poetry. **alias:** not merely "another" but "of a completely different and unfamiliar kind" (*OLD* s.v. *alius* 7). Entellus has exhibited a superhuman strength granted him by the god.

467. **dixitque et:** emphatic combination of the conjunctions *-que* and *et* (very uncommon in prose) marks the act that follows the word as instantaneous.

468-73. ≈ *Il.* 23.695–9.

468. **ast:** archaic* for *at.* **illum:** Dares, whom Aeneas has just been addressing.

471. **galeamque ensemque:** the second prize (367). *-que . . . -que* not regular Latin usage, but is modeled on Greek τε . . . τε, a conspicuous feature of Homer's epic style introduced into Roman epic by Ennius and used frequently by Vergil (e.g. 1.18 *tenditque fovetque*).

hic victor superans animis tauroque superbus
"nate dea, vosque haec" inquit "cognoscite, Teucri,
et mihi quae fuerint iuvenali in corpore vires 475
et qua servetis revocatum a morte Dareta."
dixit, et adversi contra stetit ora iuvenci
qui donum astabat pugnae, durosque reducta
libravit dextra media inter cornua caestus
arduus, effractoque inlisit in ossa cerebro: 480
sternitur exanimisque tremens procumbit humi bos.
ille super talis effundit pectore voces:
"hanc tibi, Eryx, meliorem animam pro morte Daretis
persolvo; hic victor caestus artemque repono."

---

473. **superans animis:** "triumphant in spirit" (Page); but *supero*, in addition to the idea of "overcoming" obstacles of various kinds, (*OLD* s.v. 1–5), also means "to have in abundance or surplus, or as a residue" (*OLD* s.v. 5–7); and *animis* (ablative of place where, which is idiomatic in expressions of emotion (AG §429.3)) in the plural often denotes anger or animosity (*OLD* s.v. *animus* 11; cf. 454 n.). Entellus, then, is not just proud of his victory, but is not quite ready to stop fighting, and he takes out his unspent aggression on his prize.

475. **mihi quae:** for the word order cf. *sed* 5 n.

476-81. Vergil's metrical artistry is on display in these lines. The relatively unmarked movement of the first two lines perhaps suggests the placid and unsuspecting nature of the bullock just before the sacrifice. The slow, largely spondaic movement of 479 mimics the slow rise of Entellus' fist, while the rapid dactyls of 480 suggest the sudden blow that follows. The final line begins with a single verb of dactylic shape (*sternitur*, "it is felled") in the first foot, which effectively arrests any further movement as soon as the line has begun; when the line does begin to move again, it suggests the lifeless quivering (*tremens*) of the beast, which gives out in a jerky clausula (481 n.).

479. **libravit:** not "swung" but "poised" the hand before delivering the blow.

480. **arduus:** predicate adjective, grammatically modifying the subject of *libravit* (479) but logically referring to the gloved fist that he raised up high; cf. 278 n. The enjambment* of this word effectively extends the sense of equipoise developed in the previous line. **cerébro:** cf. 413 n., *tenebris* 11 n.

481. **procumbit humi bos:** a one-syllable word at line-end always produces an odd, choppy effect. Servius greatly disapproved of this line, but most modern readers have admired the way in which *bos* at once completes the sentence and puts a definitive end both to the irregular movement of the line and to the animal's death-throes.

482. **ille:** Entellus; see 75 n.

483-4. Entellus' words make explicit a metaphorical* equivalency, which is implied throughout the games and throughout the *Aeneid*, between ritual animal sacrifice and the results of contests, whether sporting or military, between human beings.

Protinus Aeneas celeri certare sagitta   485
invitat qui forte velint et praemia dicit,
ingentique manu malum de nave Seresti
erigit et volucrem traiecto in fune columbam,
quo tendant ferrum, malo suspendit ab alto.
convenere viri deiectamque aerea sortem   490
accepit galea; et primus clamore secundo
Hyrtacidae ante omnis exit locus Hippocoontis;
quem modo navali Mnestheus certamine victor
consequitur, viridi Mnestheus evinctus oliva.
tertius Eurytion, tuus, o clarissime, frater,   495

Fourth Event: The Archery Match (485–544)

Vergil's fourth event is Homer's seventh (*Il.* 23.850–83), though the very end of the episode owes something to Homer's eighth and last event, the javelin-throw, as well (534 n.). The arrangement of this and the next two episodes is notable: the archery contest (485–544 = sixty lines) is followed by the Troia (545–603 = fifty-nine lines) and then by the burning of the ships (604–663 = sixty lines). This measured, balanced arrangement marks a turning point in the long narrative of the events of this day.

485-99. *A dove tied by a string to a mast is the mark. Four competitors draw lots for the order in which they will shoot.*

486. **velint:** cf. 291 n.

487. **ingentique manu:** cf. 241 n.

488. **traiecto in fune:** while the general sense is obvious (the bird was tethered to the mast), it is unclear whether the Latin means that the tether (*fune*) was looped (*traiecto*) around the mast or around the bird.

490. **convenere:** perfect indicative of *convenio* (= *convenerunt*, cf. 8 n.).

490-2. In taking lots, a token (*sortem*, the lot: cf. 132 n.) was cast (*deiectam*) into an urn or (as here) a helmet (*galea*), which was shaken until one lot leapt out (*exit* 492). The order in which the lots emerged determined each contestant's place (*locus*, here used by metonymy* for the lot itself) in the order of the competition.

493. **modŏ:** cf. 25 n. Construe closely with *victor*, "recently the winner," as if the latter were a perfect active participle, "having just won", since that form does not exist in Latin (except in the case of deponent verbs: cf. 14 n.).

493-8. **Mnestheus ... Eurytion ... Acestes:** all again (cf. 492 n.) by metonymy* for the lot of each contestant. For the *eu* diphthong in Eurytion's name cf. *Mnestheus* 116 n.

493-4. **Mnestheus ... Mnestheus:** "Vergil often uses epanalepsis* or the syntactically unnecessary repetition of a word in one line of a word from the previous line in order to create pathos or suggest strong emotion" (O'Hara on 4.24–6). Here perhaps the figure mimics the jubilant cries of Mnestheus' crew, still excited from their close finish in the boat race and eager for their captain to have another chance at victory, as his lot appears; cf. Perkell on 3.523–4.

Pandare, qui quondam iussus confundere foedus
in medios telum torsisti primus Achivos.
extremus galeaque ima subsedit Acestes,
ausus et ipse manu iuvenum temptare laborem.
tum validis flexos incurvant viribus arcus   500
pro se quisque viri et depromunt tela pharetris,
primaque per caelum nervo stridente sagitta
Hyrtacidae iuvenis volucris diverberat auras,
et venit adversique infigitur arbore mali.
intremuit malus micuitque exterrita pennis   505
ales, et ingenti sonuerunt omnia plausu.
post acer Mnestheus adducto constitit arcu

---

496. **Pandare:** Pandarus was incited (*iussus*) by Athena to shoot Menelaus and so break the truce between the Greeks and Trojans (*Il.* 4.86–103).

499. **manu iuvenum temptare laborem:** almost like the English expression "to try one's hand at something," but the grammar is different, *laborem* being the direct object of *temptare* and *manu* an ablative of means.

500-18. *The first three contestants: Hippocoon hits the mast, Mnestheus cuts the cord, Eurytion hits the dove.*

500. A golden line*. **validis ... incurvant viribus:** alliteration* expresses both the effort that goes into drawing the bow and the gradual bending of the bow itself.

501. **pro se quisque viri:** "the men, each with all his might" (= 12.552). **pharetris:** cf. *pharētram* 311. For the artificial lengthening of, and resulting shift of the word accent* to, the second syllable cf. *tenebris* 11 n.

505-6. **intremuit ... micuitque:** assonance* of the two verbs reinforces the sense that the first action produced the second. **micuitque:** the manuscripts all read *timuitque*, which is redundant with *exterrita* ("it was fearful, having been terrified") and unexpected in conjunction with *pennis* ("it was fearful with or in respect to its wings"). The difficulty can largely be glossed over in English paraphrase ("it was terrified and showed its fear by beating its wings," *vel sim.*), but the expression remains very odd Latin. D. A. Slater's conjecture *micuitque* is both paleographically plausible (because *mic-* could easily have been converted into *tim-* by a copyist's error) and gives better sense ("it thrashed in terror with its wings"). Some editors accept the manuscript reading on the principle of *lectio difficilior potior*, ("the more difficult reading is the stronger one"), meaning that scribes are unlikely to have changed the easily understood *micuitque* into the slightly more puzzling *timuitque*. **plausu:** the meaning is debated. The clausula of 505 *micuitque exterrita pennis* ≈ 215 *plausumque exterrita pennis*, where *plausum* is the "flapping" of a bird's wings (similarly *plaudentem* 516). In the corresponding passage of Homer, however, the archer who cuts the string is cheered (*Il.* 23.869), so that *plausu* here may mean the audience's applause.

507. **adducto ... arcu:** only the tips of the bow are drawn back towards the archer. Elsewhere (9.632) the arrow is said to be drawn back in this way, or the arms of oarsmen (141).

alta petens, pariterque oculos telumque tetendit.
ast ipsam miserandus avem contingere ferro
non valuit; nodos et vincula linea rupit 510
quis innexa pedem malo pendebat ab alto;
illa Notos atque alta volans in nubila fugit.
tum rapidus, iamdudum arcu contenta parato
tela tenens, fratrem Eurytion in vota vocavit,
iam vacuo laetam caelo speculatus et alis 515
plaudentem nigra figit sub nube columbam.
decidit exanimis vitamque reliquit in astris
aetheriis fixamque refert delapsa sagittam.
 Amissa solus palma superabat Acestes,
qui tamen aërias telum contendit in auras 520
ostentans artemque pater arcumque sonantem.
hic oculis subitum obicitur magnoque futurum

---

508. **alta:** = *alta loca* (cf. 167–8 n.).

509-10. **ipsam ... nodos:** asyndeton*. The emphatic position of the words marks the antithesis*: "the bird *itself*... he could not hit, *but*...."

511. **quīs:** archaic* for *quibus* (AG § 150c). **pedem:** "retained" accusative of specification with *innexa* (cf. 135 n.).

512. **illa:** see 75 n. **Notos atque ... in nubila:** for the postponed preposition cf. 2.654; 6.416, 692.

514. **in vota vocavit:** Eurytion appeals to his brother Pandarus as a patron of archers, much as the boxer Entellus regarded his teacher Eryx (483).

516. A silver line*.

517-18. **decidit ... aetheriis:** in Stoic thought the ether, or fine fiery substance that surrounds the universe, was considered to be the source of all life (cf. Ganiban on 1.608, Johnston on 6.724–51). At death the soul, which is composed of this substance, quits the body and returns to its native place. Thus here the bird's body becomes separated from the soul (*examinis*) that gives it life, which it leaves (*vitam reliquit*) in heaven before falling back to earth.

519-44. *The last contestant, Acestes, shoots into the air. His arrow takes fire, vanishing like a shooting star. Aeneas accepts the startling omen and awards first prize to Acestes.*

520. **contendit:** *contendit* and *contorsit* are both well attested in the manuscripts. *Contendit* is perhaps preferable as the (slightly) *difficilior lectio* (cf. 505–6 n.), since it was less commonly used with *telum* than was *contorsit*—and thus more likely to have been "corrected" by a scribe to *contendit*.

521. **ostentans:** participle of attendant circumstance (AG §496), "in displaying," but verging towards a purpose construction, "to display." **patēr:** cf. *datūr* 284 n. Construe as a predicate nominative with adverbial force (cf. *cita* 32–3 n.) suggesting the dignity with which Acestes made his display (cf. *heros* 1.196, also describing Acestes; *dea*, of Venus, 1.412). For the theme of fatherhood cf. 14 n., 130 n.

augurio monstrum; docuit post exitus ingens
seraque terrifici cecinerunt omina vates.
namque volans liquidis in nubibus arsit harundo 525
signavitque viam flammis tenuisque recessit
consumpta in ventos: caelo ceu saepe refixa
transcurrunt crinemque volantia sidera ducunt.
attonitis haesere animis superosque precati
Trinacrii Teucrique viri, nec maximus omen 530
abnuit Aeneas, sed laetum amplexus Acesten
muneribus cumulat magnis ac talia fatur:
"sume, pater; nam te voluit rex magnus Olympi
talibus auspiciis exsortem ducere honores.

522-4. Vergil never specifies how the prophets explained the meaning of the portent or what was the event that it foretold. Accordingly, scholars have debated these questions since antiquity. The likeliest interpretation at least for the latter point is that the portent foretold the foundation of Segesta with Acestes as its first king; cf. 706–7 n. The imagery parallels Anchises' interpretation of the flames about Ascanius' head, confirmed by the appearance of a shooting star (2.679–704), a clear analogue of the *sidus Iulium* of 43 BCE, which was said to betoken the apotheosis of Julius Caesar; but unlike Anchises' portent, the connection between this omen and the *sidus Iulium* is impressionistic and indirect.

524. A golden line*. **seraque:** predicate adjective modifying *omina* with adverbial force (cf. *cita* 32–3 n.): interpretation followed long after the event.

526. **signavitque viam flammis:** cf. *signantemque vias* (2.697); the phrase denotes the trail that the shooting star left behind it, not a path that it indicated for others to follow.

527. **refixa:** since the ancients thought that stars were "fixed" (*sidera quae affixa dicimus mundo,* Pliny, *Nat. Hist.* 2.28), they regarded shooting stars as having come "unfixed" (Hor. *Epod.* 17.5).

528. **crinem:** a standard metaphor* for the (equally metaphorical) "tail" or "trail" of a shooting star or comet (cf. Greek κομήτης, "having long hair").

529. **haesere:** perfect indicative of *haereo* (= *haeserunt,* cf. 8 n.). **precati:** = *precati sunt* (cf. 23–4 n.).

530-1. **nec ... abnuit:** litotes*. Aeneas warmly welcomes the omen. An ominous word or event was, if bad, immediately deprecated, or, if good, welcomed, so as to avoid the evil and make sure of the good.

534. **exsortem:** applied to persons this word usually means "having *no* share in" (6.428), but applied to things, such as prizes, it means "specially chosen" in that it is not subject to competition or lottery (cf. 490–2 n.). Vergil seems innovatively to combine these two meanings: Acestes, effectively "having no share in" the competition itself, nevertheless wins a "specially chosen" prize as a result of his exceptional performance. Cf. the prize awarded by Achilles to Agamemnon at the conclusion of Patroclus' funeral games (*Il.* 23.884–97).

ipsius Anchisae longaevi hoc munus habebis,   535
cratera impressum signis, quem Thracius olim
Anchisae genitori in magno munere Cisseus
ferre sui dederat monimentum et pignus amoris."
sic fatus cingit viridanti tempora lauro
et primum ante omnis victorem appellat Acesten.   540
nec bonus Eurytion praelato invidit honori,
quamvis solus avem caelo deiecit ab alto.
proximus ingreditur donis qui vincula rupit,
extremus volucri qui fixit harundine malum.
    At pater Aeneas nondum certamine misso   545

535-8. As often in Homer, heroic gifts gain prestige by having a distinguished pedigree. More specifically, at the end of the chariot race Achilles gives Nestor, who has not competed, a vessel that had belonged to Patroclus himself (*Il.* 23.615–23). Similarly, a gift once given to Anchises would be an especially distinguished prize if awarded at a festival in his honor.

535. **ipsĭŭs:** cf. 55 n.

536. **crātéra:** a Greek form, τὸν κρατῆρα (accusative masculine singular) from ὁ κρατήρ, a large vessel for mixing wine with water for use at a symposium. **impressum signis:** "embossed with figures" and so possibly of metal, like the prize earlier awarded for third place in the boat race, silver *cymbia* (267 n.), although in Vergil's time clay vessels that imitated more expensive metal ware by means of mold-made figures in relief were quite common.

537. **in magno munere:** "as a particular reward"; the prose idiom would be *in magni muneris loco*. **Cisseus:** father of Hecuba (7.320, 10.705) according to Euripides (says Servius); of Theano according to Homer (*Il.* 11.223), who makes Hecuba daughter of Dymas (*Il.* 16.718). For the *eu* dipthong in cf. *Mnestheus* 116 n.

538. ≈ 572. **ferre:** 247–8 n. **sui:** reflexive pronoun, objective genitive (AG §348, 349a, 350) depending on *monimentum* (not possessive adjective modifying *amoris*).

541. **praelato invidit honori:** the usual construction is *invidere aliquid alicui* "to begrudge a thing (accusative) to a person (dative)," but this construction is not uncommon (*OLD* s.v. *inuideo* 2a).

544. **volucri qui:** for the word order cf. *sed* 5 n.

Fifth Event: The Troia (545–603)

This equestrian event is for display, not competition, and corresponds to nothing in any surviving poetic source. In it the motifs of genealogy, as expressed through the etymology* of names (cf. 114–23 n.), and institutional aetiology* reappear. The very name of this Troy game (*Troia* or *lusus Troiae*) stands as a powerful link between ancient Trojan and contemporary Roman cultural identity (cf. 596–603 n.). There may however be an ironic gap in perspective between the backward-looking satisfaction that Aeneas takes in recalling the Trojan origins of this game and the narrator's forward-looking emphasis on its Roman future (569–70 n.).

545-59. Aeneas sends for Ascanius to bring up his youthful band of horsemen.

545. **certamine misso:** 286 n.

custodem ad sese comitemque impubis Iuli
Epytiden vocat, et fidam sic fatur ad aurem:
"vade age et Ascanio, si iam puerile paratum
agmen habet secum cursusque instruxit equorum,
ducat avo turmas et sese ostendat in armis   550
dic" ait. ipse omnem longo discedere circo
infusum populum et campos iubet esse patentis.
incedunt pueri pariterque ante ora parentum
frenatis lucent in equis, quos omnis euntis
Trinacriae mirata fremit Troiaeque iuventus.   555
omnibus in morem tonsa coma pressa corona;
cornea bina ferunt praefixa hastilia ferro,

---

546. **Iuli:** Ascanius' new, dynastic name (cf. Ganiban on 1.267–8: "Iulus, as an alternate name for Ascanius, was probably invented in the late Republic to associate Ascanius with the Julian *gens* (i.e. the family of Julius Caesar and thus also Augustus") occurs here for the first time in this book. It is found only twice more, almost immediately below (569–70 n.).

547. **Epytidēn:** Homer uses this patronymic* (cf. 45 n.) to describe Periphas, an (already) aged herald in the service of Anchises, as a "son of Epytus" (*Il.* 17.323–4). Vergil too mentions an Epytus, perhaps to be regarded as another son, at 2.340. The name is related to the Greek verb ἠπύω, "to call, summon, or invoke," and the form is Greek, as well (masculine accusative singular of the first decelension), τὸν Ἐπυτίδην from ὁ Ἐπυτίδης.

548-51. **Ascanio ... dic:** more prosaically, *dic Ascanio [ut] ducat* . . . . For the jussive subjunctive without *ut* after the imperative see AG §449c. **Ascanio:** the narrator has just called the boy by his dynastic, proto-Roman name, Iulus (546 n.), but Aeneas continues to use his son's Trojan name (569–70 n.). **avo:** dative of reference (AG §376–80), "in his grandfather's honor" (cf. *patri* 603). **turmas:** originally perhaps quite general in meaning, under Augustus the Equestrian order was formally organized by *turmae,* as were the cavalry units attached to legions of infantry in the Roman army.

553. **incedunt:** cf. 68 n. **ante ora parentum:** = 6.308, where Aeneas in the underworld sees the shades of young people who had been placed on the funeral pyre while their parents watched (cf. *Geo.* 4.477); and upon first entering the narrative during the storm in book 1, the hero expresses envy of those who died at Troy *ante ora patrum* (95). Of the three passages, only here is it possible to imagine the elders taking pleasure in the spectacle that takes place before their eyes; cf. 576 n.

555. **Trōi̯aeque:** cf. *Troia* 61 n.

556. **omnibus:** dative of reference (AG §376–80). **in morem:** suggests order and uniformity as opposed to disorder (cf. *sine more* 694), though here the phrase may be proleptic* – Vergil wishes this occasion to be understood as the original enactment of what would become a traditional pageant (cf. 596–603 n.). **tonsā comā pressā coronā:** note how the ablative phrase surrounds the nominative, just as a crown encircles each boy's hair. It is uncertain whether *tonsa* denotes a particular kind of "close-trimmed" wreath or is merely a decorative epithet*.

557. **bina:** cf. 61–2 n. **ferunt:** the understood subject is *pars,* "some" (cf. 108 n.).

pars levis umero pharetras; it pectore summo
flexilis obtorti per collum circulus auri.
tres equitum numero turmae ternique vagantur   560
ductores; pueri bis seni quemque secuti
agmine partito fulgent paribusque magistris.
una acies iuvenum, ducit quam parvus ovantem
nomen avi referens Priamus, tua clara, Polite,
progenies, auctura Italos; quem Thracius albis   565
portat equus bicolor maculis, vestigia primi
alba pedis frontemque ostentans arduus albam.

---

558. **pháretras:** cf. 311 n.

559. **obtorti:** an etymological* hint at *torques* (from *torqueo*), the name of this common military decoration.

560-79. *The boys advance in three companies headed by Priam, Atys, and Ascanius.*

560-1. There are three companies of twelve riders, each with a leader. For the distributive *terni* used instead of cardinal *tres,* cf. 85 n. *Seni* on the other hand is the true distributive used in multiplication (cf. 61-2 n., AG §137c). In both ways distributives were employed by poets to avoid a prosaic tone, *terni* "three apiece," and *bis seni,* "twice six," evidently sounding more elegant than the more straightforward *tres,* "three," and *duodecim,* "twelve."

561. **ductores:** the boy-captains named in 563-72.

562. **magistris:** each company also had an adult trainer, of whom Epytides was apparently the chief (579).

563. **ducit quam:** for the word order cf. *sed* 5 n.

564. **avi:** a Greek boy typically received his grandfather's name, and here as elsewhere in the *Aeneid* the customs of the heroic age are Greek. According to Roman custom the eldest son traditionally bore the same *praenomen* as his father.

565. **auctura:** the attributive future active participle expressing likelihood or certainty (AG §499.1) – "destined to increase" the Italian race (by the number and fame of his descendants). **Ítalos:** cf. *Italia* 18 n.

566. **bicolor . . . :** "dappled with patches of white." **vestigia primi . . . pedis:** a grandiloquent epic periphrasis* – the horse's prints are not to be distinguished here from its hooves. *Primi pedis* denoted not the forefoot but the front of the hoof (or "pastern" as it is called by horsemen); *stare in primis pedibus* means "to stand on tip-toe" and *primi digiti* are "finger-tips."

567. **arduus:** grammatically a predicate adjective modifying *equus* (566) but logically referring to the *frontem . . . albam* that the horse displays on high; cf. 278 n.

alter Atys, genus unde Atii duxere Latini,
parvus Atys pueroque puer dilectus Iulo.
extremus formaque ante omnis pulcher Iulus 570
Sidonio est invectus equo, quem candida Dido
esse sui dederat monimentum et pignus amoris.
cetera Trinacriis pubes senioris Acestae
fertur equis.
excipiunt plausu pavidos gaudentque tuentes 575
Dardanidae, veterumque agnoscunt ora parentum.
postquam omnem laeti consessum oculosque suorum
lustravere in equis, signum clamore paratis

---

568. **Atys ... Atii:** etymological* connections between Trojan and Roman names appear in this last episode of the games narrative, as they did in the first (114–23 n.). Augustus' mother was the daughter of Marcus Atius Balbus and Julia, sister of Gaius Julius Caesar. In making Atys the friend of Iulus, Vergil projects the linkage between the *gens Atia* and the *gens Iulia* into the legendary past.

568-9. **Atys ... Atys:** emphatically repeated in the same metrical *sedes* in consecutive lines; cf. 493–4 n., 569–70 n.

568. **duxere:** perfect indicative of *duco* (= *duxerunt,* cf. 8 n.).

569-70. **Iulo ... Iulus:** cf. the treatment of Atys' name in the preceeding lines. Here the repetition is made even more emphatic by occupying the final position and by polyptoton*. The dynastic name Iulus occurs just three times in this book, only in this episode (cf. 546 n.) and only in the voice of the narrator, who elsewhere uses the boy's Trojan name, Ascanius (74, 597, 667), as do Aeneas (548–51 n.) and, indeed, Ascanius himself (673).

570-2. Iulus' mount is a gift to him from Dido. Mention of Dido (cf. *Elissae* 3 n.) and of the Trojans' sojourn in Carthage have been oblique throughout most of this book (cf. 38 n., 51 n.). Here, however, her name is directly linked with the important themes of memory, good faith, and love (*monimentum et pignus amoris* 572). Conington-Nettleship (1858–83) on 571 speculate that this could be the same horse that Ascanius rode at 4.157, when he went with the hunting party that was the beginning of Dido and Aeneas' affair. Perhaps it is more than coincidence that Iulus' appearance on horseback here as well precedes another of Juno's attempts to block the Trojans from reaching Italy (cf. 604–40 n.). Even more poignantly, in book 11 (72–5) a richly-worked cloak, made by Dido with her own hands and given to Aeneas, is used as a burial shroud in Pallas' funeral. On the relationship between Pallas' funeral and the games held in honor of Anchises see the introduction to this book.

572. ≈ 538.

576. **Dardanidae:** cf. 45 n. **ora parentum:** cf. 553 n.

578. **lustravere:** perfect indicative of *lustro* (= *lustraverunt,* cf. 8 n.), "they traversed" (*OLD* s.v. 3; cf. 3.385); an interesting word choice because *lustrare* commonly means "to review (troops)" (cf. 6.681), and these "troops" are indeed being reviewed by the onlookers; but the troops, not the onlookers, are the subject of the verb.

> Epytides longe dedit insonuitque flagello.
> olli discurrere pares atque agmina terni 580
> diductis solvere choris, rursusque vocati

580-603. *After moving in procession round the ring, the riders put on a display of military horsemanship, in which the movements are as intricate as the Labyrinth and as lively as those of a school of dolphins. The tradition was passed on first to Alba Longa, then to Rome.*

580-7. The movement of the companies is illustrated by the following chart:

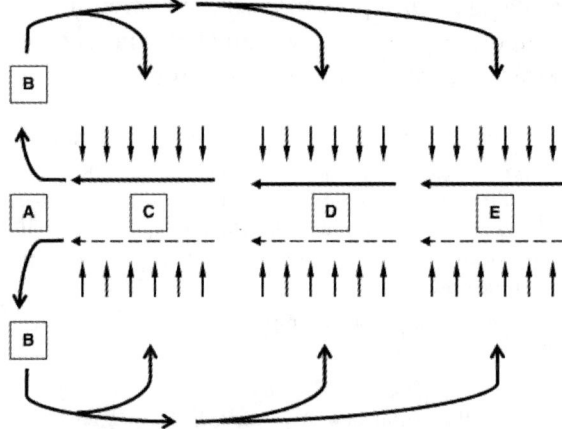

Figure 2: equestrian maneuvers of the Troia

Three companies of twelve each first ride down the middle of the circus in two lines (*agmina*), eighteen pairs (*pares*) of riders side-by-side, until the lead riders of the first two companies reach position A. Then all the riders turn ninety degrees to the left or right and gallop apart until they reach the outer edges of the circus (position B). Then they face about and charge one another, the two halves of each company converging on positions C, D, and E, respectively. After this they continue to perform intricate maneuvers in mock battle to demonstrate their skillful horsemanship and expert training.

580. olli: = *illi* (cf. 10 n.). **pares:** because each pair of riders in the *agmen* would become a pair of opponents in the charge. **terni:** the youths grouped into three companies (or *turmae* 550, 560) on either side, here called *agmina* because they are still advancing in double file; cf. 90 n.

581. choris: the six halves of these three companies. What the three *ductores* do is not stated. Since it seems unlikely that they would join one half of their company against the other, they may stand outside the "combat."

582-7. The first maneuvers described in 580–2 are simple, but they are followed here by "fresh charges" and "fresh retreats," in the course of which the two opposing divisions and their various parts wheel in and out in what seems to be a more elaborate manner, if one judges by the pair of similes* that follows (588–95). Of course in this "mimicry of war" there could be no actual charge, but just when the two squadrons were meeting the actual shock would be avoided by skillful wheeling in and out of the six companies.

convertere vias infestaque tela tulere.
inde alios ineunt cursus aliosque recursus
adversi spatiis, alternosque orbibus orbis
impediunt pugnaeque cient simulacra sub armis;   585
et nunc terga fuga nudant, nunc spicula vertunt
infensi, facta pariter nunc pace feruntur.
ut quondam Creta fertur Labyrinthus in alta
parietibus textum caecis iter ancipitemque
mille viis habuisse dolum, qua signa sequendi   590
frangeret indeprensus et inremeabilis error:
haud alio Teucrum nati vestigia cursu
impediunt texuntque fugas et proelia ludo,
delphinum similes qui per maria umida nando

582. **convertĕre ... tulĕre:** perfect indicatives of *converto* (contrast the present infinitive *convértĕre*) and *fero* (= *converterunt* and *tulerunt*, respectively; cf. 8 n.).

588-95. A double simile* comparing the intricacy of the riders' movement to the form of the Labyrinth, the legendary maze that the mythical Daedalus built as a prison for the Minotaur, and their sportiveness (*ludo* 593) to the capering of dolphins. The similes anticipate a pair of important ecphrastic* passages. In one, Aeneas sees a representation on Apollo's temple at Cumae of the human sacrifice that took place in the Labyrinth (6.20–30). In the second, a school of dolphins propitiously encircle the zone on Aeneas' shield where Augustus' victory at Actium is depicted (8.671–4). The similes thus bring out two aspects of the Troy game that are major themes in this book and in the poem, namely, the pathos of individual self-sacrifice that young men are called to make in war, and the success that such instances of sacrifice make possible.

589. **parietibus:** naturally pronounced as five short syllables (*părĭĕtĭbŭs*); but even when final *-us* is lengthened by a following consonant, as here, a sequence of four shorts cannot occur in dactylic verse. Vergil therefore resorts to the license of treating the first *i* as a consonant (*i̯*, sounded as English *y*; cf. *gĕnṵă* 432 n.), thereby artificially lengthening the first syllable and eliminating the second to produce a word of acceptable dactylic shape (*pārĭ̯ĕtĭbŭs*; cf. *ábĭ̯ĕtĕ* 663).

590. **quā:** = *ut eā* ("so that there"), introducing a relative clause of purpose (AG §531.2).

591. **inremeabilis error:** ≈ 6.27 = Cat. 64.114 *inextricabilis error*, both also of the Labyrinth, the "maze" itself being called (by metonymy*) the wandering that it causes.

592. **Teucrum:** = *Teucrorum* (cf. 45 n.). **nati:** cf. 383 n.

594. **delphinum similes:** the archaic* construction *similis* + genitive (AG §385c2) occurs only here in Vergil.

Carpathium Libycumque secant. 595
hunc morem cursus atque haec certamina primus
Ascanius, Longam muris cum cingeret Albam,
rettulit et priscos docuit celebrare Latinos,
quo puer ipse modo, secum quo Troia pubes;
Albani docuere suos; hinc maxima porro 600
accepit Roma et patrium servavit honorem;
Troiaque nunc pueri, Troianum dicitur agmen.
hac celebrata tenus sancto certamina patri.

596-603. This sentence suggests a continuity of tradition that is not supported by other evidence. The intricacy of the maneuvers performed in this ceremony have been connected with a pair of archaic* verbs, *amptruare* and *reamptruare,* having to do with dance. These may be cognate with the Etruscan word *truia,* which is inscribed over images of horsemen and a labyrinth on a sixth century oenochoe found at Tragliatella, and which has nothing to do with Troy. Therefore, while the ceremony may well have ancient origins, they would be Etruscan rather than Trojan. But Roman antiquarians, eager to establish a connection between Rome and Troy, may well have connected *truia* with *Troia.* The ceremony was first introduced at Rome by Sulla (Plut. *Cato Min.* 3) — i.e. not until the early first century BCE. It was "revived" by Julius Caesar (Suet. *Iul.* 39), regularized by Augustus (Suet. *Aug.* 43), and continued by his successors.

598. **priscos ... Latinos:** the phrase is technical, describing the early inhabitants of the district around Alba as opposed to the later Latin League (Livy 1.3).

599. **modō:** ablative of *modus* with (both instances of) *quō,* "in what way, how"; cf. the adverbial form *quōmŏdŏ.* **secum quo:** for the word order cf. *sed* 5 n. **Trŏĭă:** cf. 38 n.

600. **docuere:** perfect indicative of *doceo* (= *docuerunt,* cf. 8 n.).

601. **honorem:** cf. 58 n.

602. **Trŏĭaque ... Trŏĭánum:** cf. 61 n.

603. **hac ... tenus:** tmesis* for *hactenus.* **celebrata:** = *celebrata sunt* (cf. 23–4 n.). **patri:** cf. *avo* 550 n.

604–761: *The Burning of the Ships and its Aftermath*

The burning of the ships was a regular part of the Trojan legend, but practically every detail of it is subject to variation in the different tellings, including the location of the event, its place in the sequence of Trojan wanderings, how and why it came about, and even whose ships were burned. All that remains constant is that a group of Trojan women burn a number of ships. In fashioning this episode, Vergil adopts details from one or another version of the story to create an original episode with a traditional air.

Note the balanced arrangement of episodes that narrate the aftermath of the disaster (cf. 485–544 n.):

664–679	News from the ships reaches the men	16 lines
680–699	Jupiter sends a storm to quench the flames	20 lines
700–718	Aeneas takes council with Nautes	19 lines
719–745	Anchises appears to Aeneas in a dream	27 lines
746–761	Aeneas arranges to divide his followers	16 lines

Episodes in this section are much shorter than in the Games narrative (cf. 104–603 n.). One effect of this change is to quicken the narrative and to convey a sense that events are beginning to move impetuously towards a denouement.

Bibliography: Bertram (1971), Pavlovskis (1975–76), Holt (1979–80), Nethercut (1986), Gruen (1992, 6–51), Nugent (1992), Farrell (1997), Oliensis (2001), Casali (2010) 43–6.

> Hinc primum Fortuna fidem mutata novavit.
> dum variis tumulo referunt sollemnia ludis,   605
> Irim de caelo misit Saturnia Iuno
> Iliacam ad classem ventosque aspirat eunti,

604-40. Juno sends Iris to the beach where the Troian women mingle ritual lamentations for Anchises with regrets for their own troubles. Disguising herself, Iris reminds the women of their ceaseless wanderings, urging them to burn the ships and so make sure of remaining in Sicily.

604. **fidem:** construe *apo koinou** as "retained" accusative of specification with *mutata* (on which cf. 19-20 n.) and direct object of *novavit*. In Latin, "to renew" or "make new" often means not "to restore" to original glory from a run-down condition, but "to change," usually for the worse (cf. *res novae*, "political revolution").

606. = 9.2 ≈ 4.694. **Irim:** the normal accusative form in Latin, modeled on a few third-declension i-stem nouns (AG §67, 75). **Saturnia:** Juno, together with all the other elder Olympians, were children of Saturnus and Rhea; but Vergil uses *Saturnius* only twice, of Neptune (cf. 799 n.) and Jupiter (4.372), whereas Juno is *Saturnia* sixteen times (e.g. 1.23), making it her principal epithet* in the *Aeneid*. On its implications cf. 12.830–1, Lyne (1989) 173–7.

multa movens necdum antiquum saturata dolorem.
illa viam celerans per mille coloribus arcum
nulli visa cito decurrit tramite virgo.   610
conspicit ingentem concursum et litora lustrat
desertosque videt portus classemque relictam.
at procul in sola secretae Troades acta
amissum Anchisen flebant, cunctaeque profundum
pontum aspectabant flentes. heu tot vada fessis   615
et tantum superesse maris, vox omnibus una.
urbem orant, taedet pelagi perferre laborem.

---

608. **multa movens:** = 3.34; "making many moves" (cf. *transversa fremunt* 19–20 n.), "setting many (things) in motion," i.e. "plotting" (Page). **dolorem:** "retained" accusative of specification (cf. 135 n.) with *saturata*. Juno's *dolor* and its causes are explained at 1.9 and 1.25–8.

609. **illa:** Iris; see 75 n. **per mille coloribus arcum:** the separation of the preposition from its object is common in poetry, but is here made easier by the fact that *mille coloribus* (descriptive ablative or ablative of quality, AG §415) is equivalent to an attribtive adjective such as *multicolorem*—so Conington-Nettleship (1858–83)—meaning "thousand-colored."

610. **cito . . . tramite:** the ablative phrase conveys the manner of Iris' swift departure, but also the means by which she traveled, namely the "path" traced by the rainbow across the sky. **virgo:** pleonastic* after *illa* (609), perhaps stressing the feminine element (cf. 613–15 n.).

611. **lustrat:** "crosses" here and not "sees" or "reviews" (578 n.).

613-15. The women have not taken part in the games either as participants or as spectators, but have passed this time in ritual lamentation for Anchises. This arrangement corresponds to the normal practice of funerary observance in ancient cultures and to the thematic opposition between male and female throughout the *Aeneid,* in which men are generally aligned with fated success and women with the forces that tend to delay the realization of that success; see Nugent (1992). The women's laments for Anchises are blended with tears for themselves, like the tears of Briseis and the other captives at *Iliad* 19.301–3, ostensibly for Patroclus but also for their own sorrows. On the problematic status of women in epic more generally, cf. Keith (2000), Hinds (2000).

613. **Troadĕs:** short final syllable as in Greek rather than long as in Latin. **acta:** from *acta, -ae* (not *ago, agere*), a Greek loan word (ἡ ἀκτή, "shore") used several times by Cicero but occurring only here in Vergil and never again in poetry before the Flavian period.

614-15. The slow movement of these lines (both entirely spondaic except in the fifth foot) suggests the lugubrious atmosphere of the women's activities, in sharp contrast to the festive nature of the men's celebrations.

615-16. **tot vada . . . superesse:** accusative + infinitive of exclamation (AG §462).

616. **omnibus:** dative of indirect object with understood *est* (cf. 353 n.).

ergo inter medias sese haud ignara nocendi
conicit et faciemque deae vestemque reponit;
fit Beroe, Tmarii coniunx longaeva Dorycli,   620
cui genus et quondam nomen natique fuissent,
ac sic Dardanidum mediam se matribus infert.
"o miserae, quas non manus" inquit "Achaica bello
traxerit ad letum patriae sub moenibus ! o gens
infelix, cui te exitio Fortuna reservat ?   625
septima post Troiae excidium iam vertitur aestas,
cum freta, cum terras omnis, tot inhospita saxa
sideraque emensae ferimur, dum per mare magnum
Italiam sequimur fugientem et volvimur undis.
hic Erycis fines fraterni atque hospes Acestes: 630
quis prohibet muros iacere et dare civibus urbem ?
o patria et rapti nequiquam ex hoste penates,

---

618. **haud ignara nocendi:** "not unskilled (i.e. "well skilled," litotes*) in working ill." For this use of the gerund cf. AG §504.

620. **Beroē:** not the Latin diphthong *oe.* **Dorȳclī:** cf. *Dórȳclī* 647; cf. *tenebris* 11 n.

621. **cui:** dative of possession with *fuissent.* The verb is subjunctive because the clause is causal, giving not an explanatory remark by the narrator, but the *thought* that induced Iris to assume the shape of Beroë (informal indirect discourse, AG §592.3). Iris thinks that Beroë, as one who had seen better days, is sure to be discontented.

622. **Dardanidum:** from *Dardanis -idis,* f., not the archaic* genitive (as at 2.242 and 10.4) of *Dardanides, -ae.* m. (cf. 45 n.).

624. **traxerit:** subjunctive in a relative causal clause (AG §535e, 540c) explaining *miserae.*

626. **septima ... aestas:** Beroë here repeats the words that Dido had spoken one year previously (1.755), when the seventh summer had just passed; now the eighth summer is approaching. Scholars since the time of Servius have regarded the repetition as a chronological inconsistency and, possibly, an indication of the poem's unfinished state. For a review of the question and a critical response, see Dyson (1996). **Trōiae:** cf. 61 n.

627-8. **freta ... terras ... saxa | sidera:** all governed by *emensae* which denotes the "measuring out" of the many geographical features that the Trojans have passed by on their wanderings. **sidera:** metonymy* for the different regions that lie under the various constellations (*OLD* s.v. *sidus* 5b).

629. **Ītaliam:** cf. 18 n.

631. **iacere:** idiomatic for "laying" foundations of all kinds.

nullane iam Troiae dicentur moenia? nusquam
Hectoreos amnis, Xanthum et Simoenta, videbo?
quin agite et mecum infaustas exurite puppis.   635
nam mihi Cassandrae per somnum vatis imago
ardentis dare visa faces: "hic quaerite Troiam;
hic domus est" inquit "vobis." iam tempus agi res,
nec tantis mora prodigiis. en quattuor arae
Neptuno; deus ipse faces animumque ministrat."   640
haec memorans prima infensum vi corripit ignem
sublataque procul dextra conixa coruscat
et iacit. arrectae mentes stupefactaque corda
Iliadum. hic una e multis, quae maxima natu,
Pyrgo, tot Priami natorum regia nutrix: 645

---

633. **iam:** "at last." **Trōiae:** cf. 61 n. Iris/Beroë plays on the women's hope that their city (like that of Helenus, 3.349–52) is to be a new Troy, which is just what her mistress Juno fears as well. The frequent aetiological* and etymological* motifs in this book encourage such a view. But with this episode begins a process of leaving behind, both literally and figuratively, relics of the old Troy and of emphasizing the Italian and Latin qualities of the new Rome (12.819–42).

636. **Cassandrae:** it is strange that Iris/Beroë cites Cassandra as the source of this prophecy: Apollo granted Cassandra the gift of prophecy as a love offering, but when she rejected his advances, he retaliated by adding the curse that her prophecies, though correct, would never be believed (cf. 2.246–7, 3.182–8). Here the prophecy is false, but is believed nonetheless.

637-9. **visa ... tempus ... mora:** understand *est* (cf. 23–4 n.) with each. The omission of the word in three successive lines creates an atmosphere of breathless impetuosity bordering on frenzy; cf. 641–53 n. **Trōiam:** cf. 61 n.

641-63. *After Iris flings the first torch herself, a woman named Pyrgo recognizes that she is not Beroë but some divine being. The goddess then soars heavenward, which causes a fury among the women who immediately set upon the ships with fire.*

641. **vi:** ablative of manner, "with violence," modifying *corripit* and best construed as if it were an adverb, "violently" (AG §412b). On *vis* vs. *vires* cf. 67–8 n., 454 n.

643-4. Unusual but beautiful prosody: two early pauses in each line, a diaeresis after *et iacit* (643) and a caesura* after *Iliadum* (644) suggest first the pause which follows a vigorous effort, then the pause of astonishment. Repeated omission of the verb "to be," extending even to the subjunctive (cf. 348 n.) as well as to verbs of speaking (645 n.), continues the frenzied atmosphere of the episode.

643. **stupefacta:** = *stupefacta sunt* (cf. 23–4 n.).

644. **quae:** = *quae erat* (cf. 23–4 n.).

645. **Pyrgo:** construe with understood *dixit*. The character and her name (< Greek πῦρ "fire") were clearly invented for this episode. **tot:** Priam famously had fifty sons and fifty daughters (cf. Ganiban on 2.501).

"non Beroe vobis, non haec Rhoeteia, matres,
est Dorycli coniunx; divini signa decoris
ardentisque notate oculos; qui spiritus illi,
qui vultus vocisque sonus vel gressus eunti.
ipsa egomet dudum Beroen digressa reliqui   650
aegram, indignantem tali quod sola careret
munere nec meritos Anchisae inferret honores."
haec effata.
at matres primo ancipites oculisque malignis
ambiguae spectare rates miserum inter amorem   655
praesentis terrae fatisque vocantia regna:
cum dea se paribus per caelum sustulit alis

---

646. **vobis:** ethic dative of reference (AG §380); equivalent to a parenthetical "I tell you." **Rhoeteïa:** by metonymy* for "Trojan" (see Vocabulary).

647. **Dórўcli:** the natural quantity and accent* (cf. 620 n.).

648-9. **ardentisque ... oculos:** so Achilles recognizes the disguised Athena as a goddess by her blazing eyes (*Il.* 1.199). **qui spiritus ... qui vultus:** the pronoun *quis* is regular in such expressions, but Vergil sometimes uses the adjective *qui* instead (9.723, *Geo.* 1.3), with no difference in meaning. However, while all surviving manuscripts give *qui* in 648, about half change to *quis* in 649, forcing editors to choose whether Vergil remained consistent in this passage or started with the less common and ended with the more common form. **spiritus:** "spirit" in the sense of an impressive, energetic, confident demeanor (*OLD* s.v. 7b–d). **illi:** dative of possession with understood *sit,* a rare instance of an omitted subjunctive (required by the construction, which is an indirect question). The choice of pronoun is emphatic: the Beroe that Pyrgo is describing is distinct from the one she knows.

650. **Bérŏēn:** a Greek accusative (τὴν Βερόην from ἡ Βερόη).

651. **tali quod:** for the word order cf. *sed* 5 n. **careret:** subjunctive because the causal clause states the motive of someone other than the speaker (AG §540 n.1), here Beroë (the real one, not Iris in disguise), whom Pyrgo paraphrases.

653: **effata:** = *effata est* (cf. 23–4 n.).

654. **matres:** fatherhood is a major theme in this book in respect of the observances devoted to Anchises, of Aeneas' progress in filling the paternal role that Anchises has vacated, and in respect of the lines of descent between eponymous Trojan ancestors and the Roman *gentes* that they will found. But in contrast to the *patres,* who will marry Italian brides and father Trojan-Italian children, these women are destined to remain in Sicily (715–18). The only mother who really counts as such in this book, as in the poem as a whole, is Venus: see Nugent (1992), Farrell (1997).

655. **spectare:** historical infinitive (AG §463) here denoting a continuous action (contrast 685–6 n.) – the women simply "gazed" in astonishment until suddenly startled by the flight of Iris, when they break out into a sudden cry (expressed in the indicative *conclamant* (660)).

656. **fatis:** ablative of cause (AG §404), "the (Italian) realms that call them *because of their destinies*."

ingentemque fuga secuit sub nubibus arcum.
tum vero attonitae monstris actaeque furore
conclamant, rapiuntque focis penetralibus ignem 660
(pars spoliant aras), frondem ac virgulta facesque
coniciunt. furit immissis Volcanus habenis
transtra per et remos et pictas abiete puppis.
 Nuntius Anchisae ad tumulum cuneosque theatri
incensas perfert navis Eumelus, et ipsi 665
respiciunt atram in nimbo volitare favillam.

---

658. **secuit . . . arcum:** *secare* is used frequently of vigorous active movement with an accusative that denotes the substance *over* which, not *through* which, the cutting takes place (6.899 *secat viam*). Thus Iris "cuts a rainbow" across the sky as she goes.

659. **monstris:** for the "poetic plural" cf. *vinaque* 98 n. In contrast to the *monstrum* of Acestes' bowshot (522–4 n.), the meaning of this *monstrum* seems clear: some god wants the women to burn the ships. But the women act impulsively and without anticipating the ultimate outcome: see 706–7 n.

661-2. **pars spoliant:** collective singular subject of a plural verb (AG §317d2, 108 n.). A prior *pars*, subject of *rapiunt* (660), is to be inferred. **aras:** the *quattuor arae* mentioned at 639–40. **frondem . . . coniciunt:** develops and explains *spoliant aras*. The women take the garlands that decorated the altars and the firewood to be used for burning sacrificial victims, and use these as kindling for the ships instead. Their act is thus related in a perverse way to the important theme of sacrifice.

662. **furit immissis Vulcanus habenis:** a heady mixture of images – the fire god Vulcan (a standard instance of metonymy* for the element fire) "rages" like an insane person or a wild beast "with loosened reins" (a common metaphor* from horseracing: cf. 146 n.).

663. **pictas ăbĭĕtĕ puppis:** (for the pronunciation and scansion cf. 589 n.) "painted ships of pine," enallage* for "ships of painted pine." The ablative of material (AG §403.2), which regularly takes a preposition or at least a verb of making or constructing; but poetic usage is freer, and here the position of *abiete* between *pictas* and *puppes* allows it to be used as virtually equivalent to the adjective *abiegnas* (cf. 266 n., 609 n.).

664-79. News of the fire reaches Aeneas, and Ascanius gallops off to stop the women. They come to their senses and flee, panic-stricken, as the men arrive and try to quench the flames.

664-5. **Nuntius . . . Eumelus:** otherwise unknown, but a Greek warrior of the same name takes part in Homer's chariot race (*Il.* 23.288, etc.), and that is probably why Vergil uses the name here. It is impossible to say whether *nuntius* is an appositive ("the messenger E.") or an adverbial predicate nominative ("acting as messenger (*or*) taking the message"; cf. *cita* 32–3 n.). In either case, the words go closely together, but stand in hyperbaton* at opposite ends of the entire phrase, artfully framing it. For the *eu* diphthong in Eumelus' name cf. *Mnestheus* 116. **cuneos:** the wedge-shaped divisions of the seats in a theater. Vergil writes here as if the games took place in an artificial Augustan-era theater (cf. 288–9 n., 340–1 n.). **incensas . . . navis:** "the burning of the ships" (cf. *commissos . . . ludos* 113 n.) for "news of the . . . " by ellipsis*.

    primus et Ascanius, cursus ut laetus equestris
    ducebat, sic acer equo turbata petivit
    castra, nec exanimes possunt retinere magistri.
    "quis furor iste novus ? quo nunc, quo tenditis" inquit,   670
    "heu, miserae cives? non hostem inimicaque castra
    Argivum, vestras spes uritis. en, ego vester
    Ascanius !" — galeam ante pedes proiecit inanem,
    qua ludo indutus belli simulacra ciebat.
    accelerat simul Aeneas, simul agmina Teucrum.   675
    ast illae diversa metu per litora passim
    diffugiunt, silvasque et sicubi concava furtim
    saxa petunt; piget incepti lucisque, suosque
    mutatae agnoscunt excussaque pectore Iuno est.

---

667. **cursus ut:** for the word order cf. *sed* 5 n.

669. **magistri:** 560–1 n. That the *ductores* and *magistri* are not the same is shown by 668, where the *magistri* vainly try to control Ascanius (cf. 133 n.).

670. **quis:** subject of an understood *est* (cf. 23–4 n.).

672. **Argivum:** = *Argivorum* (cf. 45 n.).

675. **Teucrum:** = *Teucrorum* (cf. 45 n., 592, 690). For the *eu* diphthong cf. *Mnestheus* 116.

676-7. **ast:** cf. 468 n. **illae:** cf. 75 n. **diversa ... per litora passim | diffugiunt:** "they scatter over different parts of the shore"; normal Latin idiom would require *diversae* (modifying *illae*) "they scatter *in different directions* along the shore." Perhaps an instance of enallage*.

677. **sicubi:** The women behave like frightened animals at the approach of the men, seeking "the forests and (literally) if there are rocky hollows anywhere" (i.e. "whatever rocky hollows there are"). The entire clause introduced by *sicubi* (= *si* + *alicubi*, "if anywhere") is parallel to *silvas,* the direct object of *petunt* (678). For the conditional clause containing an indefinite pronoun or adverb cf. 363 n.

677-8. **concava ... saxa:** nominative, subject of an understood *sunt*. The meaning is not "hollow rocks," but caves and crannies in rocky areas.

678-9. **piget incepti lucisque:** an impersonal verb of feeling (AG §354b), "it troubles" (in a general sense, *piget* is often used in place of *pudet*, "it causes shame," and *paenitet*, "it causes regret"), constructed with an accusative of the person affected — here understand *illas* from *illae* 675 — and a genitive of the cause of the feeling — here *incepti* (perf. part. of *incipio* used substantively, as often, to mean "an attempt" or "an undertaking"), with *lucis* ("light") expressing the consequence that now they do not want anyone to see them. The narrator momentarily adopts the women's point of view: the revulsion that they now feel reflects their true attitude, which is really the same as that of their men (*suos*), whom they now recognize (*agnoscunt*) — after returning (*mutatae*: cf. 19-20 n., 606 n.) to their normal state of mind. **excussaque pectore Iuno est:** the narrator returns to his own, privileged perspective to assign responsibility for the destructive act to Aeneas' divine antagonist. *Pectore* is a collective singular instead of *pectoribus* (which is much less common in Vergil), but it may connote that the women were acting as one under Juno's influence.

Sed non idcirco flamma atque incendia viris   680
indomitas posuere; udo sub robore vivit
stuppa vomens tardum fumum, lentusque carinas
est vapor et toto descendit corpore pestis,
nec vires heroum infusaque flumina prosunt.
tum pius Aeneas umeris abscindere vestem   685
auxilioque vocare deos et tendere palmas:
"Iuppiter omnipotens, si nondum exosus ad unum
Troianos, si quid pietas antiqua labores
respicit humanos, da flammam evadere classi
nunc, pater, et tenuis Teucrum res eripe leto.   690
vel tu, quod superest, infesto fulmine morti,

680-99. *Aeneas prays for Jupiter either to send the Trojans help or to annihilate them on the spot, and a great storm of rain extinguishes the flames.*

681. **posuere:** perfect indicative of *pono* (= *deposuerunt*, cf. 8 n.)..

682. **stuppa:** tar was used to seal the joints of the hull against leakage, and though the timbers themselves were wet (*udo . . . robore* 681) the tar would continue to smolder and could burst again into flames. **lentusque:** "lingering."

683. **est:** from *edo*, not *sum*; see Glossary. **toto descendit corpore:** a slightly difficult phrase. The ablative with a verb of motion usually denotes source or manner; but since *toto corpore* seems to mean all of the ships together, the phrase must denote the place where the fire took up residence after "descending" upon it. **pestis:** the image, along with *corpore*, is appropriate to a medical description of disease, and is used elsewhere of Dido's lovesickness (4.2, 66–7).

685-6. **abscindere . . . vocare . . . tendere:** historical infinitives (AG §463), here denoting instantaneous action (contrast 655 n.). **umeris abscindere vestem:** a sign of violent emotion. **auxilio:** dative of purpose (AG §382.2).

687. **exosus:** = *exosus es* (cf. 192 n.). The compound is not found in literature before Vergil. **ad unum:** "to the last man" (*OLD* s.v. *unus* 2b).

688. **Trōiānos:** cf. 61 n. **quid:** = *aliquid* following *si;* cognate accusative (AG §390b–d) with *respicit:* "if it has *any* regard for . . . ."

690. **tenuis . . . res:** accusative plural; "slender fortunes." **Teucrum:** = *Teucrorum* (cf. 45 n., 592, 675). For the *eu* diphthong cf. *Mnestheus* 116.

691. **vel tu:** the pronoun emphasizes the direct personal character of the appeal. **quod superest:** two interpretations are possible: 1) the clause may in effect modify the verb in a way that makes an adversative transition between one thought and the next ("save us or put us to death, *which is the remaining option*"); 2) it may define the direct object of *demitte* ("put to death *what remains* (of us)" (796 n.)). The first of these requires the reader to infer a direct object from the context, such as *nos* from *Teucrum* (690) or perhaps *me* from the first-person verb *mereor* (692). **morti:** dative with the compound verb *demitte* 692 (cf. 34 n., AG §368a, 428h).

si mereor, demitte tuaque hic obrue dextra."
vix haec ediderat cum effusis imbribus atra
tempestas sine more furit tonitruque tremescunt
ardua terrarum et campi; ruit aethere toto   695
turbidus imber aqua densisque nigerrimus Austris,
implenturque super puppes, semusta madescunt
robora, restinctus donec vapor omnis et omnes
quattuor amissis servatae a peste carinae.
   At pater Aeneas casu concussus acerbo   700
nunc huc ingentis, nunc illuc pectore curas
mutabat versans, Siculisne resideret arvis
oblitus fatorum, Italasne capesseret oras.
tum senior Nautes, unum Tritonia Pallas
quem docuit multaque insignem reddidit arte   705

---

693. **vix ... cum:** cf. 84 n., 159–60 n.

694. **sine more:** "without restraint" (cf. *in morem* 556, "according to form").

695. **ardua terrarum:** "the lofty places of the earth," i.e. mountains. Unlike other phrases in which *loca* is to be understood (cf. 168 n.), here the partitive genitive (AG §346.3) creates a grand periphrasis*; cf. Williams (1960) *ad loc.*

697. **implenturque super:** tmesis* for the prosaic *superimplenturque*, "and are filled to overflowing."

698. **restinctus:** *restinctus est* (cf. 23–4 n.). **donec:** for the word order cf. 5 n.

700-18. *Aeneas considers giving up his quest and settling in Sicily. The seer Nautes urges him to go on, but to leave behind the women and old men, the infirm, and the timid to found a city in Sicily with the help of Acestes.*

701. **nunc huc ... nunc illuc:** a variation on *huc illuc* (408 n.; cf. 431 n.). **curas:** direct object of both *mutabat* and *versans*.

702-3. **Siculisne ... Italasne:** alternative plans expressed as indirect questions, each introduced by *-ne* and in apposition to *curas* 701. For the quantity of *Ītalasne* cf. *Ītaliam* 18 n. **resideret ... capesseret:** secondary sequence determined by *mutabat* 701.

704. **unum:** whether by itself, as here, or with the superlative and similar expressions (e.g. 1.15 *magis omnibus unam*, 2.426 *iustissimus unus*, 3.321 *felix una ante alias*), *unus* can be used to mean "one above all others (or) in particular" (*OLD* s.v. 8). **Tritonia:** an epithet* of Pallas Athena in Latinized form (cf. *Tritonis, -idos* 2.226), variously explained by Servius (on 2.171) and perhaps deriving ultimately from the Homeric τριτογένεια, the meaning of which is uncertain (cf. Kirk on *Il.* 4.513–16).

(haec responsa dabat, vel quae portenderet ira
magna deum vel quae fatorum posceret ordo)—
isque his Aenean solatus vocibus infit:
"nate dea, quo fata trahunt retrahuntque sequamur;
quidquid erit, superanda omnis fortuna ferendo est.   710
est tibi Dardanius divinae stirpis Acestes:
hunc cape consiliis socium et coniunge volentem;
huic trade amissis superant qui navibus et quos
pertaesum magni incepti rerumque tuarum est;

706. **haec:** feminine nominative singular, Pallas (cf. 704).

706-7. **vel . . . vel:** alternative explanations expressed as indirect questions depending on *responsa* (a "poetic plural"; cf. *vinaque* 98 n.). The burning of the ships is considered to be a *monstrum,* a divine message requiring interpretation: cf. 523 n., 659 n.

707. **deum:** = *deorum* (cf. 45 n.).

708. **isque:** i.e. *Nautes* (704). The pronoun is very infrequent in poetry. **Aenean:** a Greek form, τὸν Αἰνείαν (masculine accusative singular) from ὁ Αἰνείας. **solatus:** = *consolatus* (cf. 402–3 n.) or, in effect, *consolans,* because the participle of a deponent verb is often treated as equivalent to a present active form.

709. **nate dea:** cf. 383 n. **trahunt retrahuntque:** the phrase accurately expresses the repetitive quality of the Trojan's wanderings to this point, particularly since this is their second stop on Sicily with Acestes; but besides actual repetitions and reversals of course, it encompasses any series of adventures that the fates may have in store.

710. **omnis fortuna:** "every(thing that) fortune (gives us)" or "every (kind of) fortune (no matter how bad)." **ferendo:** ablative of the gerund (AG §507.1) combining the ideas of manner ("patiently") and, especially, means ("by enduring (or) endurance"). **ęst:** prodelision (cf. elision*) of *est* at line end is common and should be distinguished from other occurrences of a final monosyllable; cf. 481 n.

712. **consiliis:** dative of purpose (AG §382.2) by analogy with common phrases like *locum castris capere* (*OLD* s.v. *capere* 9a–b). *Socium* normally takes the objective genitive.

713-14. **amissis superant qui navibus:** a somewhat difficult phrase, even if the general meaning is clear. Servius considers *superant* here as equivalent to *supersunt* or *superfluunt,* which suggests that he takes *amissis . . . navibus* as dative (which is clearly the case at 2.643 *captae superavimus urbi,* "we have survived the taking of the city"; cf. *OLD* s.v. *supero* 5b). This would recommend construing the present passage as "those who survive the loss of the ships." But unlike the fall of Troy, no one perished when the ships were burned, and Nautes' advice is hardly to leave behind all the survivors. Logically, he must mean "(those) who exceed (our transport capacity) after the loss of the ships," with *amissis . . . navibus* as ablative absolute. On the word order *amissis . . . qui* cf. *sed* 5 n. **quos pertaesum . . . est:** the impersonal verb *taedet* (here with the intensifying prefix *per-*) governs the objective genitive, *incepti rerumque,* and the accusative of the person affected, *quos* (AG §221b). In the present system active forms of *taedeo* are normally used, but in the perfect system, as here, passive forms are common. The impersonal construction accounts for the neuter form *pertaesum* (as also at 4.18).

longaevosque senes ac fessas aequore matres 715
et quidquid tecum invalidum metuensque pericli est
delige, et his habeant terris sine moenia fessi;
urbem appellabunt permisso nomine Acestam."
    Talibus incensus dictis senioris amici
tum vero in curas animo diducitur omnis. 720
et Nox atra polum bigis subvecta tenebat:
visa dehinc caelo facies delapsa parentis
Anchisae subito talis effundere voces:
"nate, mihi vita quondam, dum vita manebat,
care magis, nate, Iliacis exercite fatis, 725
imperio Iovis huc venio, qui classibus ignem
depulit, et caelo tandem miseratus ab alto est.
consiliis pare quae nunc pulcherrima Nautes
dat senior; lectos iuvenes, fortissima corda,
defer in Italiam. gens dura atque aspera cultu 730
debellanda tibi Latio est. Ditis tamen ante

---

716. **quidquid:** the neuter includes men, women, and children alike (cf. 1.601–2 *quidquid ubique est | gentis Dardaniae*).

717. **habeant . . . sine:** 163 n.

718. **Acestam:** Vergil connects the Greek name of the town, Egesta (Lat. *Segesta*), with the name of Acestes. Cf. Thuc. 6.2, Cic. *Ver.* 2.4.72.

719-45. Aeneas remains unsure, but that night Anchises appears in a dream, bidding him follow the counsel of Nautes. In Italy he is to find the Sibyl of Cumae and under her guidance visit Anchises in Elysium to learn what fate has in store for him and his descendants.

719-20. Aeneas' confidence is so shaken by the loss of the ships that even Nautes' sound and friendly advice leaves him more doubtful than ever.

721. **polum:** metonymy* for *caelum*.

722. **visa:** = *visa est* (cf. 23–4 n.). **caelo . . . delapsa:** though Anchises himself is below in Elysium (735), the vision comes from above, being sent by Jupiter (726).

724-5. **nate . . . nate:** cf. 383 n. and Cat. 64.215 *nate, mihi longa iucundior unice vita*.

725. **care magis:** = *carior*. **nate . . . fatis:** = 3.182.

728. **pulcherrima:** agrees grammatically with *quae*, but logically modifies its antecedent, *consiliis*. This treatment of adjectives is emphatic, but idiomatic in Latin prose as well as poetry.

729. **corda:** the seat of courage (from Latin *cor* via French *coeur*, "heart"); synecdoche* for *viri* (cf. 318 n.).

730. **Ītaliam:** cf. 18 n.

infernas accede domos et Averna per alta
congressus pete, nate, meos. non me impia namque
Tartara habent, tristes umbrae, sed amoena piorum
concilia Elysiumque colo. huc casta Sibylla   735
nigrarum multo pecudum te sanguine ducet.
tum genus omne tuum et quae dentur moenia disces.
iamque vale; torquet medios Nox umida cursus
et me saevus equis Oriens adflavit anhelis."
dixerat et tenuis fugit ceu fumus in auras.   740
Aeneas "quo deinde ruis ? quo proripis ?" inquit,
"quem fugis ? aut quis te nostris complexibus arcet ?"
haec memorans cinerem et sopitos suscitat ignis,
Pergameumque Larem et canae penetralia Vestae
farre pio et plena supplex veneratur acerra.   745

---

732. **infernas ... domos:** Vergil always gives *domus* second-declension endings, as here, except in the genitive singular (*domūs* 1.356 etc.).

733. **congressus ... meos:** *congressus* is a prosaic word, but perhaps sounded less so as a "poetic plural" (cf. *vinaque* 98 n.). It is constructed with the genitive, with possessive adjectives (as here), and with *cum* + the ablative to mean "meeting(s) with me." **nate:** see 383 n.

735. **colō:** the final syllable is not elided before *huc,* an instance of hiatus* (here without correption*; cf. *Ilio* 261 n.).

736. **nigrarum:** cf. 96–7 n. **multo ... sanguine:** ablative of price (AG §416).

738. **iamque vale:** = 2.789, 11.827; *Geo.* 4.497; cf. 49 n.

741. **deinde:** cf. 14 n. The tone is exactly that of English "then" or "now" in indignant questions. **proripis:** supply *te,* the omission of which connotes the speaker's agitation.

742. **quem fugis?** = 6.466, Aeneas' final words to Dido, echoing her *mene fugis* 4.314; cf. *Ecl.* 2.60 with Clausen (1994) *ad loc.*

743-5. For sacrifice after a vision cf. 3.176–7, 8.542.

744. **canae penetralia Vestae:** the goddess is "white-haired" because she (like her Greek counterpart, Hestia) was considered the eldest of the Olympians. In the Roman state cult, Vesta was closely associated with the Penates, whose name is related to *penetralia,* "arcane objects" that were thought to have come with Aeneas from Troy and eventually to Rome.

745. **farre pio:** = *mola salsa,* a mixture of meal and salt that was sprinkled on altars during sacrifices (cf. 4.517). It was regularly offered to the Penates (Hor. *Carm.* 3.23.20) and was thought to expiate ill-omened dreams ([Tibullus] 3.4.9).

Extemplo socios primumque accersit Acesten
et Iovis imperium et cari praecepta parentis
edocet et quae nunc animo sententia constet.
haud mora consiliis, nec iussa recusat Acestes.
transcribunt urbi matres populumque volentem   750
deponunt, animos nil magnae laudis egentis.
ipsi transtra novant flammisque ambesa reponunt
robora navigiis, aptant remosque rudentisque,
exigui numero, sed bello vivida virtus.
interea Aeneas urbem designat aratro   755
sortiturque domos; hoc Ilium et haec loca Troiam
esse iubet. gaudet regno Troianus Acestes

746-61. *Aeneas announces his plan to Acestes and his followers. They make lists of those who are to stay behind; then the others repair the fleet while Aeneas marks out the new town.*

746-8. Where Nautes' advice had deepened Aeneas' doubt (719–20 n.), hearing the same advice from his father restores the hero's resolve. **quae . . . constet:** indirect question depending on *edocet,* parallel to the direct objects *imperium* and *praecepta* 747.

749. **haud mora:** construe with understood *est* (cf. 23–4 n.), as always with this common Vergilian phrase. **consiliis:** dative of indirect object (cf. 353 n.).

750. **transcribunt:** ≈ *adscribunt,* the normal technical term for enrolling citizens in a colony (*OLD* s.v. *ascribo* 2b). The change of prefix seems to reflect the transferral of these individuals from Aeneas' leadership to that of Acestes. The subject must be inferred from *socios* (746). **matres:** accusative of direct object.

751. **deponunt:** "they put (them) ashore" as if literally taking them off the ships (Servius). **nil:** cognate or adverbial accusative (AG §390d, n. 2) with *egentis.* **magnae laudis:** genitive of want (AG §356) with *egeo,* which also takes the ablative of separation. Such verbs take the genitive in Greek, which has no ablative, and probably for this reason the construction appealed to the Roman poets who imitated them. **egentis:** accusative in agreement with *animos.*

752. **ipsi:** i.e. Aeneas' *socii* (cf. 750 n.).

753. A hypermetric* line.

754. **virtus:** possibly intended as a collective noun, as if *viri fortes,* in apposition to *exigui* ("few in number, but (*a band of*) *courageous men* keen for war"); but it is easy to understand *est* (cf. 23–4 n.) and infer a possessive so as to render "few in number, but *their* courage *is* keen for war."

755-7. In his note on this passage Servius describes in detail the ritual that the Romans observed in founding a new city. Cf. Vergil's descriptions of the foundations of Carthage (1.420–9) and of Pergamum in Crete (3.132–9). **sortiturque:** on assignment by lot cf. 132 n. **domos:** by metonymy* for "building plots." Aeneas is just laying out the city and distributing land; the houses themselves did not yet exist. For the ending cf. 732 n. **Trōi̯am . . . Trōi̯anus:** cf. 61 n. **regno:** Acestes' settlement is for the first time called a "kingdom."

indicitque forum et patribus dat iura vocatis.
tum vicina astris Erycino in vertice sedes
fundatur Veneri Idaliae, tumuloque sacerdos   760
ac lucus late sacer additur Anchiseo.

---

758. **forum:** here "an assembly," the thing being called the place where it occurs (by metonymy*).

759-61. The cult of Aphrodite at Eryx was famous (Thuc. 6.46.3, Theoc. 15.100) long before it was imported to Rome as the cult of Venus Erycina in 215 BCE. Thereafter it contributed to the Venus cults promoted by Sulla and Pompey as well as to the cult of Venus Genetrix adopted by Julius Caesar and then by Augustus. See Galinsky (1968), Gruen (1992).

761. **lucus late sacer:** Anchises receives a hero's *temenos* at the goddess' cult site. A *lucus* is not a densely planted grove (a *nemus*), but a more open area defined and surrounded by trees, and generally one that is consecrated, so that, strictly speaking, *sacer* is pleonastic* and emphatic. The adverb *late* stands by enallage* for the adjective *latus*, modifying *lucus* logically, but *sacer* grammatically. Vergil sometimes gives a single noun multiple modifiers for special effect (e.g. 3.658 *monstrum horrendum, informe, ingens*, of the Cyclops Polyphemus) but in general he prefers to distribute attributives more evenly throughout a sentence. By using *late*, he avoids the somewhat plodding effect that *lucus latus* would have produced, and further enhances the idea of consecration, so that the *lucus* becomes not merely "broad and holy," but "broadly holy" or "holy throughout its length and breadth," "a wide space of consecrated ground." **additur:** = *additus est*. **Ānchīsēō:** a solemnly spondaic* line ending adds to the religious aura that surrounds the hero's tomb. *Anchiseus* (possessive adjective instead of noun in the genitive; cf. *Hectorei* 190 n.) occurs only here.

762–871: The Trojans Sail from Sicily to Italy

This brief concluding section (90 lines) of departure balances the similarly brief (103 lines) opening section of arrival.

Venus' responsibility for Aeneas' welfare has been evident throughout the book in subtle ways (19-20 n., 23-4 n., 412 n.; cf. 1.667). Now, as the book concludes, her influence becomes overt as she is shown bargaining with Neptune to secure safe passage to Italy for Aeneas and his people (779-826). Thus the reader is aware, even if Aeneas is not, that he would have been lost without her protection. The bargain that Venus strikes involves a human sacrifice as Neptune demands one life in return for the safety of all the rest. The death of Palinurus thus draws together the motifs of literal animal sacrifice (96 n.) and metaphorical* human sacrifice (96-7 n., 327-38 n., 476-81 n., 483-4 n.) that have pervaded much of the previous action in this book.

Bibliography: Putnam (1965) 64-104, Brenk (1991), Dyson (1996), Leigh (2010).

> Iamque dies epulata novem gens omnis, et aris
> factus honos: placidi straverunt aequora venti
> creber et aspirans rursus vocat Auster in altum.
> exoritur procurva ingens per litora fletus;   765
> complexi inter se noctemque diemque morantur.

762-78. *The wind blows fair, and after a sad parting from their comrades Aeneas offers sacrifice and the fleet sets sail.*

762. **iamque dies:** cf. 49 n. There *dies* is nominative, but here it is the accusative of duration of time (AG §423.2). **novem:** a span of nine days separates the day of the games from the events that precede (64-5 n.) and follow it. The religious observances that mark both periods establish a ritual atmosphere for all the events of the book. **epulata:** = *epulata est* (cf. 192 n.). The verb *epulor* denoted public, ceremonial banqueting, often with religious significance (cf. *dapes* 92 n.), as opposed to *cenare,* which is used of private dinner parties. **aris:** ablative, not dative: the altars are where sacrifice occurs, but they do not receive it. Poetry freely uses the ablative of place where without preposition (AG §429.4).

763. **factus:** = *factus est* (cf. 23-4 n.). Although *facio* seems a colorless verb, it is the *mot juste* for making sacrifice (*OLD* s.v. 24). **honos:** archaic* for *honor*, i.e. "sacrifice" (*OLD* s.v. *honor* 2b) and cf. 58 n.

764: **creber et:** for the word order cf. *sed* 5 n. *Creber* is a predicate adjective with adverbial force (cf. *cita* 32-3 n.) grammatically modifying *Auster* but logically referring to the participle *aspirans*.

765. **procurva:** = *curva;* a Vergilian coinage*, occurring only here in classical Latin.

766. **noctemque diemque:** not accusative of duration of time but direct object of *morantur.*

    ipsae iam matres, ipsi, quibus aspera quondam
visa maris facies et non tolerabile numen,
ire volunt omnemque fugae perferre laborem.
quos bonus Aeneas dictis solatur amicis   770
et consanguineo lacrimans commendat Acestae.
tris Eryci vitulos et Tempestatibus agnam
caedere deinde iubet solvique ex ordine funem.
ipse caput tonsae foliis evinctus olivae
stans procul in prora pateram tenet, extaque salsos   775
proicit in fluctus ac vina liquentia fundit.
certatim socii feriunt mare et aequora verrunt;   778
prosequitur surgens a puppi ventus euntis.   777
    At Venus interea Neptunum exercita curis

767-9. **ipsae . . . ipsi:** the repetition emphasizes that even those of both sexes who had not wanted to continue the journey regret having to separate themselves from their friends and relatives and to forego their share in the prize that might have been theirs; cf. 70 n.

768. **visa:** = *visa erat* (cf. 23–4 n.)

769. **perferre:** the prefix indicates willingness to struggle on *through to the end*.

773. **deinde:** cf. 14 n. **ex ordine:** = *rite*, "solemnly," according to Servius, as if casting off were simply a continuation of the preliminary rites (cf. *ex more* 244).

774-8. These lines are substantially composed out of other passages in Vergil's poetry. Some consider the repetitions to be place-holders, assuming that Vergil would have rewritten the lines if he had lived. It seems possible, however, that verbal repetition is meant to underline the ritual quality of the actions described in these lines.

774. ≈ *Geo.* 3.21.

775-6. **extaque . . . fundit:** ≈ 237–8.

777-8. The manuscripts are evenly divided on the ordering of these two lines. The arrangement 778–777 (as printed here), however, seems to describe a more natural sequence of events: first the men start rowing; then a breeze follows/accompanies them as they go (*euntis*).

777. = 3.130.

778. = 3.290. **certatim:** the note of competition links the resumption of the voyage to the interlude of the games (*certamina* 604).

779-826. *Venus, fearful that Juno might rouse another storm, appeals to Neptune to bring Aeneas in safety to the Tiber. Neptune promises to help Aeneas as he has in the past, but demands that one life be sacrificed in recompense for Aeneas' safe passage. Then he drives over the sea to calm it, followed by his train of sea-deities.*

After Aeneas makes sacrifice and departs, the scene shifts to a negotiation on the divine plane, by means of which Venus obtains for Aeneas what he hoped to secure by sacrifice. Viewed from one angle, the shift of scene conforms to the epic motif of double motivation, by virtue of which every action has both human and divine causes. From a slightly different point of view, Aeneas' piety is contrasted with the ruthlessness of the gods as the conventional

adloquitur talisque effundit pectore questus: 780
"Iunonis gravis ira neque exsaturabile pectus
cogunt me, Neptune, preces descendere in omnis;
quam nec longa dies pietas nec mitigat ulla,
nec Iovis imperio fatisque infracta quiescit.
non media de gente Phrygum exedisse nefandis 785
urbem odiis satis est nec poenam traxe per omnem
reliquias Troiae: cineres atque ossa peremptae
insequitur. causas tanti sciat illa furoris.

---

animal sacrifice that he performs is repeated, at Neptune's insistence and with Venus' approval, in the sacrifice of Palinurus (see Leigh (2010)).

781-98. Venus' speech is remarkably manipulative, focusing mainly on Juno's opposition to the Trojans (whom, according to Homer, both Aphrodite/Venus and Poseidon/Neptune supported) and on her more recent arrogant interference in Neptune's own realm (the storm scene in book 1).

781. **Iunonis:** the first word sets the tone for Venus' entire speech. **exsaturabile:** elsewhere only at Statius *Theb.* 1.214; cf. *exsaturata* 7.298 (again with reference to Juno). Lyne (1989) 173–7 detects in *exsaturabile* an intricate and sinister pun involving Juno's most common epithet*, Saturnia (cf. 606 n.) and the carnivorous behavior of her father, Saturnus (= Cronus), in early Greek myth (e.g. Hesiod, *Th.* 453–62); cf. 785–6 n.

782. **descendere:** by using this verb ("to stoop") Venus emphasizes the humility of her plea and the desperateness of her situation.

783. *pietas nec mitigat ulla:* no *pietas* (on Aeneas' part) appeases Juno.

784. **infracta:** the prefix is intensive.

785-6. **non . . . satis est:** the city of Troy is spoken of as the heart that Juno plucks out of the body of the Phrygian people and devours (*exedisse*) before proceeding to outrage the maimed and mutilated remains. The imagery recalls a passage of Homer in which Zeus tells Hera that she would not be satisfied (n.b. *satis* and cf. 781 n.) until she "ate Priam and the sons of Priam raw" (*Il.* 4.34). Achilles, too, tells Hector that he wishes his anger would drive him to devour Hector's corpse (*Il.* 22.346–7), which he then mistreats as Juno is said to have mistreated the Trojans. **traxe:** = *traxisse* by syncope* (4.605–6 n.). The image of "dragging" recalls Achilles' dragging Hector's body around the walls of Troy.

787. **rēliquias:** for the lengthening of the first syllable cf. *Ītaliam* 18 n. *Reliquias* is the direct object of *insequitur* 788, denoting both what remains of the Trojan people (as elsewhere, e.g. 1.30) i.e. "survivors" (*OLD* s.v. *reliquiae* 3) and, continuing the imagery of the previous lines, "the remains or relics of a dead person, esp. after cremation" (*OLD* s.v. 2). **Trŏiae:** cf. 61 n. **cineres atque ossa:** appositive to *reliquias* (cf. 47).

788. **sciat:** jussive subjunctive, dismissive in tone – her reasons (*causas*) are for her to know, because no one else can understand them. There is some irony* in this, since the epic begins with the narrator asking his Muse to tell him the causes of Juno's anger (1.8), which he then traces back to, among other events, the judgment of Paris (1.27), by which Venus (through bribery) – and not Juno – was named fairest of goddesses.

ipse mihi nuper Libycis tu testis in undis
quam molem subito excierit: maria omnia caelo   790
miscuit Aeoliis nequiquam freta procellis,
in regnis hoc ausa tuis.
per scelus ecce etiam Troianis matribus actis
exussit foede puppis et classe subegit
amissa socios ignotae linquere terrae.   795
quod superest, oro, liceat dare tuta per undas
vela tibi, liceat Laurentem attingere Thybrim,
si concessa peto, si dant ea moenia Parcae."
tum Saturnius haec domitor maris edidit alti:

---

789. **tu testis:** construe with *es,* omission of which is not common in the second person (cf. 192 n.), but is here made possible by the emphatic use of the pronoun.

790. Venus here paraphrases Neptune's own words (1.133–4) to remind him of his earlier indignation.

791. **Aeoliis:** because they were caused by Aeolus' letting loose the winds at Juno's request (1.65–75).

793. **per scelus:** "wickedly," to be construed with the ablative absolute *matribus actis.* **Trōiánis:** cf. 61 n.

794-5. **classe . . . amissa:** Venus exaggerates, since only a portion of the fleet was lost.
subegit . . . linquere: Aeneas is to be understood as the subject accusative of *linquere.*
ignotae linquere terrae: another distortion, since the Trojans had visited Sicily previously and regard it as hospitable country (23–4 n.). *Linquere* with direct and indirect object means "to leave something to the mercy or control of something else" (*OLD* s.v. *linquere* 6).

796. **quod superest:** "as for the rest," a transitional formula (cf. 691 n.).

796-7. **liceat . . . liceat:** i.e. to Aeneas and his remaining followers. **dare tuta . . . vela tibi:** elsewhere (e.g. 1.35) *dare vela* alone means "to set sail" (cf. 139 n.), and that idiom should be borne in mind; but the indirect object *tibi* (like *fatis* 3.9 and *ventis* 4.546) almost requires that *dare* be translated as "give." Venus asks Neptune that the Trojans might entrust their sails to him instead of to the fates or the winds (i.e. that they might sail under his protection).

798. **ea moenia:** i.e. walls by the Tiber, which has just been mentioned (*Thybrim* 797).

799. **Saturnius:** while Juno is frequently called *Saturnia* (606 n.), Neptune is *Saturnius* only here, perhaps to signal that he is a match for his sister; perhaps also, in view of his startling demand at 814–15, to suggest that all of Saturn's children share something of the same bloodthirsty temperament (cf. 781 n.).

"fas omne est, Cytherea, meis te fidere regnis, 800
unde genus ducis. merui quoque; saepe furores
compressi et rabiem tantam caelique marisque.
nec minor in terris, Xanthum Simoentaque testor,
Aeneae mihi cura tui. cum Troia Achilles
exanimata sequens impingeret agmina muris, 805

800-15. Neptune's response is gracious and receptive to Venus' request, emphasizing their like-mindedness. But after granting Aeneas safe passage, he mentions almost casually, but pointedly, that he will require one life in compensation for this favor.

800. **fas omne est:** "it is entirely right." **Cytherĕa:** the long *e* of the penult represents the Greek diphthong ει in Κυθέρεια. The island of Cythera was the site of an important cult of Aphrodite because it was there that she was born of the sea-foam (Hesiod, *Th.* 192–3). Neptune, as god of the sea, aptly addresses Venus by this cult-title to suggest their affinity. **meis te fidere regnis:** the infinitive depends on the impersonal construction *fas est:* "it is right to . . . " (AG §454; cf. §452), with *te* as subject accusative. The case of *meis . . . regnis* is uncertain, because *fidere* takes either the dative of indirect object (§AG 367) or the ablative (of place where, according to AG § 431), with no difference in meaning.

801. **merui:** in addition to the confidence that Venus would naturally have in Neptune as the god of the element in which she was born, he has "earned" her trust by protecting Aeneas from shipwreck. **saepe:** the Trojans have survived two storms at sea (1.81–156, 3.192–210) and have avoided another (5.8–34). In book 1 the reader knows for certain that it was Neptune who saved the Trojans. Book 3 is narrated by Aeneas, who cannot inform his audience what divine forces may lie behind natural phenomena. In this book, when Palinurus faces the first storm he wonders out loud what Neptune has in store (14)—a question that will be shockingly answered in this episode (814–15, 840), at least for the reader; but neither Palinurus nor Aeneas will ever know the whole truth (6.341–62). So, with *saepe* the reader glimpses as Aeneas cannot how constantly the gods' favor sustains him.

802-11. Neptune recalls the contest between Aeneas and Achilles as described by Homer (*Il.* 20.156–351). Achilles' contest with the river Xanthus in fact takes place after his duel with Aeneas (*Il.* 21.136–382).

804-810. **cum . . . cum:** the verbs of both of these *cum* clauses (for the first, *impingeret, daret, gemerentque,* and *posset* 805–7; for the second, *cuperem* 810) are imperfect subjunctives to express action simultaneous with that of the main verb (*rapui* 810); but the force of the first clause is circumstantial (AG §546), while that of the second is concessive (AG §549): when the Trojans could do nothing to stop Achilles, Neptune saved Aeneas from him, even though the god wanted the city destroyed. There are no explicit verbal markers to help make this distinction; the reader must infer that the second clause is concessive from knowing that, in the *Iliad,* Poseidon (the Greek Neptune) favored the Greeks and opposed the Trojans.

804-5. **Aeneae:** objective genitive (AG §348), modified by *tui* and depending on *cura*. **mihi:** dative of possession (AG § 373) with understood *est* (cf. 23–4 n.). **Trŏi̯a:** trisyllabic (though the final syllable is lost in elision* before *Achilles*). **agmina:** "troops" (cf. 90 n.), governed in common by *sequens* and *impingeret*. As often, a circumstantial participle is best rendered as a parallel main verb—"when Achilles *was pursuing* the exhausted Trojan troops *and pinning* them . . . ."

milia multa daret leto, gemerentque repleti
amnes nec reperire viam atque evolvere posset
in mare se Xanthus, Pelidae tunc ego forti
congressum Aenean nec dis nec viribus aequis
nube cava rapui, cuperem cum vertere ab imo   810
structa meis manibus periurae moenia Troiae.
nunc quoque mens eadem perstat mihi; pelle timores.
tutus, quos optas, portus accedet Averni.
unus erit tantum amissum quem gurgite quaeres;
unum pro multis dabitur caput."   815
his ubi laeta deae permulsit pectora dictis,
iungit equos auro genitor, spumantiaque addit
frena feris manibusque omnis effundit habenas.
caeruleo per summa levis volat aequora curru;
subsidunt undae tumidumque sub axe tonanti   820
sternitur aequor aquis, fugiunt vasto aethere nimbi.

806-8. In recalling this scene from the *Iliad*, Neptune "quotes" the words of the river Xanthus (21.218–20), which had previously been paraphrased in Latin by Catullus (64.357–60).

806. **dare leto:** "put to death" (cf. 139 n.).

809. **Aenean:** cf. 708 n.

810. **nube cava:** cf. 1.516. At *Iliad* 20.321 Neptune saves Aeneas by bringing a mist over the eyes of Achilles. **cum:** concessive.

811. **periurae moenia Troiae:** "Neptune and Apollo built the walls of Troy; when King Laomedon cheated them of their promised reward, they destroyed the city" (Perkell on 3.3). For the pronunciation of *Trŏi̯ae* cf. 61 n.

813. **tutus:** construe as an adverb: "safely" or "in safety" (136–7 n.).

814. **unus erit . . . quem:** ≈ <u>unus erit quem</u> *tu tolles in caerula caeli* | *templa* (Ennius, *Annales* fr. 54–5 in Skutsch (1985), fr. 63–4 in Warmington (1935–40); cf. Ovid, *Met.* 14.806, *Fast.* 2.485). The Ennian context refers to the apotheosis of Romulus, whose fate contrasts sharply with that of the sacrificial victim Palinurus. On the word order *amissum quem* cf. *sed* 5 n.

815. **caput:** = *vita,* as often in Latin.

816. **laeta:** proleptic* – his words soothed her soul and so made it glad.

817. **auro:** ablative of means, "with gold"; equivalent in sense to *aureo iugo,* "with a golden yoke." **genitor:** cf. 14 n.

821. **sternitur aequor aquis:** ≈ 8.89. **aequor:** the level surface (cf. *aequus*) of either water or land (141 n.; cf. *Geo.* 1.50); perhaps proleptic* in view of the verb *sternitur* – the surface of the water is calmed and so becomes level. **aquis:** variously explained as dative of reference or ablative of place where.

tum variae comitum facies, immania cete,
et senior Glauci chorus Inousque Palaemon
Tritonesque citi Phorcique exercitus omnis;
laeva tenent Thetis et Melite Panopeaque virgo,   825
Nisaee Spioque Thaliaque Cymodoceque.

---

822. **tum:** cf. 455 n. Construe with understood *sequuntur* or some similar verb. **cētē:** a Greek form, τὰ κήτη (neuter nominative plural) from τὸ κῆτος, "whales" or "sea monsters" of any sort.

823-6. A catalogue of minor sea divinities in Neptune's retinue. Pliny the Elder (*Nat. Hist.* 36.5.26) describes a painting by Scopas that hung in the Circus Flaminius, in which were depicted Neptune, Thetis, Achilles, Nereids riding on dolphins, whales (or seahorses), Tritons, the "chorus" of Phorcus, sea-monsters, and other marine creatures. The panel was probably known to Vergil and may have helped to inspire this highly pictorial passage. But stimulus to the visual imagination is equalled by the musical sequence of exotic names, many of them clearly borrowed from specific literary sources (see notes). Apart from such decorative functions, catalogues in the *Aeneid* lend emphasis at key points in the narrative and ease transitions between episodes.

823. **Glauci:** a Boeotian fisherman who was changed into a sea-god (Ovid, *Met.* 14.1–74) and became a sort of typical "old man of the sea." **Inōūsque:** possessive adjective instead of genitive (cf. *Hectorei* 190 n.), "Ino's (son)." Ino (alias Leucothoe or Leucothea), is a Theban princess who, being pursued by her insane husband, Athamas, threw herself from a cliff into the waves below and was transformed into a minor sea-goddess (Ovid, *Met.* 4.416–562). **Palaemon:** son of Athamas and Ino who shared his mother's fate; also known as Melicertes (*Geo.* 1.437) and identified with the Roman god Portunus (241 n. with Servius *ad loc.*).

824. **Tritones:** Triton is a single individual at 1.144 and 6.173, but he "became 'pluralized' in works of art" (Williams (1960) on 823 f.). The fact that Pliny too speaks of *Tritones* in the Scopas panel (cf. 823–6 n.) may be a sign that Vergil had this particular image in mind. **Phorcique:** Hesiod (*Theog.* 237) and Homer (*Od.* 13.96) know a sea-god named Phorcys, a third-declension name; other writers use the second-declension form Phorkos (Latin *Phorcus*), which Vergil adopts here.

825-6. **laeva:** = *laeva loca* (cf. 168 n.). **Thetis . . . Cymodoceque:** in a famous Homeric catalogue (*Il.* 18.39–49) Thetis, sea-goddess and mother of Achilles, is accompanied by twenty-four nymphs, daughters of the sea-god Nereus, including the six named here. **Panopaeaque virgo:** 240, *Geo.* 1.437.

826. This line is formed from two halves of the lines that begin Homer's catalogue of Nereids (*Il.* 18.39–40).

Hic patris Aeneae suspensam blanda vicissim
gaudia pertemptant mentem; iubet ocius omnis
attolli malos, intendi bracchia velis.
una omnes fecere pedem pariterque sinistros,   830
nunc dextros solvere sinus; una ardua torquent
cornua detorquentque; ferunt sua flamina classem.
princeps ante omnis densum Palinurus agebat
agmen; ad hunc alii cursum contendere iussi.
iamque fere mediam caeli Nox umida metam   835
contigerat, placida laxabant membra quiete
sub remis fusi per dura sedilia nautae,
cum levis aetheriis delapsus Somnus ab astris

827-71. *As the fleet sails with fair winds, the god Sleep, taking the shape of a sailor, tries to persuade Palinurus to abandon his post and enjoy some rest. When Palinurus refuses, the god first throws him into a profound sleep and then casts him overboard. Aeneas wakes, discovers the loss of his pilot, and takes his place.*

The death of Palinurus continues a pattern that begins with the loss of Creusa at the end of book 2 and the deaths of Anchises and Dido in books 3 and 4, respectively. Here death is most explicitly figured as the sacrifice of a blameless victim. The theme of sacrifice, which is so prominent in this book, thus culminates in one of the most troubling and seemingly arbitrary and unnecessary deaths in the entire poem. See especially Putnam (1965), Feldherr (1995).

827. **suspensam blanda:** a splendid instance of what Horace (*Ars Poet.* 47–8) calls *callida iunctura*, ("clever juxtaposition"). The words contrast sharply, illustrating how Aeneas' anxiety begins giving way to the enticement of hope. **suspensam:** cf. 4.9.

829. **malos:** from *malus, -i,* "mast" (not *malus -a -um,* "bad, evil"). **intendi:** 403 n.

830-1. **una . . . pariter . . . una:** emphasizes the way in which the whole fleet acts together. **fecere pedem:** *pedes* are the sheets or ropes at the bottom of a sail, by which it can be adjusted for tacking. **fecere . . . solvere:** perfect indicatives of *facio* (= *fecerunt*) and *solvo* (*solverunt*), respectively (cf. 8 n.). **sinūs:** cf. 16 n.

832. **sua:** 53–4 n. Stronger than the simple possessive (*eius*), the reflexive form indicates an especially close relationship: the winds are so favorable that they seem to belong to the fleet.

834. **ad hunc:** "towards him." **cursum:** direct object of *contendere*. **iussi:** *iussi sunt* (cf. 23–4 n.).

835-8. **iamque fere . . . cum:** 49 n., 159–60 n., 327 n. **mediam . . . metam:** the personified Night in her chariot (721) is supposed to ascend the sky, like the sun, and at midnight half her course is done and she begins to descend; the midpoint in her journey is therefore compared to the turning post that marks the half-way point of a chariot race. In this context the imagery inevitably recalls the position of the Trojan fleet at the opening of the book (cf. 1–2 n. *medium . . . tenebat . . . iter*) and the drama of the boat-race around its all-important turning post (for *meta*, cf. 129 n., 159).

838. A golden line*. **lĕvis:** predicate adjective with adverbial force (cf. *cita* 32–3 n.), grammatically modifying *Somnus* but logically referring to the participle *delapsus*.

aëra dimovit tenebrosum et dispulit umbras,
te, Palinure, petens, tibi somnia tristia portans   840
insonti; puppique deus consedit in alta
Phorbanti similis funditque has ore loquelas:
"Iaside Palinure, ferunt ipsa aequora classem,
aequatae spirant aurae, datur hora quieti.
pone caput fessosque oculos furare labori.   845
ipse ego paulisper pro te tua munera inibo."
cui vix attollens Palinurus lumina fatur:
"mene salis placidi vultum fluctusque quietos
ignorare iubes? mene huic confidere monstro?

---

839. **áĕră:** accusative (cf. 13 n.).

840. **te, Palinure:** Vergil is more restrained in using apostrophe* than later epic poets, and more deliberate than is Homer. This instance must rank as one of the most effective in the entire poem.

841. **insonti:** unexpected and very emphatic by enjambment* and by caesura* in the second foot. Vergil makes it as clear as possible that Palinurus has done nothing to deserve this death. **deus:** suggests the divine power that Somnus will bring to bear on Palinurus. It is not to be a fair fight.

842. **Phorbanti:** this Phorbas is otherwise unkown. At Hom. *Il.* 14.490 a Phorbas is named as the father of Ilioneus, but no direct reference to the Homeric passage seems intended. Vergil prefers to give minor characters Homeric names rather than to introduce new names into the epic tradition. **loquelas:** often suggests soft, insinuating speech; cf. Lucr. *DRN* 1.39, an often imitated passage in which the poet asks Venus herself to seek peace for the Romans by blandishing *loquelas* on her lover Mars — thus preventing unnecessary deaths rather than causing one, as the *loquelae* of Somnus (who is presumably Neptune's agent acting with Venus' complicity) do here.

843. **Iăsĭdē:** four syllables; a Greek form, ὦ Ἰασίδη (masculine vocative singular) from the patronymic* ὁ Ἰασίδης, "son of Iasius"; contrast the *-ē* of the Latin second-declension vocative (cf. *Menoete* 166 n.). A son of Jupiter, Iasius was one of the founders of the Trojan race (cf. Perkell on 3.168); Palinurus (like Iapyx, 12.392) was one of his descendants.

845. **furare:** imperative of the deponent verb *furor, furari*. **labori:** dative of separation (AG §381), common with verbs meaning "to take."

847. **cui:** dative with *attollens* (cf. 34 n.). Construe as a connective relative: "but to him . . . ." **vix . . . :** "scarcely lifting his eyes," i.e. keeping them steadily fixed on the prow and the star he was steering by, without attending to his interlocutor. The explanation "with scarcely lifted eyes," as though they were already feeling the drowsy influence of the god, is forced and inconsistent with the very energetic reply which follows.

848-49. **mene . . . mene:** emphatic by position and by anaphora*: "Are you telling *me* . . . ?" **iubes:** construe with both *me ignorare* and *me confidere*.

Aenean credam (quid enim?) fallacibus auris   850
et caeli, totiens deceptus fraude sereni?"
talia dicta dabat, clavumque adfixus et haerens
nusquam amittebat oculosque sub astra tenebat.
ecce deus ramum Lethaeo rore madentem
vique soporatum Stygia super utraque quassat   855
tempora, cunctantique natantia lumina solvit.
vix primos inopina quies laxaverat artus,

---

850. **Aenean:** cf. 708 n. Emphatic by position, as if to say, "even assuming I might be reckless about my own safety, could I ever expose *Aeneas* to such risk?" **quid enim?:** the parenthesis contributes to the vivid, almost colloquial character of Palinurus' speech.

851. **et:** = *etsi*, to be construed with *deceptus*: "even though (I have been) deceived . . . ." **caeli:** manuscripts and editors are divided between *caeli* and *caelo*. The former, "entrust Aeneas to the false winds even (*et*) when so often deceived by the treachery of a clear sky" (note that this entails taking *et* as an intensive adverb, as for instance in *timeo Danaos et dona ferentis*, 2.49), gives better sense than the latter, "entrust Aeneas to the false winds and (*et*) the sky after being so often deceived by fair weather," which entails taking the adjective *sereno* ("fair") substantively ("fair weather").

852. **dicta dabat:** = *dicebat* (cf. 139 n.).

853. **nusquam:** a very strong negative (*OLD* s.v. 5) with no reference to place as such. **amittebat:** cf. *datūr* 284 n. **sub astra:** "directed up towards (*OLD* s.v. *sub* 21) the stars" by which he was steering.

854. **Lethaeo rore:** Lethe is the river of forgetfulness in the Greek mythological underworld (6.749–50). Here the waters of Lethe cause Palinurus to fall into a deep sleep and thus, very much against his will, to "forget" his duty.

855-6. **vique soporatum Stygia:** a complex, powerful phrase, launched by this book's third and final instance of *vis*, "violence" (67–8 n., 454 n.). *Sopor* as compared with *somnus* is "a deep and overpowering sleep" or one "applied to the sleep of death" (*OLD* s.v.); and while the verb *soporo* everywhere else means "to put to sleep," Vergil alone uses only the participle (here and in the very similar 6.420) to mean "endowed with soporific properties." Finally, Styx, the river of death, encircles the underworld. To cross it is to die (cf. 6.134); Palinurus' fate, to die without being allowed to cross it, is still worse (6.367–76). **utraque . . . tempora:** 233 n. **cunctantique . . . :** "and despite his efforts (i.e. his struggles to keep awake) loosens his swimming eyes." *Solvit* stands in opposition to *tenebat* (853), which describes an "intent" gaze.

857-9. **laxaverat . . . et proiecit:** "an example of parataxis*, wherein two independent clauses are placed side by side without a subordinating conjunction" (Ganiban *ad* 2.172; cf. AG §268); here the effect is softened somewhat by the coordinating conjunction *et* ("peace (*quies*) had scarcely relaxed his limbs, *and* he (*Somnus*) threw (the helmsman) overboard," where *cum inversum* (see 84 n., and with *vix . . . et* cf. *vix . . . cum* 693 n.) might have been expected ("peace had scarcely relaxed his limbs *when* Somnus threw him . . . ").

857. **primos . . . artus:** "peace had scarcely relaxed *his first limbs*" may be understood as an instance of enallage* for "peace had scarcely *first begun to relax* his limbs" (with the adjective *primos* "replacing" the adverb *primum*); but the notion of peace as seeping

et superincumbens cum puppis parte revulsa
cumque gubernaclo liquidas proiecit in undas
praecipitem ac socios nequiquam saepe vocantem;   860
ipse volans tenuis se sustulit ales ad auras.
currit iter tutum non setius aequore classis
promissisque patris Neptuni interrita fertur.
iamque adeo scopulos Sirenum advecta subibat,
difficilis quondam multorumque ossibus albos   865
(tum rauca adsiduo longe sale saxa sonabant),
cum pater amisso fluitantem errare magistro
sensit, et ipse ratem nocturnis rexit in undis

---

gradually through the body and so having got control of just his *primos artus,* i.e. the first *parts of* his limbs that it encounters, is very powerful.

858-9. **cum . . . cumque:** cf. *in . . . inque* 2.51; *perque . . . perque* 1.537, 2.364, 4.671. The repeated pronoun adds force. The conjunction is not required (cf. 2.358 *per tela per hostes*), "but it also adds a certain vehemence to the style" (Page).

861. **ales:** predicate adjective modifying *ipse,* best construed as an adverbial phrase (cf. *cita* 32–3 n.) modifying *sustulit:* "he lifted himself (*se*) on (*his*) wings."

862. **iter:** cognate accusative with *currit* (AG §390).

864-7. **iamque adeo . . . cum:** 49 n., 159–60 n., 268–70 n.

864. **scopulos Sirenum:** the Sirens were mythical creatures whose beautiful singing enticed sailors into shipwreck against the rocky shores of their islands. Vergil follows Apollonius (and Hellenistic scholarship generally) in locating these islands somewhere near the bay of Naples; but in the *Argonautica* (4.885–919; cf. Nelis (2001) 205–9), Aphrodite Erycina rescues Butes, the only Argonaut to leap overboard under the influence of the Sirens' song, while here Venus Erycina conspires in the death of Palinurus. Cf. 865–6 n.

865-6. **quondam . . . tum:** the Sirens were *once* a danger because of their song; Odysseus alone heard their song and nevertheless sailed safely by (*Od.* 12.37–54, 153–200). According to post-Homeric tradition, the Sirens became distraught at Odysseus' success and hurled themselves into the sea; *then* (including in particular the time when Aeneas approached them) the only sound to be heard was that of waves crashing against the rocks. **rauca:** perhaps modifying *saxa,* as either an attributive or (more likely) a predicate adjective ("the noisy rocks resounded" vs. "the rocks resounded noisily," cf. *cita* 32–3 n.; possibly better construed as modifying the internal accusative of *sonabant* ("the rocks *make rough noises*"; cf. 19 n.). In all three cases the roughness is explained by the incessant pounding of the waves (*adsiduo . . . sale,* ablative of cause; on *sale* cf. 848 n.), and the quality of the sound is expressed in the hissing sibilants of *ad*s*iduo . . . s*ale *s*axa *s*onabant.

868. **ipse ratem . . . rexit . . . undis:** Aeneas takes his helmsman's place. The act invites two opposite interpretations. On the one hand, it may symbolize Aeneas' continued growth as a leader; on the other, it repeats what Gyas did when he pitched Menoetes overboard, tried to steer the ship himself (cf. 176 n. *ipse . . . ipse*), and went from first place to last in the boat race.

multa gemens casuque animum concussus amici:
"o nimium caelo et pelago confise sereno, 870
nudus in ignota, Palinure, iacebis harena."

870-1. Aeneas pronounces an epitaph for his lost comrade, one that is dignified and in keeping with the traditions of the genre.

870. **nimium . . . confise:** Williams (1960) on line 850 observes that "It is a most effective piece of poetic irony* that Aeneas in his last farewell to Palinurus attributes his death to the very thing that he had most resolutely refused to do." The gap between human and divine perspectives remains enormous.

871. **nudus:** "unburied." On the consequences of not receiving burial see 6.322–30. The contrast between the unfortunate helmsman's fate and the elaborate honors paid to Anchises, who rests in a proper grave, is extremely stark.

Appendix A: Vergil's Meter[1]

1. Basic concepts. Dactylic hexamater was the meter of Homer and later Greek epic. Once it was adopted by the influential Latin poet Ennius in his *Annales* (second century BCE),[2] it became the meter of Roman epic as well. As the name indicates, "dactylic hexameter" literally describes a line that contains six (Gr. *hex*) measures (Gr. *metra*) or, more commonly, "feet."[3] The individual feet consisted of one long syllable, conventionally noted by a symbol (–) called a "macron" (from the Greek word for "long"), followed by two short ones, each noted by the symbol (◡) called a "breve" (from the Latin word for "short"). The feet were called "dactyls" because their shape resembles the structure of a finger (*dactylos* in Greek): the bone from the main knuckle to the first joint is longer than the two bones leading to the fingertip (– ◡◡). The first syllable of a dactylic foot is always long, and this regularity preserves a sense of metrical beat within the line. But because short syllables in Greek and Latin take about half as long to pronounce as long ones, a long syllable could substitute for the two short ones in any of the first four feet.[4] The resulting foot (– –) was called a "spondee" from the Greek word for "pouring a libation to the gods," because the slow movement of spondaic verse was regarded as suitable for such solemn occasions. The fifth foot is almost always a dactyl, so that the basic character of the verse reasserts itself as the end of the line approaches.[5] The end itself is signaled by the unique character of the sixth foot, which is actually truncated (or, in metrical terminology, catalectic), i.e. the final short syllable of the sixth foot is omitted. The syllable that follows the initial long is allowed to be either long or short, and is marked

---

[1] For more on Vergil's meter, see Jackson Knight (1944) 232–42, Duckworth (1969) 46–62, Nussbaum (1986), and Ross (2007) 143–52.

[2] The earliest Latin epics by Livius Andronicus and Naevius were composed in Saturnian verse, a meter that is not fully understood.

[3] This word probably originated with choral meters, i.e. dance meters, and then applied to other meters, like the dactylic hexameter, that were not meant for dancing.

[4] More technically the two short syllables of a dactyl are "contracted" into one long syllable, and a spondee is formed.

[5] Very rarely a spondee occurs in the fifth foot, in which case character of the line is felt to be so altered that it is called "spondaic."

with a symbol (x) called "anceps" (Latin for "two-headed," i.e. "undecided"). Therefore, the end of a line was largely regularized as – ⏑⏑ / –x, so that no matter what pattern of dactyls and spondees may be found in the first four feet, the end of almost every line is quite regular. The general scheme of the Latin dactylic hexameter can thus be notated as follows:

$$-\underset{1}{\smile\smile} \;/\; -\underset{2}{\smile\smile} \;/\; -\underset{3}{\smile\smile} \;/\; -\underset{4}{\smile\smile} \;/\; -\underset{5}{\smile\smile} \;/\; -\underset{6}{\mathrm{x}}$$

Here, a solidus (/) separates metrical feet, and places where two short syllables may be replaced by a single long one are marked with the notation ⏓.

A general idea of the dactylic hexameter rhythm can be felt in the opening of Longfellow's *Evangeline*:

Thís ĭs thĕ /fórĕst prĭ/mévăl. Thĕ /múrmŭrĭng /pínes ănd thĕ /hémlŏcks
      1   2   3   4   5   6 x

béardĕd wĭth /móss, ănd ĭn /gármēnts /gréen, ĭndĭ/stínct ĭn thĕ /twílĭght,
      1   2   3   4   5   6 x

stánd līke /Drúĭds ŏf /éld, wĭth /vóicēs /sád ănd prŏ/phétĭc,
      1   2   3   4   5   6 x

stánd līke /hárpērs /hóar, wĭth /béards thāt /rést ŏn thĕɪr /bósŏms.
      1   2   3   4   5   6 x

In the first line, five dactylic feet are followed by a final disyllabic foot; in each successive line, the substitution of spondees for dactyls in the first four feet becomes more and more frequent, until line 4 is entirely spondaic up to the fifth foot. The different patterns found in these four lines begin to suggest something of the verse-form's flexibility. A difference between Latin and English verse, however, is that in English, the first syllable in each foot must not only be long, but must also bear the natural accent* of the word, and that there must be no other word accent in any foot, apart from the first syllable. In Classical Latin meter, however, metrical feet are based not on word *stress* but on the *quantity* of individual syllables (i.e. whether they are long or short). Thus, in Latin, a word's natural accent will not always fall on the first syllable of a foot.

2. *Scansion.* In learning to read a line of Latin metrically, it is important to learn how to *scan* it, i.e. to identify its pattern of long and short syllables. A syllable can be *long* in two ways: *by nature*, if it contains either a vowel that

is inherently long or a diphthong;[6] or *by position*, if it contains a naturally short vowel followed either by a double consonant (*x* or *z*) or, in most cases, by two consonants, even if one or both consonants are found in the next word.[7] In general, all other syllables are *short*.[8] If, however, a word ending in a vowel, diphthong, or *-m* is followed by a word that begins with a vowel, diphthong, or *h* + vowel, the first vowel or diphthong is *elided*. Elided syllables are not marked long or short but are tied to the syllable that follows, which receives its normal value as either long or short. *Elision* occurs frequently in Vergil.[9]

Here are a couple of examples to illustrate these rules:

haud equidem sine mente, reor, sine numine divum   (*Aen.* 5.56)

This is a very easy line to scan. As we will see, it is entirely dactylic, and it contains no elisions, so that every vowel counts in some way. Since the last foot contains only two syllables, and the next-to-last foot is almost always dactylic, we may begin by marking off the last two feet:

haud equidem sine mente, reor, sine ′nūmĭnĕ ′dīvŭm
                                           5   6

That leaves four feet, which means there must be at least four additional long syllables at the beginning of each. Three vowels in the first four feet are followed by a pair of consonants, so that the length of these syllables is unmistakably clear:

haud equidēm sine mēnte, reŏr, sine ′nūmĭnĕ ′dīvŭm
                                             5   6

---

6   One can determine if a vowel is long by nature by looking the word up in a dictionary to see if it has a macron over it or by checking inflected endings in a grammar (for example, some endings, like the first and second declension ablative singular (-*a*, -*o*), are always long; others, like the second declension nominative neuter plural (-*a*), are always short). The standard Latin diphthongs include *ae, au,* and *oe,* but note that in Greek names and other Greek words, these same combinations may be treated as separate vowels. Such instances are generally noted in the commentary.

7   An exception to this general rule: if a short vowel is followed by a mute consonant (*b, c, d, g, p, t*) and a liquid (*l* or *r*), the resulting syllable can be either short or long. Cf. 2.663 where *patris* and *patrem* are short and long respectively: *natum ante ora pătris, pātrem qui obtruncat ad aras.* It should also be noted that *h* is a rough breathing mark, not a true consonant; it therefore does not help make a vowel long by position.

8   Rarely, however, a short syllable is lengthened in arsis*.

9   Rarely, however, a final vowel is left unelided in *hiatus**.

Here a bit of arithmetic is helpful. If there are four feet, and all are spondiac, then there will be eight syllables in all (4 x 2); if they are all dactylic, there will be twelve syllables (4 x 3). So the number of syllables remaining must be in that range (or we will have made some mistake). Remembering that diphthongs (like *au* in *haud*) count as a single vowel, and that the *u* that follows *q*, as in *equidem*, does not count as a vowel, we find that there are in fact twelve vowels in all:

$$h\underset{1}{au}d\;\underset{2}{e}qu\underset{3\;4}{i}d\underset{5\;6}{e}m\;s\underset{7}{i}n\underset{8}{e}\;m\underset{9\;10}{e}nt\underset{}{e},\;r\underset{}{e}\underset{}{o}r,\;s\underset{11\;12}{i}n\underset{}{e}$$

So the remaining four feet must be entirely dactylic. We may already know that the *au* in *haud* is long by nature, because it's a diphthong, and in any case the first syllable of the line will always be long. If we put it together with the three other long syllables that we identified and subtract those four from the total of twelve, the remainder is eight, and all of these must be short. That leaves us with this perfectly scanned line:

$$h\bar{au}d\;\breve{e}qu\acute{i}d\breve{e}m\;s\breve{i}n\breve{e}\;m\bar{e}nt\breve{e},\;r\bar{e}\breve{o}r,\;s\breve{i}n\breve{e}\;n\bar{u}m\breve{i}n\breve{e}\;d\bar{i}v\breve{u}m$$

The next example is a little more complicated:

> interea medium Aeneas iam classe tenebat   (*Aen.* 5.1)

We can start the same way, by assuming that the fifth and sixth feet conform to the general pattern:

$$\text{interea medium Aeneas iam}\;\overset{}{cl\bar{a}ss\breve{e}}\;\overset{}{t\breve{e}n\bar{e}b\overset{x}{a}t}$$

Again this works well: the *a* in *classe* is long by position, and we may know that the *e* that precedes the personal endings of second-conjugation verbs is long by nature if the ending has at least two syllables (as it always does in the imperfect -*ēbam*, -*ēbās*, etc.). In any case, we once again have four feet to scan, and this time we seem to have more than twelve vowels, which should be impossible. But if we look more carefully, we should realize that the *i* in *iam* is a consonant, not a vowel. Just realizing that, by the way, gives us another foot, because the *a* in *iam* itself is followed by a consonant cluster (*m* + *cl*), so that it is long by position; and since it is the final syllable of its foot, that foot must be a spondee, so that the preceding syllable must be long, as well. And in fact, the last syllable of *Aeneas* is long both by nature and by position, since the *a* is followed by *s* + consonantal *i* (or *j*). That gives us:

interea medium Aeneās iam classe tenebat
                        4   5   6

Now, looking over the remaining three feet for any vowels that are long by nature or by position, we notice two: the *i* of *interea* and the diphthong *Ae* in *Aeneas*. Since there is only one syllable between this *ae* and the beginning of the next foot, that syllable must be long as well, because the pattern – ᵕ – (which is called a "cretic") cannot occur in dactylic verse. That gives us one more foot:

interea medium Aēnē ās iam classe tenebat
                    3   4   5   6

Only two feet left; but there still seem to be too many syllables, because the most we can use now is six, and in *interea medium* there are seven vowels. But, once again, we should now notice, if we have not already, that *medium* ends in a vowel plus *m* and the word that follows it, *Aeneas*, begins with a diphthong, which is a kind of vowel. That situation almost always produces an elision (noted by a small circle under the elided vowel) which means that the final *um* in *medium* does not make a syllable; and this leaves us with six vowels to distribute evenly over the remaining two feet, which therefore must be dactyls:

intĕrĕā mĕdĭu̥m Aēnē ās iam classe tenebat
 1   2   3   4   5   6

This is obviously not the way that the ancient Romans read poetry, and it is not the way that you will eventually read it, either. In fact, you should always practice reading Vergil, preferably aloud, according to a natural dactylic pattern. There will be times, especially at the beginning, when you will not be able to figure out the metrical pattern of a line, and this is where applying the more mechanical process of scansion outlined here can help. In addition, if you make it a habit to scan a few lines every day, eventually you will become more familiar with the most likely and possible patterns of dactylic verse, and you should develop a better sense of natural quantity, as well; and this will help you to read the poetry with real enjoyment of its natural sound and its artistry, which are among its most beautiful characteristics.

3. *Internal pauses.* The flow of a line is affected not only by its rhythm but also by the placement of word breaks, of which there are two kinds. A word break between metrical feet is called a *diaeresis* (Greek, "a pulling apart" by

the seams).¹⁰ A word break in the middle of a foot is called a *caesura* (Latin, "a cutting"). Diaereses are largely avoided, because if too many word endings fall at the ends of metrical feet, the line will sound choppy. But they can also be used to good effect. In the following line

ēt iăcĭt. ‖ ārrēc´taē mēn´tēs stŭpĕ´fāctăquĕ ‖ cōrdă   (*Aen.* 5.643)

There are two *diaereses* (‖), one after *iacit* and the other after *stupefactaque*.¹¹ The first one is obviously more significant, because Vergil has chosen it as the place to end a sentence that began in a previous line before stopping here. This is a device called enjambment*, which is used to create emphasis. Conversely, the second diaeresis between the fifth and sixth feet is a very frequent occurrence in hexameter poetry. It seldom coincides with a syntactical pause and in general does nothing to impede the movement of the line to its conclusion.

There will be more to say about diaereses later on. But if we look back at the line we considered previously, we notice that caesurae (marked with a ᵞ) are found in the second, fourth, and fifth feet:

īntĕrĕ´ā ᵞ mĕdĭu̯m ‖ Āēnē´ās ᵞ i̯ām ‖ clāssĕ ᵞ tĕ´nēbăt   (*Aen.* 5.1)

When a caesura falls after a long syllable (like the first and second caesurae above, following *intereā* and *Aeneās*), it is called "strong"; if it falls after a short syllable (like the third one, following *classĕ*), it is called "weak." A strong caesura does not necessarily entail a longer pause than a weak caesura: the terminology relates to the "strong" or "weak," i.e. long or short, character of the syllable that precedes it.

It is no accident that caesurae occur more frequently than diaereses. When a word break falls at the end of a foot, particularly early in the line, it tends to arrest the movement of the verse, while ending a word in the middle of a foot creates an opportunity to pause without compromising a sense of

---

10 When a *diaeresis* occurs just before the fifth foot, it is often called a *bucolic diaeresis* because this type of diaeresis was used frequently in pastoral poetry: e.g. *nos patriam fugimus; tu, Tityre,* ‖ *lentus in umbra* (Vergil, *Eclogues* 1.4).

11 Note, however, that in the combinations *qu*, *gu*, or *su* + vowel (e.g. *-que*, *sanguis*, *suesco*), the *u* does not count as a vowel but is treated as part of the the preceding consonant, so that the combinations themselves count as a single consonant for the purposes of scansion.

forward movement.¹² There is almost always at least one important caesura in any given line (which may be strong or weak, though in Latin strong caesurae are more common), and it often coincides with a sense break and is called the *main* or *principal caesura*.¹³ It most frequently falls in the third foot, but also occurs not uncommonly in the second or fourth (or sometimes both). In the example given above, it is easy to imagine a strong pause after *interea* (just as one would pause in English after beginning a sentence with "Meanwhile... ") and a slighter pause after *Aeneas* (which serves to emphasize the subject of the sentence). Such pauses shape the movement of each verse by breaking it into two (or more) parts.

4. *Metrical ictus and word accent.* In addition to metrical length, words also have a natural accent.¹⁴ In poetry, this accent may coincide or clash with the metrical stress (*ictus**) that falls on the first syllable of each foot.¹⁵ Coincidence of word accent and metrical stress produces fluidity in the verse; clashing of word accent (´) and metrical stress (1 through 6) creates tension. For example, once again at the opening of book 5, we find this:

---

12 It took Roman poets some time to learn this lesson. Here is a line written by Quintus Ennius, the first poet to write Latin hexameters:

spársīs" hástīs" lóngīs" cámpūs" spléndĕt ĕt" hórret

(*Scipio* fr. 6 Warmington (1935–40))

There is a diaeresis following every foot, while on the other hand there is only a single, insignificant caesura in the fifth foot. The result is an exceptionally choppy line, an effect that is intensified by the fact that the first four feet are all spondees, which produces a slow-moving sequence of nine long syllables in a row, with no ictus clash anywhere in the line (see the following section). In addition, the first three words of the line have the same ending (*īs*... *īs*... *īs*), as do, in effect, the last three (*et*... *et*... *et*). It is unfair to criticize Ennius without having more of the context: possibly he meant this line to contrast sharply with others around it. But Vergil and other poets of his time used these effects much more sparingly, and avoided combining them as Ennius does here.

13 Readers may differ on where (or even if) there is a main caesura in a given line.

14 Disyllabic words have their accent on their initial syllable: *cáris, dábant, mólis*. If, however, words are three syllables or longer, the word accent falls on the penultima (second to last syllable), if it is long (*ruébant, iactátos*) but on the antepenultima (the syllable preceding the penultima), if the penultima is short (*géntibus, mária, pópulum*).

15 Classical Latin speakers would presumably have pronounced the word accents in reading lines, while still maintaining the basic rhythm of hexameter. Otherwise, the ictus would have transformed the basic sound of the word.

Intĕrĕā́ mĕdĭŭm Aenḗās iām clāssĕ́ tĕnḗbāt   (*Aen.* 5.1)

In the first half of this line — in fact, before the caesura that falls in the fourth foot — the natural accent of the words *interea*, *medium*, and *Aeneas* never falls on the first syllable of a metrical foot; but in the the fifth and sixth feet, the natural accent of *classe* and *tenebat* does so. This is a very common pattern in Latin hexameter verse. The pattern found in the first half of the line is known as "ictus clash," because the natural accent of the words is said to clash with an important metrical pattern of the hexameter, the ictus that falls on the first syllable of each foot. This ictus clash is said to "resolve" itself in the second half of the line, where ictus and accent coincide.[16] We can represent this pattern of ictus clash (≠) and resolution (=) as follows:

Intĕrĕā́ mĕdĭŭm Aenḗās iām clāssĕ́ tĕnḗbāt

This coincidence of ictus and accent in the fifth and sixth feet is another factor that allows the basic character of dactylic verse to assert itself as each line draws to a close. In creating clashes, the placement of *strong caesurae* is particularly important. For example, "if a word of two or more syllables ends after the first long syllable of a foot (that is, producing a strong caesura), there will be a clash between accent and ictus in that foot," because the final syllable of such words is not accented.[17] The strong caesurae after *interea* and *Aeneas* in the line quoted above display this principle well.

5. *Variation from line to line.* Vergil looked beyond the individual hexameter as a compositional unit.[18] The dactylic hexameter suggests a natural pause at line end, and it was understandable for poets to complete the expression of a thought by the end of a verse (i.e. "end-stopped" verses*). For example, consider the following passage from Ariadne's soliloquy in poem 64 of Catullus, one of Vergil's most important Latin predecessors:

---

16 Vergil sometimes avoids such resolution for special effect, though he does so rarely. For example, in the following line, a clash between ictus and word accent occurs in the final two feet:

stĕrnĭtŭ́r ēxănĭ́mīsquĕ trĕ́mēns prōcúmbĭt hŭ́mī bṓs (5.481).

17 Ross (2007) 146. For word accentuation, see n. 14 (above).
18 The hexameters of the *Eclogues* and *Georgics* function much more frequently than those of the *Aeneid* as individual units of thought.

nunc iam nulla viro iuranti femina credat,
nulla viri speret sermones esse fideles;
quis dum aliquid cupiens animus praegestit apisci,
nil metuunt iurare, nihil promittere parcunt:
sed simul ac cupidae mentis satiata libido est,
dicta nihil metuere, nihil periuria curant.   (Cat. 64.143–8)

Here, each individual hexameter forms a unit for the expression of a thought. This is not to claim that Catullus' lines (or those of Vergil's other predecessors) are all end-stopped in this way, or that Vergil did not compose such lines. Nonetheless, in the *Aeneid* he displayed a stronger tendency to express ideas beyond the confines of the single hexameter. Enjambment* (the continuation of the sense or a syntactic unit from one line to the next), for example, takes on an increased importance, and this is related to Vergil's characteristically paragraphic or periodic style[19] — one that develops ideas over several lines, and has the effect of moving the reader through the narrative at a more dynamic pace. The opening of book 5 is an excellent example. Here are lines 1–7 scanned and with enjambment (≫), end-stopped clauses (|) and sentences (||), and major diaereses (//) and caesurae (ʸ) all marked:

Intĕrĕā, ʸ mĕdĭu̯m // Āenēās i̯ām // clāssĕ tĕnēbăt, |
cērtŭs ĭtēr ʸ flūctūsquę̆ ātrōs Ăqui̯lōnĕ sĕcābăt |
moēnĭă̆ rēspĭcĭēns, ʸ quaē // i̯ām īnfēlīcĭs Ēlīssăe ≫
cōnlūcēnt flāmmīs. ʸ quaē // tāntu̯m āccēndĕrĭt īgnĕm ≫
cāusă̆ lătēt; ʸ dūrī māgnō sĕd ămōrĕ dŏlōrĕs ≫
pōllūtō, ʸ nōtūmquĕ̆ fŭrēns quīd // fēmĭnă̆ pōssĭt, |
trīstĕ pĕr // āugŭrĭu̯m ʸ Tēucrōrŭm // pēctŏră̆ dūcŭnt. ||

Note that the book begins with a metrically and syntactically self-contained line, which Vergil could have let stand as a complete sentence. The second line extends the first, but repeats it in certain significant ways: they share the same major caesura in the second foot, and they end with verbs of similar shape and ending (*tenebat, secabat*). It is as if Vergil wished at the very beginning of the book to establish the basic pattern of his verse form before beginning to vary it (an effect that is emphasized by observance of the bucolic diaeresis in line 1), and perhaps also to re-establish a sense of

---

19   See, e.g., the discussion in Gransden (1976) 45.

normality after the tumultuous events of book 4. He does not end the sentence, however, but continues it into line 3, which differs from the first two lines both in the placement of its major caesura (in the third instead of the second foot) and especially in the fact that the sentence we are reading is in no way sytactically complete at the end of the line. This establishes a pattern of enjambment that sweeps the reader along to the major caesura of line 4, which is also in the third foot, where the first sentence finally comes to an end. Vergil then resumes with a new sentence that carries over the end of line 4, pauses at the major caesura of line 5 (but not at the end of that line), again at the major caesura and at the end of line 6, before giving us in line 7 the completion of a complex sentence in another metrically and syntactically self-contained line (again with observance of the bucolic diaeresis) that rounds out a brilliantly composed, two-sentence paragraph. The result is a forceful, metrically varied, and memorable introduction to book 5.

Appendix B: Stylistic Terms

Vergil's skillful use of language is a defining element of his artistry. He often employs rhetorical figures and stylistic devices to reinforce the content of his poetry. Careful attention should therefore be paid *both* to what Vergil says *and* to how he says it. The following list defines many of the terms (primarily rhetorical, stylistic, and metrical) that are encountered in studying Vergil and that are used in the commentary. For more information on the terms, see Lanham (1991), Brogan (1994), and Lausberg (1998). Fuller information on Vergilian style can be found in Jackson Knight (1944) 225–341, Camps (1969) 60–74, O'Hara (1997), and Conte (2007) 58–122. Stylistic analyses of Vergilian passages are presented in Horsfall (1995) 237–48 and Hardie (1998) 102–14. NB: all line references are to the *Aeneid* unless otherwise noted.

Aetiology (Gr. "investigation of causes"): the study of the origin or cause of a name, event, custom, ritual, etc. Explanations of how something came into being are important elements of Hellenistic poetry, represented most significantly by Callimachus' influential *Aetia* ("Causes" or "Origins"), and thus *aetiology* became an important component of Latin poetry as well. The interest in *aetiology* can be seen in numerous passages in the *Aeneid*: e.g. the explanation of the origin of the enmity between Rome and Carthage (4.615–29) or of the *lusus Troiae* (5.545–603 n.). *Aetiology* is also an important component of numerous wordplays through the epic, see O'Hara (1996).

Alliteration: the repetition of a letter or sound in neighboring words, though the term today is most often used for the repetition of initial consonants. (For the repetition of vowel sounds, see *assonance*; for consonants more generally, see *consonance*.) *Alliteration* is frequent in Vergil and employed for a variety of purposes: e.g. to emphasize words, to suggest connections between words, to create effects such as *onomatopoeia* and *paronomasia*, or simply to please the ear. Some examples: *cavum conversa cuspide* (1.81, of Aeolus striking a mountain), *magno misceri murmure* (4.160, of a storm) and *suadent . . . sidera somnos* (2.9, of stars at night).

Anaphora (Gr. "bringing back"): the repetition of a word at the beginning of consecutive sentences or clauses. It is commonly used, e.g., to convey emphasis, emotion, or stylistic elevation. Consider Dido's scornful questions in her reply to Aeneas at 4.369–70: <u>num</u> *fletu ingemuit nostro?* <u>num</u> *lumina flexit?* | <u>num</u> *lacrimas victus dedit aut miseratus amantem est?* ("Did he sigh as I cried? Did he turn his eyes (toward me)? Did he, yielding, shed tears or pity his lover?"). Cf. also the famous lines from the *Georgics* describing Orpheus' lament for Eurydice: <u>te</u>, *dulcis coniunx,* <u>te</u> *solo in litore secum* | <u>te</u> *veniente die,* <u>te</u> *decedente canebat* ("Of you, sweet wife, of you on the lonely shore, of you at day's rising, of you at day's setting he used to sing to himself," *Geo.* 4.465–6). Here *anaphora* is combined with other features (e.g. *apostrophe* and *asyndeton*).

Antithesis (Gr. "opposition"): the juxtaposition of contrasting ideas usually within a balanced or parallel construction. In *Aeneid* 7.312, Juno expresses her decision to rely on the power of the underworld to achieve her will as follows: *flectere si nequeo superos, Acheronta movebo* ("If I am unable to bend the heavenly gods, Acheron I will incite"). The *antithesis* of *superos* (i.e. heaven) and *Acheronta* (i.e. hell) adds clarity, force, and emotion to Juno's decision. Cf. also <u>novo veterum</u> *errore locorum* ("by a <u>new error</u> concerning ancient places," 3.181).

Apo koinou (Gr. "in common"): describing a construction in which two clauses or phrases syntactically share a word or phrase. E.g. *nec nos obniti contra nec tendere tantum* | *sufficimus* (5.21–2), wherein *contra* should be understood with both *obniti* and *tendere*, i.e. "we are able neither to fight against nor to make enough headway (against)." Cf. also *miratus . . . adventum sociasque rates occurrit Acestes* (5.35–6), wherein *adventum sociasque rates* must be shared as the direct object of both *miratus* and *occurrit*, i.e. "Acestes marveled at the arrival of the allied ships and went to meet (them)" (in this translation, *adventum sociasque rates* is construed as a *hendiadys*, see commentary note).

Aposiopesis (Gr. "becoming silent"): the abrupt stopping of a sentence or a thought, usually to suggest the overwhelming emotional state of the speaker. E.g. *iam caelum terramque meo sine numine, venti,* | *miscere et tantas audetis tollere moles?* | *quos ego – ! sed motos praestat componere fluctus* ("Now, winds, do you dare to intermingle the sky and land without my command, and to raise such great upheavals (of water)? You whom I –! But better to subdue the waves that you've stirred up," 1.133–5). Here, Neptune suddenly cuts short his rebuke of the winds.

Apostrophe (Gr. "turning away"): a sudden shift of address to a figure (or idea), absent or present. E.g. *improba Amor, quid non mortalia pectora cogis!*

(4.412). In this line, the narrator Vergil suddenly addresses *Amor*, emphasizing the role the god had played in Dido's disastrous love for Aeneas. *Apostrophe* occurs as early as Homer, but in the Hellenistic period it became a characteristic feature. Vergil uses it more discerningly, usually to heighten the emotional register or to vary the pace of a passage. In general, cf. Behr (2005).

Archaic, archaism: the use of a form or expression that is old or no longer current. It can be introduced for a variety of effects. Quintilian (*Inst.* 8.3.24) writes that "age confers dignity, because words which not everyone would have used give style a more venerable and distinguished air. Vergil, with his perfect judgment, used this Ornament with unique skill. *Olli, quianam, moerus, pone,* and *pelligerent* produce a sprinkling of that authoritative air of antiquity, which is impressive also in picture, and which no art can reproduce" (Russell, Loeb).

Arsis, lengthening in: the lengthening of a final short syllable of a word when it occurs in *arsis* (i.e. at the first long syllable of a hexameter foot, which receives the *ictus*, the metrical stress), and is followed by a strong caesura (cf. 1.651 *Pergama cum peterēt* . . . ; 4.64 *pectoribūs* . . .).

Assonance (Lat. "answer with the same sound"): the repetition of vowel sounds in neighboring words or phrases. Latin is rich in vowel sounds, making *assonance* a natural and frequent poetic feature. E.g. *nate dea, quo fata trahunt retrahuntque, sequamur* ("Goddess-born, let us follow where fate draws us to and draws us back," 5.709) and *quinquaginta atris immanis hiatibus Hydra* ("the monstrous Hydra with her fifty black, gaping mouths," 6.576). See also *alliteration* and *onomatopoeia*, which often makes use of assonance.

Asyndeton (Gr. "unconnected"): the omission of conjunctions (e.g. *et, -que, aut, sed*) between words, phrases, or clauses. *Asyndeton* can convey effects such as emphasis, suddenness, and vehemence. One of the most famous Latin examples is Caesar's *veni, vidi, vici*. Vergil uses *asyndeton* frequently both on a small scale with individual words (e.g. *eiectum litore, egentem,* "cast out on the shore, begging," 4.373), and on a larger scale with clauses, as when Aeneas scans the sea after the storm that begins the epic: *navem in conspectu nullam, tris litore cervos | prospicit errantis* (1.184–5). This last example lacks a conjunction between *nullam* and *tris,* and can be further classified as *adversative asyndeton* because contrast is implied: "He sees not one ship but three stags wandering on the shore."

Caesura (Lat. "a cutting"): a word break *within* a metrical foot. *Caesurae* (plural) are often described as strong or weak: a *strong caesura* is one that falls after the first syllable of a foot; a *weak caesura* is one that falls after the second syllable of a *dactylic* foot. The most important *caesura* in any given line often coincides with a sense break and is called the *main* or *principal caesura* (indicated by ‖ below). It most frequently falls in the third foot, but also occurs not uncommonly in the second or fourth (or sometimes both). For example, in 1.750:

$$\text{mūltă sŭ}^{/}\text{pēr Prĭă}^{/}\text{mō rŏgĭ}^{/}\text{tāns, ‖ sŭpĕr}^{/}\text{Hēctŏrĕ}^{/}\text{mūltă}^{x}$$

there are *strong caesurae* after the initial *super*, after Priamo, and after *rogitans*; a *weak caesura* occurs after the initial *multa*. (*Weak caesurae* are also described as *trochaic*, since the initial two syllables before the word break form a *trochee*, as in the first *mūltă* above.) The *main caesura* may be taken as falling after *rogitans*, where there is also a syntactical pause. For further discussion and additional examples, see the appendix on "Vergil's Meter."

Chiasmus: (Gr. "crossing"): an arrangement of words whereby parallel constructions are expressed in reverse word order. E.g. *expletus dapibus vinoque sepultus* (3.630). The word "chiasmus" is derived from the Greek letter "chi" because if the parallel constructions are split in half and placed one over the other, an X is formed when the syntactically related words are connected:

expletus   dapibus
X
vinoque   sepultus

Chiasmus is a type of *hyperbaton*.

Coinage. See **Neologism**.

Correption. See **Hiatus**.

Dactyl: a metrical foot comprised of one long syllable followed by two short ones (–⏑⏑). See the appendix on "Vergil's Meter."

Diaeresis (Gr. "division"): a word break between metrical feet. For example, in 4.1:

$$\text{Āt rē}^{/}\text{gīnă gră}^{/}\text{vī ĭam}^{/}\text{dūdūm}^{‖}\text{saūcĭă}^{/}\text{cūră}^{x}$$

Diaereses (plural) occur after *iamdudum* and *saucia*. When a *diaeresis* occurs after the fourth foot (i.e. just before the fifth foot), it is often called a *bucolic diaeresis* because this type of *diaeresis* was used frequently in pastoral poetry; e.g.:

nōs pătrĭ́ăm fŭgĭ́mūs; tū, Tī́tўrĕ, ‖lēntŭs ĭn ū́mbră̆ (Vergil, *Ecl.* 1.4)

For further discussion and additional examples of *diaeresis*, see the appendix on "Vergil's Meter."

Ecphrasis (Gr. "description"), **ecphrastic:** a detailed and vivid description of an object, person, or event, though in a more restricted sense the term *ecphrasis* was applied to a detailed description specifically of a work of art. On *ecphrasis* in Vergil, see Fowler (1990 and 1991), Thomas (1983), Barchiesi (1997), Putnam (1998).

Elision: if a word ending in a vowel, diphthong, or vowel + –*m* is followed by a word that begins with a vowel, diphthong, or *h*, the first vowel or diphthong is *elided*. As a result the two syllables merge and are scanned as one. For example, in 1.3 there are two *elided* syllables (marked by the vowels u̯ and ẹ):

lītŏră̆, mū́ltu̯m īllẹ ́ĕt tēr ́rīs iāc ́tātŭs ĕt ́āltŏ̆

For further discussion and additional examples, see the appendix on "Vergil's Meter." For *prodelision*, see 5.710 n.

Ellipsis (Gr. "leaving out"): the omission of a syntactically necessary word (or words) that can be inferred from the context. For example, when Laocoon rushes down from the citadel to warn the Trojans about the wooden horse, his speech is prefaced with the phrase *et procul* ("and from far off," 2.42). Here some verb of speaking such as *clamat* has been omitted but can be easily inferred, and the *ellipsis* may help convey the frantic nature of Laocoon's actions. *Ellipsis*, however, also can serve to create "the charm of brevity and novelty" (Quintilian, *Inst.* 9.3.58, Russell, Loeb).

Enallage (Gr. "interchange"): the distortion of "the syntactic relations among words: one element of the phrase, often the adjective, is referred not to the element to which it belongs by a logical or grammatical connection, but to another one more or less near by" (Conte (2007) 70). E.g. *fida . . . fraterna Erycis* (5.24): here, "the trustworthy, brotherly shores of Eryx" really means "the trustworthy shores of (your) brother Eryx") since *fraterna* modifies *litora* grammatically but *Erycis* in sense. This type of *enallage* is also referred to as *transferred epithet* or *hypallage*. But other types of syntactic exchanges fall under the category of *enallage* as well. Consider the phrase *volvere casus* (lit. "to roll misfortunes," 1.9). Here Vergil has reversed the real syntactic relationship between the words as we must imagine them (*volvi casibus*, "to be enveloped" or "overwhelmed by misfortunes"), if the phrase is to make sense. As these examples show, *enallage* forces us to stop momentarily and puzzle out the semantic and syntactic connections. It occurs much more frequently in the *Aeneid* than in Vergil's other works and can thus be construed as an element of stylistic elevation. See the discussion of these examples and of *enallage* as a defining aspect of Vergil's style in Conte (2007) 70–5. The term *hypallage* is often used interchangeably with *enallage*.

End-stopped Lines: see Enjambment.

Enjambment (Fr. "crossing over," "spanning"): the continuation of the sense or a syntactic unit from one line to the next. This feature is frequent in Vergil and plays with our expectations that thoughts and clauses will be contained within the individual hexameter line. As a result, enjambed words are given more emphasis, which can be heightened if some kind of pause follows, as in Ilioneus' appeal to Dido (1.524–5): *Troes te miseri, ventis maria omnia vecti, | oramus* ("(It is) you (that) we, wretched Trojans, carried by the winds over every sea beseech"). *Oramus* ("we beseech") has been enjambed, and is followed by a strong *caesura*, which bestows still more emphasis to the verb. Such *enjambment* of the main verb for emphasis is particularly characteristic of Vergil. Lines without *enjambment* are called *end-stopped*.

Epanalepsis (Gr. "taking up again"): the "syntactically unnecessary repetition of a word or phrase from a previous line, to add emphasis, ornament, or pathos, producing the effect of lingering over a word or idea" (O'Hara 1997: 253), as in 4.25–6: *... adigat me fulmine ad <u>umbras</u> | pallentis <u>umbras</u> Erebo* ("may he hurl me with lightning to the shades, | the pale shades in Erebus"). Consider also 2.405–6, in which Cassandra is being dragged away from Pallas' temple with her hands bound: *ad caelum tendens ardentia <u>lumina</u> frustra, | <u>lumina</u>, nam teneras arcebant vincula palmas* ("directing her burning eyes to the sky in vain, | her eyes, because bonds were constraining her soft palms," 2.405–6). In both examples, Vergil emphatically repeats a word at the end of one line and the beginning of the next. *Epanalepsis* is used less often in Vergil's poetry than, e.g., in Catullus 64.

Epithet (Gr. "added"): an adjective or descriptive phrase that accompanies or substitutes for a name. The use of epithets goes back to the *Iliad* and *Odyssey* (e.g. "rosy-fingered" Dawn and "gray-eyed" Athena), where they are important compositional elements for oral poetry such as Homeric epic. In

Vergil they become literary devices that help create epic tone. Just as Homer's Odysseus is "of many turns" (Gr. *polytropos*), and Achilles "swift-footed" (Gr. *podas okus*), Aeneas is *pius* (e.g. 1.220, 305, 708, etc.), an *epithet* underscoring the importance of *pietas* for his heroic characterization. Some other examples in Vergil: *Iuppiter <u>omnipotens</u>* (e.g. 5.687), <u>*infelix*</u> *Dido* (e.g. 1.749), and <u>*regia*</u> *Iuno* (e.g. 4.114).

Etymology: the (study of the) derivation of a word. The word *etymology* itself, e.g., is from Gr. *etumos* ("true") and *logos* ("word"). *Etymologies* were particularly characteristic of Hellenistic writers and important for Vergil. E.g. at 5.117 (see n.), the name of the Trojan *Mnestheus* is taken as the etymology of the Roman clan *Memmii*. Often we can see Vergil engaging in etymological wordplay (cf. *paronomasia**): e.g. at 1.261-2, we find *fabor . . . fata*, perhaps suggesting the etymological connection between the words. But sometimes wordplay can playfully suggest false etymologies: e.g. 4.71 *teris . . . terris*. In 3.693 *Plemyrium undosum*, Vergil might be seen as engaging in bilingual etymological wordplay by applying a Latin epithet (*undosum*) to a Greek noun (Gr. *plemmyris*, "flood-tide"), thus suggesting the derivation of the epithet. On etymological wordplay, see especially O'Hara (1996).

Golden Line and Variations: in dactylic hexameter, an artful arrangement of two adjective/substantive phrases with a verb in between. It usually takes the form of abVAB, wherein V is a verb/participle, while A and B represent the interlocked (lower-case) adjective and (upper-case) noun phrases. E.g.:

> a   b   V   A   B
> egressi optata potiuntur Troes harena   (1.172)

The variation abVBA is often called a **silver line**, in which the two adjective-noun phrases are not interlocked; rather one phrase frames the other. E.g.:

> a   b   V   B   A
> cetera populea velatur fronde iuventus   (5.134)

The term "golden line" is not an ancient one but dates to the seventeenth century, most famously in Dryden's preface to his *Sylvae* (1685).

Hendiadys (Gr. "one through two"): the expression of one idea through two terms joined by a conjunction. E.g. *sanguine . . . et virgine caesa*, "with blood and a slaughtered maiden" really means "with the blood of a slaughtered maiden"; in *spargens rore levi et ramo felicis olivae* (6.230), *rore . . . ramo* really means "dew from the bough."

Hiatus (Lat. "gaping," "yawning"): the "gap" created when two syllables, which would normally be elided (see *elision* above), are not, usually when the preceding syllable receives special emphasis. E.g. 4.667:

> lamentis gemituque et femineo ululatu

Here, *hiatus* occurs between *femineo* and *ululato* (i.e. there is no elision between the final -*o* of *femineo* and the initial *u*- of *ululatu*.) A long vowel in *hiatus* is sometimes shortened, an occurrence that is called *correption*. This is a regular license in Greek poetry, but is used by Roman poets only occasionally, sometimes where Greek words are involved, particularly names, as in the following example:

> Glaucō ět Pănŏpēaĕ ět Īnōō Mělĭcěrtĕ (*Geo.* 1.437)

Here there are two instances of *hiatus* before *et,* only the second of which involves *correption* (i.e. shortening of the diphthong -*ae*).

Hypallage: see **Enallage.**

Hyperbaton (Gr. "transposed"): any distortion of normal word order. Because Latin is a highly inflected language, there is much latitude in altering word arrangements without sacrificing clarity of meaning. Indeed *hyperbaton* is a central element of Latin poetry. It includes simple distortions, such as *anastrophe* and *tmesis*, but can also involve more formalized patterns such as interlocking word order (*synchysis*, e.g. *mixtoque undantem pulvere fumum*, 2.609), *chiasmus*, enclosing noun-adjective phrases (e.g. <u>magnum</u> *reginae sed enim miseratus* <u>amorem</u>, 4.28), and so-called *golden lines* (e.g. *aurea purpuream subnectit fibula vestem*, 4.139).

Hyperbole (Gr. "excess"), **hyperbolic:** exaggeration, used for emphasis or some other effect. E.g. Aeneas, as he gazes at the murals of the Trojan War at Carthage, "wets his face with a copious flood (of tears)," <u>largo</u> *. . . umectat* <u>flumine</u> *vultum* (1.465); or consider the gust of wind that "lifts the waves to the stars," *procella . . . fluctusque ad sidera tollit* (1.102–3). See Quintilian (*Inst.* 8.6.67–76), who concludes that "Hyperbole only has positive value when the thing about which we have to speak transcends the ordinary limits of nature. We are then allowed to amplify, because the real size of the thing cannot be expressed, and it is better to go too far than not to go far enough" (8.6.76, Russell, Loeb).

Hypermetric line: a line in which an extra final syllable elides with the initial syllable of the following line. E.g. 1.332-3:

> iactemur doceas; ignari hominumque locorumqu*e*
> erramus vento huc vastis et fluctibus acti:

Here, the final syllable (*-que*) of *locorumque* elides (see above) with the initial vowel of *erramus* at the start of the following line. Most examples in Vergil involve elision of *-que* at line end, as here (though cf. *Geo.* 1.295). At times, such lines can add to the poetic texture of an event, as at 2.745-6:

> quem non incusavi amens hominumque deorumqu*e*,
> aut quid in eversa vidi crudelius urbe?

Here the hypermetric *-que* in *deorumque* elides with *aut* in the following line and helps convey Aeneas' fury as he searches for Creusa. Hypermetric lines do not occur in Homer, though Vergil's Latin epic predecessors such as Ennius and Lucretius employed them. As Austin (1955) on 4.558 writes: "it was Virgil who first used [hypermetric lines] for artistic purposes."

Ictus (Lat. "stroke," "blow"): the special metrical emphasis that the first syllable of each foot receives. The dynamic interplay between *ictus* and *word accent* is central to Vergil's metrical artistry. See the appendix on "Vergil's Meter."

Irony (Gr. "dissembling"): saying one thing but with its opposite somehow implied or understood. For example, in *Aeneid* 1 Venus, disguised as a huntress, tells her son Aeneas that his comrades and fleet are safe, and adds the following clause to qualify her prediction: *ni frustra augurium vani docuere parentes* ("unless for nothing my parents have falsely taught augury (to me)," 1.392). This line is playfully ironic because Venus is a goddess (her father being the king of the gods), and knows that her revelations are truthful. *Dramatic irony* results when the reader or spectator possesses information unknown to a character and consequently interprets the character's words or actions in a different light. Thus when Dido tells the Trojans that they should consider her city their own (*urbem quam statuo, vestra est,* 1.573), there is dramatic irony, since we as readers know not only that Dido's generosity will bring about her downfall, but also that Aeneas' descendants, the Romans, will eventually conquer Carthage.

Litotes (Gr. "simplicity"): the description of something by negating its opposite. Because it provides emphasis through understatement, *litotes* can be considered the opposite of *hyperbole* and is not unusual in Vergil. So, when Pallas (Minerva) is described as *non aequae Palladis* ("not favorable,"

1.479), Vergil conveys through *litotes* that she is actually "hostile" or "angry." Cf. also *nec abnuit* ("not reject," i.e. accept, 5.530–1), *non digna* ("not worthy," i.e. unworthy, 2.144), *non immemor* ("not unmindful," i.e. remembering, 5.39).

Metaphor (Gr. "transference"): the application of a word or phrase from one field of meaning to another, thereby suggesting new meanings. E.g. *At regina gravi iamdudum saucia cura | vulnus alit venis et caeco carpitur igni* ("But the queen long since hurt by grievous love feeds the wound with her veins and is consumed by an unseen fire," 4.1–2). Dido's passion for Aeneas is figured here as a wound (*vulnus*) and as fire (*igni*).

Metonymy (Gr. "change of name"): the substitution of one word for another somehow closely related. In Vergil, *metonymy* often involves names, qualities, or attributes. For example, *Bacchus* can stand in for "wine" (3.354) and *Ceres* for "bread" (1.701). But *metonymy* can involve other types of relationships, such as those between cause and effect (e.g. *labores* for "things produced by labor," 2.306), and between possessor and thing possessed (e.g. *Vcalagon* for "Ucalegon's house," 2.312). See also *synecdoche*, which is a type of *metonymy*.

Neologism (Gr. "new word" or "utterance"): a newly coined word. E.g. 3.430 *circumflectere*; 5.765 *procurva* (instead of *curva*); 6.638 *virecta* (from *virere*). Because such words would presumably have seemed unusual to a contemporary reader/hearer, they would have had a special poetic resonance. *Neologism* is also referred to as *coinage*.

Onomatopoeia (Gr. "making of a word" or "name"): the use or formation of words that imitate natural sounds. Individual words may be *onomatopoetic*, as *ululaunt* at 4.168. Onomatopoetic effects can be found in phrases as well. For example, in *fit sonitus spumante salo* ("a sound arises from the spuming sea," 2.209), the *alliteration* of *s* imitates the sound of the sea; in *quinquaginta atris immanis hiatibus Hydra* ("the monstrous Hydra with her fifty black, gaping mouths," 6.576), the use of *a* suggests the gaping of the Hydra's mouths. As is clear from these examples, *onomatopoeia* often involves devices such as *alliteration*, *assonance*, and *consonance*.

Oxymoron (Gr. "pointedly foolish"): the juxtaposition of seemingly contradictory words. For example, in *animum pictura pascit inani* ("he feeds his spirit on empty paintings," 1.464), the idea of feeding (*pascit*) on something that is empty (*inani*) seems paradoxical. Cf. also *festina lente* ("hurry slowly,"

Gr. *speude bradeos*), a proverb, we are told, that Augustus especially liked (Suetonius, *Augustus* 25.4).

Parataxis (Gr. "placing side by side"): the sequential ordering of independent clauses (as opposed to *hypotaxis*, the subordination of one clause to another). A famous example is Caesar's *veni, vidi, vici*. An example from *Aeneid* 2: *vix positum castris simulacrum: arsere coruscae | luminibus flammae arrectis...* (2.172-3). Though the two halves of the sentence are independent, in sense one is subordinated to the other: "scarcely had the image been placed..., (when) glittering flames blazed..." Vergil leaves it to the reader to sense such logical relationships. *Parataxis* is particularly characteristic of Vergil and epic more generally.

Paronomasia (Gr. "slight alteration of name"): a wordplay or pun, usually employing words that sound similar. Consider *cari... cura parentis* ("concern of a caring parent," 1.646), *auri... aura* ("gleam of gold," 6.204), and *părentis praeceptis... părere* ("obey your parent's instructions," 2.606-7). *Paronomasia* often makes use of word *etymology* and various sound effects such as *alliteration* and *assonance*, and is a feature of Vergilian poetry that has roots going back to Homer but that bears the special influence of the erudite work of the Alexandrian tradition. (See the list and discussion of *paronomasia* in O'Hara (1996) 60-3 with n. 316 and *passim*.)

Patronymic (Gr. "father's name"): a name formed by attaching a suffix to the name of a father or other ancestor. E.g. 5.407 *Anchisiades*, "son of Anchises," i.e. Aeneas; 3.248 *Laomedontiadae*, "descendants of Laomedon," i.e. the Trojans; 6.58 *Aeacides*, (grand)son of Aeacus," i.e. Achilles. *Patronymics* are elevated in tone and characteristic of epic poetry.

Periphrasis (Gr. "circumlocution"): the use of many words to express an idea that could be stated more succinctly, if not by just one word. It is an important element of elevated, epic style. It can be used to express something that might normally be said with language seemingly inappropriate to epic: e.g. *toto proflabat pectore somnum* ("was breathing out sleep with his whole chest," 9.326), a phrase that, according to Servius, Vergil uses to avoid the humble word *sterto* ("snore"). More commonly, it is used in Vergil as a stylistic embellishment, particularly to achieve an elevated and/or erudite tone, such as in *Iovis ales* ("Jove's bird," i.e. the eagle, 1.394), *Amphrysia vates* ("Amphrysian soothsayer," i.e. the Sibyl, 6.398), or the description of nighttime as *tempus erat, quo prima quies mortalibus aegris | incipit et dono divum gratissima serpit* ("It was the time when first quiet begins for weary mortals and creeps up on them most pleasingly by grace of the gods," 2.268–9, an example cited in Quintilian, *Inst.* 8.6.60).

Pleonasm (Gr. "excess"): redundancy, especially for the sake of emphasis. E.g. *arma virumque cano, Troiae qui primus ab oris | Italiam fato profugus Laviniaque venit | litora — multum <u>ille</u> et terris iactatus et alto . . .* (1.1–3). Here, the *ille* is technically unnecessary but draws added attention to the *vir* (1), Aeneas.

Polyptoton (Gr. "in many cases"): the repetition of a word in its inflected cases. Dido begins her address about Aeneas' effect on her to her sister Anna with clauses beginning with *quae . . . quis . . . quem . . . quam . . . quibus . . . quae* (4.9–14). Here *polyptoton* creates an artful, but grammatically varied patterning that allows for an expansive introduction to the emotional content of what Dido describes. *Polyptoton* can create other effects: at 1.684, it emphasizes the deception involved when Venus asks Amor to take on the appearance of Ascanius: *notos pueri puer indue vultus*, "as a boy (*puer*= Amor), put on the familiar appearance of the boy (*pueri*=Ascanius)." Cf. also 4.83, where Dido's visions of Aeneas at night is described: *illum <u>absens absentem</u> auditque videtque* ("absent, she hears and sees the absent one").

Prolepsis (Gr. "anticipation"), **proleptic**: the use of a word or phrase that anticipates a later event or outcome. For example, as Dido embraces Amor (disguised as Ascanius), she is called *miserae* (1.719), a word that looks forward to the tragic outcome that will result from the god's infection of her, though at the moment she appears fine. Consider also *furentem | incendat reginam* (1.659–60): here the force of *furentem* is not "set the raging queen on fire" but "set her on fire so that she rages."

Silver Line: see **Golden Line and Variations.**

Simile (Lat. "similar"): a figurative comparison between two different things. It is an important component of epic style. E.g. *uritur infelix Dido totaque vagatur | urbe furens, qualis coniecta cerva sagitta, | quam procul incautam nemora inter Cresia fixit | pastor agens telis liquitque volatile ferrum | nescius: illa fuga silvas saltusque peragrat | Dictaeos; haeret lateri letalis harundo* (4.69–73). In this simile, Dido, consumed by her love for Aeneas, is compared to a wounded stag.

Spondaic Line: a hexameter line in which the fifth foot is not a dactyl (-⏑⏑) but a spondee (- -). E.g. 2.68:

$$\text{constitit atque oculis Phrygia agmina cīrcūmsp}\overset{x}{\text{ē}}\text{xit:}$$

Vergil employs *spondaic lines* frequently and usually for special effect, perhaps as here, where Sinon is described carefully scanning the crowd of his hostile Trojan captors. Such lines often involve Greek names, as at 3.517:

    armatumque auro circumspicit Ōrī̆ōna.

Spondee: a metrical foot comprised of two long syllables (- -). See the appendix on "Vergil's Meter."

Syllepsis: see **Zeugma**.

Synchysis (Gr. "mingling," "confusion"): an arrangement of two phrases (here Aa and Bb) that interweave their members in an ABab pattern. It is also called *interlocking word order*. E.g.

    A   B   a   b

    mixtoque undantem pulvere fumum   (2.609)

Here the *synchysis* may be seen to mimic the mingling of dust and smoke that is described.

Syncope (Gr. "a cutting short"): the omission of a letter or syllable from the interior of a word. E.g., 1.201 *accestis* for *acce(ssi)stis*; 2.379 *aspris* for *asp(e)ris*; 3.50 *mandarat* for *manda(ve)rat*; 5.786 *traxe* for *trax(iss)e*; 6.58 *repostas* for *repos(i)tas*.

Synecdoche (Gr. "understanding one thing with another"): a type of *metonymy* that uses the part for the whole (or the reverse). E.g. *atque rotis summas levibus perlabitur undas* ("with his light wheels he glides over the wave-tops," 1.147). Here *rotis* ("wheels") really stands in for "chariot." Other examples include *ferrum* ("iron") for "sword," *tectum* ("covering" or "roof") for "house," *sceptrum* ("scepter") for *regnum* ("rule"). Quintilian (*Inst.* 8.6.19) says that "*synecdoche* has the power to vary the discourse, enabling the hearer to understand many things from one, the whole from the part, the genus from the species, the consequences from the antecedents, and vice versa" (Russell, Loeb).

Synizesis (Gr. "collapse"): the collapsing of two vowels into one (a diphthong or simple vowel) to allow a word to fit into a poetic meter. For example, in *dehinc* the *e* and *i* combine to form one syllable at 1.131, 256; 6.678; 9.480. Cf. also *aurea* at 1.698 and *ferrei* at 6.280, both of which scan as disyllables.

Tmesis (Gr. "cutting"): the "cutting" of the elements of a word (usually a compound word) by interjecting a word or words in between. Most often *tmesis* involves the separation of a prefix: *circum . . . fudit* (1.412), *circum . . . dati* (2.218–19), *ante . . . quam* (3.255–6), *inque salutatam* (9.288). Cf. also *quo . . . usque* (5.384) and *hac . . . tenus* (5.604). *Tmesis* involving compound verbs often has an an archaic flavor, since in Homer such prefixes function as adverbs and can stand independently, though in later usage they formed compound words. However, *tmesis* can also occur for other reasons, such as the creation of emphasis or for metrical purposes.

Transferred Epithet: see **Enallage, Hypallage**.

Trochee: a metrical foot comprised of a long syllable followed by a short one (– ˘). In the dactylic hexameter (see the appendix on "Vergil's Meter") the final foot is disyllabic and can be either a trochee or spondee. E.g. *venit* in the final foot of 1.2 (*Italiam fato profugus Laviniaque vēnĭt*) is a *trochee*.

Word accent: disyllabic words have their accent on their initial syllable: *cáris, dábant, mólis*. If, however, words are three syllables or longer, the word accent falls on the penultima (second to last syllable) if it is long (*ruébant, iactátos*) but on the antepenultima (the syllable preceding the penultima) if the penultima is short (*géntibus, mária, pópulum*). The interplay between (i.e. the clash or coincidence of) *word accent* and *ictus* is a fundamental element of Vergil's artistry. See the appendix on "Vergil's Meter."

Wordplay: see **Paronomasia**.

Zeugma (Gr. "yoking"): the governing of two (or more) words by one, as in *Troiugena . . . qui numina Phoebi, | qui tripodas, Clarii et laurus, qui sidera sentis* ("O Trojan-born, you who (perceive) the will of Phoebus, who (perceive) the tripods and laurels of the Clarian, who perceive the stars," 3.359–60), wherein all the accusative objects are dependent on *sentis* in the final clause. Sometimes the "yoking" can involve literal and metaphorical senses of a word, in which case the *zeugma* is sometimes referred to as *syllepsis* (Greek, "taking together"): e.g. *crudelis aras traiectaque pectora ferro | nudavit* (1.355–6), wherein Sychaeus figuratively "reveals" his murder at the altar (*aras*) but literally "bares" his pierced chest (*traiectaque pectora*).

Works Cited

A few standard reference works are cited by the following abbreviations:

AG *Allen and Greenough's New Latin Grammar* (see Mahoney (2001)).
OCD *The Oxford Classical Dictionary*, 3d ed. (see Hornblower and Spawforth (1996)).
OLD *Oxford Latin Dictionary* (see Glare (1996)).

The names of classical authors and texts are cited by the abbreviations used in *OCD*.

Adler, E. (2003) *Vergil's Empire: Political Thought in the Aeneid.* Lanham, MD.
Allen, G. (2000) *Intertextuality.* London.
Allen, W. S. (1989) *Vox Latina: The Pronunciation of Classical Latin.* 2d ed. Cambridge.
Anderson, W.S. (1969 first edition; 2005 second edition) *The Art of the Aeneid.* Wauconda, IL.
Armstrong, D., Fish, J., Johnston, P. A., and Skinner, M. (eds.) (2004) *Vergil, Philodemus, and the Augustans.* Austin.
Austin, R. G. (ed.) (1955) *P. Vergili Maronis Aeneidos Liber Quartus.* Oxford.
Barchiesi, A. (1984) *La traccia del modello: effetti omerici nella narrazione virgiliana.* Pisa.
——(1997) "Ecphrasis," in *The Cambridge Companion to Virgil*, ed. C. Martindale. Cambridge: 271–81.
Behr, F. (2005) "The narrator's voice: a narratological reappraisal of apostrophe in Virgil's *Aeneid*," *Arethusa* 38.2: 189–221.
Bertram, S. (1971) "The generation gap and *Aeneid* 5," *Vergilius* 17: 9–12.
Bowra, M. (1933–34) "Aeneas and the Stoic ideal," *Greece and Rome* 3: 8–21; reprinted in *Oxford Readings in Vergil's Aeneid*, ed. S. J. Harrison (1990). Oxford: 363–77.
Brenk, F. E. (1991) "Wind, waves, and treachery: Diodorus, Appian, and the death of Palinurus in Vergil," in *Mito/Storia/Tradizione: Diodoro Siculo e la Storiografia classica*, eds. E. Galvagno, C. Mole Ventura. Catania: 327–46.
Briggs, W. W., Jr. (1975) "Augustan athletics and the games of *Aeneid* V," *Stadion* 1: 267–83.
——(1981) "Virgil and the Hellenistic epic," *Aufstieg und Niedergang der römischen Welt* 2.31.2: 948–84.
Brogan, T. V. F. (ed.) (1994) *The New Princeton Handbook of Poetic Terms.* Princeton.
Cairns, F. (1989) *Virgil's Augustan Epic.* Cambridge.
Camps, W. A. (1969) *An Introduction to Virgil's Aeneid.* Oxford.
Casali, S. (2010) "The development of the Aeneas legend," in *A Companion to Vergil's Aeneid and Its Tradition*, eds. J. Farrell and M. C. J. Putnam. Malden, MA: 37–51.

Clausen, W. (1987) *Virgil's Aeneid and the Tradition of Hellenistic Poetry.* Berkeley, CA.

———(1994) *A Commentary on Virgil, Eclogues.* Oxford.

———(2002) *Virgil's Aeneid: Decorum, Allusion, and Ideology.* Munich and Leipzig. A revised and expanded version of Clausen (1987).

Coleman, R. (1977) *Virgil: Eclogues.* Cambridge.

Conington, J., and Nettleship, H. (eds.) (1858–83) *The Works of Virgil.* Three volumes. London.

Conte, G. B. (1986) *The Rhetoric of Imitation: Genre and Poetic Memory in Virgil and Other Latin Poets,* tr. C. Segal. Ithaca, NY.

———(1999) "The Virgilian paradox: an epic of drama and sentiment," *Proceedings of the Cambridge Philological Society* 45: 17–42. A revised version is included in Conte (2007) 23–57.

———(2007) *The Poetry of Pathos: Studies in Virgilian Epic.* Oxford.

Crook, J. (1996) "Political history: 30 B.C. to A.D. 14," in *The Augustan Empire: 43 B.C. – A.D. 69. The Cambridge Ancient History,* vol. X. Second edition, eds. A. Bowman, E. Champlin, and A. Lintott. Cambridge: 70–112.

Dyson, J. (1996) "The puzzle of *Aen.* 1.755–6 and 5.626," *Classical World* 90.1: 41–3.

Edmunds, L. (2001) *Intertextuality and the Reading of Roman Poetry.* Baltimore.

Farrell, J. (1991) *Vergil's Georgics and the Traditions of Ancient Epic: The Art of Allusion in Literary History.* Oxford.

———(1997) "The Virgilian intertext," in *The Cambridge Companion to Virgil,* ed. C. Martindale. Cambridge: 222–38.

———(1999) "*Aeneid* 5: poetry and parenthood," in *Reading Vergil's Aeneid,* ed. C. Perkell. Norman, OK: 96–110.

———(2001) "The Vergilian century," *Vergilius* 47: 11–28.

———(2005) "The Augustan period: 40 BC-AD 14," in *A Companion to Latin Literature,* ed. S. J. Harrison. Oxford: 44–57.

Farrell, J. and Putnam, M. C. J. (eds.) (2010) *A Companion to Vergil's Aeneid and Its Tradition.* Oxford.

Feeney, D. C. (1984) "The reconciliations of Juno," *Classical Quarterly* 34: 179–94; reprinted in *Oxford Readings in Vergil's Aeneid,* ed. S. Harrison (1990). Oxford: 339–62.

———(1991) *The Gods in Epic: Poets and Critics of the Classical Tradition.* Oxford.

———(1998a) *Literature and Religion at Rome: Cultures, Contexts, and Beliefs.* Cambridge.

———(1998b) "The appearance(s) of Mercury and the Motivation of Aeneas," in *A Woman Scorn'd: Responses to the Dido Myth,* ed. Burden. London: 105–130.

———(2007) *Caesar's Calendar: Ancient Time and the Beginnings of History.* Berkeley, CA.

Feldherr, A. (1995) "Ships of state: *Aeneid* 5 and Augustan circus spectacle," *Classical Antiquity* 14: 245–65.

———(2002) "Stepping out of the ring: repetition and sacrifice in the boxing match in *Aeneid* V," in *Clio and the Poets: Augustan Poetry and the Traditions of Ancient Historiography,* eds. D. Levene and D. Nelis. Leiden: 62–79.

Fowler, D. (1990) "Deviant focalisation in Virgil's *Aeneid*," *Proceedings of the Cambridge Philological Society* 36: 40–63; reprinted in Fowler (2000): 42–63.

———(1991) "Narrate and describe: the problem of ekphrasis," *Journal of Roman Studies* 81: 25–35; reprinted in Fowler (2000): 64–85.

———(1997) "Story-telling," in *The Cambridge Companion to Virgil*, ed. C. Martindale. Cambridge: 259–70.

———(2000) *Roman Constructions: Readings in Postmodern Latin*. Oxford.

Gale, M. (2000) *Virgil on the Nature of Things: The Georgics, Lucretius and the Didactic Tradition*. Cambridge.

Fratantuono, L. (2007) *Madness Unchained: A Reading of Virgil's Aeneid*. Lanham, MD.

Galinsky, G. K. (1968) "*Aeneid* V and the *Aeneid*," *American Journal of Philology* 89: 157–85.

———(1969) *Aeneas, Sicily, and Rome*. Princeton.

———(1988) "The anger of Aeneas," *American Journal of Philology* 109: 321–48.

———(1996) *Augustan Culture: An Interpretive Introduction*. Princeton.

———(2003) "Greek and Roman drama and the *Aeneid*," in *Myth, History, and Culture in Republican Rome: Studies in Honour of T. P. Wiseman*, eds. S. Braund and C. Gill. Exeter: 275–94.

———(ed.) (2005) *The Cambridge Companion to the Age of Augustus*. Cambridge.

Ganiban, R. (2000) *Vergil: Aeneid 2*. Newburyport, MA.

———(2009) *Vergil: Aeneid 1*. Newburyport, MA.

George, E. V. (1974) *Aeneid VII and the Aetia of Callimachus*. Mnemosyne Supplement 27. Leiden.

Glare, P. G. W. (ed.) (1996) *The Oxford Latin Dictionary*. Revised with corrections. Oxford.

Glazewski, J. (1972–73) "The function of Vergil's funeral games," *Classical World* 66: 85–96.

Gransden, K. W. *Virgil's Iliad: An Essay on Epic Narrative*. Cambridge.

Gruen, E. S. (1992) *Culture and National Identity in Republican Rome*. Ithaca, NY.

Gurval, R. A. (1995) *Actium and Augustus*. Ann Arbor.

Hardie, P. R. (1986) *Virgil's Aeneid: Cosmos and Imperium*. Oxford.

———(1991) "The *Aeneid* and the *Oresteia*," *Proceedings of the Virgil Society* 20: 29–45.

———(1993) *The Epic Successors of Virgil*. Cambridge.

———(1997) "Virgil and tragedy," in *The Cambridge Companion to Virgil*, ed. C. Martindale. Cambridge: 312–26.

———(1998) *Virgil*. New Surveys in the Classics 28. Oxford.

———(2002) "Another look at Virgil's Ganymede," in *Classics in Progress: Essays on Ancient Greece and Rome*, ed. T. P. Wiseman. Oxford: 333–61.

Harrison, S. J. (ed.) (1991) *Vergil, Aeneid 10. With Introduction, Translation, and Commentary*. Oxford.

———(ed.) (2005) *A Companion to Latin Literature*. Oxford.

Heinze, R. (1903 first edition; 1908 second edition; 1915 third edition) *Vergils epische Technik*. Leipzig and Berlin.

———(1993) *Virgil's Epic Technique*, trans. H. Harvey, D. Harvey, and F. Robertson. Berkeley, CA.

Hexter, R. (1992) "Sidonian Dido," in *Innovations of Antiquity*, eds. R. Hexter and D. Selden. London: 332–84.

Hinds, S. (1998) *Allusion and Intertext: Dynamics of Appropriation in Roman Poetry*. Cambridge.

———(2000) "Essential epic: genre and gender from Macer to Statius," in M. Depew and D. Obbink (eds.), *Matrices of Genre: Authors, Canons, and Society*. Cambridge, MA: 221–44.

Hirtzel, F. A. (ed.) (1900) *P. Vergili Maronis Opera*. Oxford.

Holt, P. (1979–80) "*Aeneid* V: past and future," *Classical Journal* 75: 110–21.

Hornblower, S. and Spawforth, A. (eds.) (1996) *The Oxford Classical Dictionary*. Third edition. Oxford.

Horsfall, N. (1995) *A Companion to the Study of Virgil*. Leiden.

Hunter, R. L. (2006) *The Shadow of Callimachus: Studies in the Reception of Hellenistic Poetry at Rome*. Cambridge.

Jackson Knight, W. F. (1944) *Roman Vergil*. London.

Johnson, W. R. (1976) *Darkness Visible: A Study of Vergil's Aeneid*. Berkeley, CA.

———(2005) "Introduction," in *Virgil: Aeneid*, trans. S. Lombardo, Indianapolis, IN: xv–lxxi.

Johnston, P. A. (1980) *Vergil's Agricultural Golden Age: A Study of the Georgics*. Leiden.

———(2012) *Vergil: Aeneid 6*. Newburyport, MA.

Jones, A. H. M. (1970) *Augustus*. London.

Keith, A. M. (2000) *Engendering Rome: Women in Latin Epic*. Cambridge.

———(2006) "Women's networks in Vergil's *Aeneid*," *Dictynna* 3: 211–33.

Kennedy, D. (1992) "'Augustan' and 'Anti-Augustan': reflections on terms of reference," in *Roman Poetry and Propaganda in the Age of Augustus*, ed. A. Powell. Bristol: 26–58.

Kirk, G. S. (ed.) (1990) *The Iliad. A Commentary. Vol. 2, Books 5–8*. Cambridge.

Knauer, G. N. (1964a) *Die Aeneis und Homer: Studien zur poetischen Technik Vergils mit Listen der Homerzitate in der Aeneis*. Göttingen.

———(1964b) "Vergil's *Aeneid* and Homer," *Greek, Roman and Byzantine Studies* 5: 61–84; reprinted in *Oxford Readings in Vergil's Aeneid*, ed. S. J. Harrison (1990). Oxford: 390–412.

Lanham, R. A. (1991) *A Handlist of Rhetorical Terms*. Second edition. Berkeley, CA.

Lausberg, H. 1998. *Handbook of Literary Rhetoric: A Foundation for Literary Study*, trans. M. Bliss, A. Jansen, and D. Orton. Leiden.

Leigh, M. (2010) "Boxing and sacrifice in the epic: Apollonius, Vergil, and Valerius," *Harvard Studies in Classical Philology* 105: 117–55.

Lewis, C. T. and Short, C. (eds.) (1962) *A Latin Dictionary*. Oxford.

Lyne, R. O. A. M. (1987) *Further Voices in Vergil's Aeneid*. Oxford.

———(1989) *Words and the Poet: Characteristic Techniques of Style in Vergil's Aeneid.* Oxford.

Mack, S. (1978) *Patterns of Time in the Aeneid.* Hamden, CT.

McGowan, M. M. (2002) "On the etymology and inflection of Dares in Vergil's boxing match, *Aeneid* 5.362–484," *Classical Philology*: 80–8.

Mahoney, A. (ed.) (2001) *Allen and Greenough's New Latin Grammar.* Newburyport, MA.

Martindale, C. (1993) *Redeeming the Text: Latin Poetry and the Hermeneutics of Reception.* Cambridge.

———(ed.) (1997) *The Cambridge Companion to Virgil.* Cambridge.

Mynors, R. A. B. (ed.) (1969) *P. Vergili Maronis Opera.* Oxford.

———(ed.) (1990) *Virgil: Georgics.* Oxford.

Nappa, C. (2005) *Reading After Actium: Vergil's Georgics, Octavian, and Rome.* Ann Arbor.

Nelis, D. (2001) *Vergil's Aeneid and the Argonautica of Apollonius Rhodius.* Leeds.

———(2010) "Vergil's library," in *A Companion to Vergil's Aeneid and Its Tradition*, eds. J. Farrell and M. C. J. Putnam. Malden, MA: 13–25.

Nethercut, W. R. (1986) "*Aeneid* 5.105: the horses of Phaethon," *American Journal of Philology* 107: 102–8.

Nisbet, R. G. M. and Hubbard, M. (eds.) (1970) *A Commentary on Horace: Odes, Book 1.* Oxford.

Nisbet, R. G. M. and Rudd, N. (eds.) (2004) *A Commentary on Horace: Odes Book III.* Oxford.

Norden, E. (1903 first edition; 1916 second edition; 1926 third edition) *P. Vergilius Maro: Aeneis Buch VI.* Leipzig and Berlin.

Nugent, S. G. (1992) "*Aeneid* V and Virgil's voice of the women," *Arethusa* 25: 255–92.

———(1999) "The women of the *Aeneid*: vanishing bodies, lingering voices," in *Reading Vergil's Aeneid*, ed. C. Perkell. Norman, OK: 251–70.

O'Hara, J. J. (1990) *Death and the Optimistic Prophecy in Vergil's Aeneid.* Princeton.

——— (1996) *True Names: Vergil and the Alexandrian Tradition of Aetiological Wordplay.* Ann Arbor.

———(1997) "Virgil's style," in *The Cambridge Companion to Virgil*, ed. C. Martindale. Cambridge: 241–58.

———(2007) *Inconsistency in Roman Epic: Studies in Catullus, Lucretius, Vergil, Ovid, and Lucan.* Cambridge.

———(2010) "The unifinished *Aeneid*?" in *A Companion to Vergil's Aeneid and Its Tradition*, eds. J. Farrell and M. C. J. Putnam. Malden, MA: 96–106.

———(2011) *Vergil: Aeneid 4.* Newburyport, MA.

Oliensis, E. (2001) "Freud's *Aeneid*," *Vergilius* 47: 39–63.

Osgood, J. (2006) *Caesar's Legacy: Civil War and the Emergence of the Roman Empire.* Cambridge.

Otis, B. (1964) *Virgil: A Study in Civilized Poetry.* Oxford.

Page, T. E. (ed.) (1894, 1900) *Virgil: Aeneid.* Two volumes. London.

Palmer, L. R. (1954) *The Latin Language.* London.

Panoussi, V. (2002) "Vergil's Ajax: allusion, tragedy, and heroic identity in the *Aeneid*," *Classical Antiquity* 21: 95-134.
———(2009) *Greek Tragedy in Vergil's Aeneid: Ritual, Empire, and Intertext*. Cambridge.
Pavlock, B. (1985) "Epic and tragedy in Vergil's Nisus and Euryalus episode," *Transactions of the American Philological Association* 115: 207-24.
Pavlovskis, Z. (1975-76) "Aeneid V: the old and the young," *Classical Journal* 71: 193-205.
Pelling, C. (1996) "The Triumviral period," in *The Augustan Empire: 43 B.C. - A.D. 69. The Cambridge Ancient History*, vol. X. Second edition, eds. A. Bowman, E. Champlin, and A. Lintott. Cambridge: 1-69.
Perkell, C. (ed.) (1989) *The Poet's Truth: A Study of the Poet in Virgil's Georgics*. Berkeley, CA.
———(1994) "Ambiguity and irony: the last resort?" *Helios* 21: 63-74.
———(1999) *Reading Vergil's Aeneid: An Interpretive Guide*. Norman, OK.
———(2002) "The golden age and its contradictions in the poetry of Vergil," *Vergilius* 48: 3-39.
———(2010) *Vergil: Aeneid 3*. Newburyport, MA.
Petrini, M. (1997) *The Child and the Hero: Coming of Age in Catullus and Vergil*. Ann Arbor.
Poliakoff, M. B. (1985) "Entellus and Amycus: Vergil, *Aen.* 5.362-484," *Illinois Classical Studies* 10: 227-31.
Pöschl, V. (1950) *Die Dichtkunst Vergils: Bild und Symbol in der Aeneis*. Innsbruck.
———(1962) *The Art of Vergil: Image and Symbol in the Aeneid*, trans. G. Seligson. Ann Arbor.
Powell, A. (ed.) (1992) *Roman Poetry and Propaganda in the Age of Augustus*. Bristol.
Putnam, M. (1965) *The Poetry of the Aeneid: Four Studies in Imaginative Unity and Design*. Cambridge, MA.
———(1979) *Virgil's Poem of the Earth: Studies in the Georgics*. Princeton.
———(1995) *Virgil's Aeneid: Interpretation and Influence*. Chapel Hill.
———(1998) *Virgil's Epic Designs: Ekphrasis in the Aeneid*. New Haven.
Richardson, L., Jr. (1992) *A New Topographical Dictionary of Ancient Rome*. Baltimore.
Rose, A. (1982-83) "Vergil's ship-snake simile (*Aeneid* 5.270-281)," *Classical Journal* 78: 115-21.
Ross, D. O. (1987) *Virgil's Elements: Physics and Poetry in the Georgics*. Princeton.
———(2007) *Virgil's Aeneid: A Reader's Guide*. Oxford.
Scullard, H. H. (1982) *From the Gracchi to Nero: A History of Rome from 133 B.C. to A.D. 68*. Fifth edition. London.
Shotter, D. (2005) *Augustus Caesar*. Second edition. London.
Skutsch, O. (ed.) (1985) *The Annals of Q. Ennius*. Oxford.
Southern, P. (1998) *Augustus*. New York.
Stahl, H.-P. (ed.) (1998) *Vergil's Aeneid: Augustan Epic and Political Context*. London.
Swallow, E. (1952-53) "The strategic fifth *Aeneid*," *Classical World* 46: 177-9.
Syme, R. (1939) *The Roman Revolution*. Oxford.

Thomas, R. (1983) "Virgil's ecphrastic centerpieces," *Harvard Studies in Classical Philology* 87: 175–84.

––––– (ed.) (1988) *Virgil: Georgics*. Two vols. Cambridge.

–––––(1999) *Reading Virgil and His Texts: Studies in Intertextuality*. Ann Arbor.

–––––(2001) *Virgil and the Augustan Reception*. Cambridge.

Traill, D. A. (2001) "Boxers and generals at Mount Eryx," *American Journal of Philology* 122: 405–13.

Van Sickle, J. (1992) *A Reading of Virgil's Messianic Eclogue*. New York.

Vernant, J.-P. and Vidal-Naquet, P. (1988) *Myth and Tragedy in Ancient Greece*, tr. J. Lloyd. New York.

Volk, K. (ed.) (2008a) *Virgil's Eclogues*. Oxford.

–––––(ed.) (2008b) *Virgil's Georgics*. Oxford.

Wallace-Hadrill, A. (1993) *Augustan Rome*. London.

Warmington, E. H. (1935–40) *Remains of Old Latin*. Revised edition. Four volumes. Cambridge, MA.

White, P. (1993) *Promised Verse: Poets in the Society of Augustan Rome*. Cambridge, MA.

–––––(2005) "Poets in the new milieu: realigning," in *The Cambridge Companion to the Age of Augustus*, ed. K. Galinsky. Cambridge: 321–39.

Wigodsky, M. (1972) *Virgil and Early Latin Poetry*. Wiesbaden.

Wilkinson, L. P. (1963) *Golden Latin Artistry*. Cambridge.

–––––(1969) *The Georgics of Virgil: A Critical Survey*. Cambridge.

Williams R. D. (ed.) (1960) *Virgil: Aeneid V*. Oxford.

Wlosok, A. (1999) "The Dido tragedy in Virgil: a contribution to the question of the tragic in the *Aeneid*," transl. of Wlosok (1976), in *Virgil: Critical Assessments of Classical Authors*, vol. 4, ed. P. Hardie. London: 158–81. Originally published as "Vergils Didotragödie: ein Beitrag zum Problem des Tragischen in der *Aeneis*," in *Studien zum antiken Epos*, eds. H. Görgemanns and E. A. Schmidt. Meisenheim: 228–50.

Zanker, P. (1988) *The Power of Images in the Age of Augustus*, trans. A. Shapiro. Ann Arbor.

List of Abbreviations

act.	= active
abl.	= ablative
acc.	= accusative
adj.	= adjective
adv.	= adverb
cf.	= *confer*, i.e. compare
comp.	= comparative
conj.	= conjunction
contr.	= contracted
dat.	= dative
def.	= defective
dep.	= deponent
f.	= feminine
freq.	= freq.
gen.	= genitive
i.e.	= *id est*, that is
imperat.	= imperative
impers.	= impersonal
ind.	= indicative
indecl.	= indeclinable
indef.	= indefinite
inf.	= infinitive
interj.	= interjection
intr.	= intransitive
interrog.	= interrogative
m.	= masculine
mod.	= modern
n.	= neuter (e.g. ádytum, -ī, n.)
n.	= note (e.g. 34 n.)
nom.	= nominative
num.	= numeral
opp.	= opposed
part.	= participle
pass.	= passive
perf.	= perfect
pers.	= person
pl.	= plural
poss.	= possessive
prep.	= preposition
pron.	= pronoun
ref.	= reflexive
rel.	= relative
semidep.	= semideponent
sing.	= singular
subj.	= subject
subst.	= substantive
superl.	= superlative
tr.	= transitive

Vocabulary for *Aeneid* 5

Except for one-syllable words, word accent is indicated by an acute sign (´). All long vowels are marked with a macron except those that are followed by **x** or **z** or by two consonants other than a mute + liquid combination (so, **dū́cō, dū́cere** but **dúxī, dúctum**). The diphthongs **ae, au, ei, eu**, and **oe** are marked with a single macron; where these same combinations do not form diphthongs, the vowels are marked separately (**ăḗnus; ăēr, ăĕris**). Otherwise, all unmarked vowels are short. A breve is also used occasionally to distinguish between words of similar spelling but different sound, metrical value, and meaning (e.g. **lēvis** "smooth" and **lĕvis** "light"). Consonantal **u** is written as **v** except in the combinations **gu, qu,** and **su** (according to convention). Consonantal **i**, or vocalic **i** treated as consonantal, is written as **i̯**. Where related words are given in parentheses at the end of each entry, the typeface signifies as follows: **boldface** for words used in *Aeneid* 5, ***bold italics*** for words used in the *Aeneid*, but not in book 5, *italics* for words Vergil uses only in the *Eclogues* or *Georgics*, and plain type for words that Vergil does not use.

ā or **ăb**, prep. with abl., *from; away from*; to denote the agent: *by, by means of.*
abdū́cō, -dū́cere, -dúxī, -dúctum, tr., *to lead back* or *away from.*
ábeō, abī́re, ábiī, ábitum, intr., *to go away* or *depart.*
ắbiēs, ắbi̯etis, f., *a fir tree* or *pine tree; fir wood* or *pine wood.* (scansion and pronunciation: 663 n., *parietibus* 589 n.)
ábnuō, abnúere, ábnuī, abnū́tum, tr., *to decline, refuse,* or *reject.*
absíndō, abscíndere, abscī́dī, abscíssum, tr., *to rend* or *tear away.*
āc, see **átque.**
accḗdō, -cḗdere, -céssī, -céssum, tr., *to go to* or *approach.*
accélerō, -ắre, -ắvī, -ắtum, intr., *to hasten; to make haste.*

accéndō, -céndere, -céndī, -cénsum, tr., *to kindle* or *light up;* fig. *to excite.*
accípiō, -cípere, -cḗpī, -céptum, tr., *to receive.*
accúrrō, -cúrrere, -cúrrī, -cúrsum, intr., *to run to* or *up to someone* or *something.*
ắcer, ắcris, ắcre, adj., *bold, active, spirited, zealous.*
acérbus, -a, -um, adj., *bitter.*
acérra, -ae, f., (lit. *made of maple*); *an incense box, pan,* or *censer.*
ắciēs, -ḗī, f., *a line of troops in battle array.*
ácta, -ae, f., *the seashore; a beach.* (= Greek ἡ ἀκτή)
acū́tus, -a, -um, adj., *pointed, sharp.* (perf. part. of *ácuō*)
ad, prep. with acc., *to, towards; at, near; according to, in accordance with, after; against.*

áddō, áddere, áddidī, ádditum, tr., *to put to* or *onto; to add to.*
addū́cō, -dū́cere -dúxī, -dúctum, tr., *to draw* or *pull something towards one.*
adeṓ, adv., *indeed.* (accent: cf. Allen (1987) 187
ádeō, adīre, ádiī, áditum, intr., *to go to* or *towards; to approach.*
ádferō, adférre, áttulī, adlā́tum, tr., *to bring to; to bring up.*
adfī́gō, -fī́gere, -fíxī, -fíxum, tr., *to fasten to; to fix firmly.*
ádflō, -flā́re, -flā́vī, -flā́tum, intr. and tr., *blow* or *breathe upon.*
adhíbeō, adhibḗre, adhíbuī, adhíbitum, tr., *hold to or towards; apply; invite to.* (**hábeō**)
adhū́c, adv., of place, *thus far;* of time, *hitherto, as yet, still.* (accent: cf. Allen 1978: 87)
áditus, -ūs, m., *an approach;* hence, *a vulnerable spot* 441.
ádi̯uvō, adi̯uvā́re, adi̯ū́vī, adi̯ū́tum, tr., *to aid* or *help; to support a claim.*
ádloquor, ádloquī, adlocū́tus sum, dep., *to speak to* or *address.*
adnī́tor, -nī́tī, -níxus sum, dep., *to lean against; to strive hard.*
adspī́rō, -spīrā́re, -spīrā́vī, -spīrā́tum, intr. and tr., *to breathe towards* or *upon.*
ádstō, adstā́re, ádstitī (no supine stem), intr., *to stand at* (or) *by.*
adsíduus, -a, -um, adj., *continuous, untiring, relentless;* literally *sitting at something.* (**sédeō**)
adsuḗtus, -a, -um, adj., *accustomed to, used to.* (perf. part. of adsuescō)
adsúltus, ūs, m., *a leaping upon; an assault.* (**sáltus**)
ádsum, adésse, ádfuī, fut. part.

adfutū́rum, intr., *to be present; to come forward* (364)
ádvehō, -véhere, -véxī, -véctum, tr., *to carry to* or *towards.*
advḗlō, -ā́re, -ā́vī, -ā́tum, tr., *to put a veil on something; to crown.*
advéntō, -ā́re, -ā́vī, -ā́tum, intr., *to come to* or *arrive.* (*freq. of* **adveniō**)
advéntus, -ūs, m., *an arrival.* (**adveniō**)
advérsus, -a, -um, adj. *turned towards; facing; opposite.* (perf. part. of **advértō**)
advértō, -vértere, -vértī, -vérsum, tr., *to turn one thing towards another;* (pass., with middle or ref. force) *to put in at.* (34 n.)
ádvocō, -ā́re, -ā́vī, -ā́tum, tr., *to call towards oneself; to summon.*
ádytum, -ī, n., *the innermost and most sacred chamber of a temple,* entered only by the priest; *the shrine of a tomb.* (83 n.)
āeger, āegra, āegrum, adj., *sick or feeble; difficult.*
ā́emulus, -a, -um, adj., *jealous, envious;* subst. *a rival.*
Āenéadēs, -dāe; gen. pl. **Āenéadum,** m. (patronymic*), *a son* or *descendant of Aeneas;* pl. *the followers of Aeneas; the Trojans;* later, *the Romans.*
Āenéās, Āenéāe; acc. **Āenéān,** m., *the son of Venus and Anchises; the hero of the* Aeneid.
ā́enus, -a, -um, adj., *made of bronze* or *copper,* often translated *brazen;* subst. **ā́ena, -ṓrum,** n. pl. *bronzes; bronze caldrons* (cf. 102 n.). (**āes**)
Āeólius, -a, -um, adj., *of* or *belonging to Aeolus, king of the winds; caused by Aeolus.* (791 n.)

aequaévus, -a, -um, adj., *equal in age.* (=aéquus + aévum)
aequális, -e, adj., *equal, generally in age; comrade.*
aéquō, -áre, -ávī, -átum, tr., *to make equal* or *even; to level;* perf. part. aequátus 844, *well-balanced.*
aéquor, aéquoris, n., *a level surface, usually the sea, but sometimes the land* or *plain;* aéquore tótō 456, *over the whole field.*
aéquus, -a, -um, adj., *equal, well matched.*
áēr, áĕris, acc. sing. áĕra, m., *air,* i.e. *the lower atmosphere, below the level of the ether (*aéthēr*); mist.*
áerĕŭs, -a, -um, adj., *made of bronze* or *copper.* (aes)
āérius, -a, -um, adj., *aerial.* (áēr)
aes, áeris, n., *copper* or *bronze.*
aestās, aestátis, f., *summer.*
aethēr, aétheris, acc. sing. aéthera, m., *the upper air* (i.e. above the áēr); *the sky.*
aethérius, -a, -um, adj., *ethereal, heavenly.*
aévum, -ī, n., *time, lifetime, time of life.*
ágger, ággeris, m., *an earthwork, pile,* or *mound* (e.g. of a tomb 44; of a road 273)
ágmen, ágminis, n., (lit. *anything moving forward); a train; a line of march; a body of men* (such as a company, troop, or fleet) *moving* or *ready to move as one* 834; *the stroke of oars* 211; *the gliding of a snake* 90. (ágō)
ágna, -ae, f., *a lamb.*
agnóscō, agnóscere, agnóvī, ágnitum, tr., *to recognize, to acknowledge.*
ágō, ágere, ḗgī, áctum, tr., *to put in motion, drive, drive on,* or *speed along; to do* or *perform; to spend* (time). iam témpus ágī rēs 638, *now is the time for action;* imperat. áge or ágite, *come, come on!*
agréstis, -e, adj., *belonging to the field; rustic.* (áger)
áịō, áit, áịebat, etc., intr. and tr. (def.), *to affirm; to say* or *speak.*
ála, -ae, f., *a wing.*
álacris, álacre, adj., *alert, brisk.*
Álba, -ae, f., *Alba Longa, a town in Latium, founded by Ascanius.*
Albánus, -a, -um, adj., *belonging to Alba;* pl. subst. *the people of Alba Longa, the Albans.*
álbus, -a, -um, adj., *white.*
Alcídēs, -ae, m. (patronymic*), *son* or *descendant of Alceus,* i.e. *Hercules.*
álēs, álitis, adj., *winged, going on wings;* m. subst. *a bird.* (ála)
álius, -a, -um, adj. and pron., *other, different; another; a match for* (someone) 378.
álmus, -a, -um, adj., *nourishing, kindly, benign.*
álō, álere, áluī, áltum, tr., *to cause to grow; to nourish, sustain.*
altáre, -is, n.; usually pl., altária, -ium, *a fixture placed on an altar* (ára) *in which offerings were burned,* or, *the burnt offerings themselves.* (cf. 53-4 n.)
áltē, adv., *highly* or *deeply; on high* 443. (áltus)
álter, áltera, álterum, adj. and pron., *the second (of two); the other;* álter . . . álter, *(the) one . . . (the) other.*
altérnus, -a, -um, adj., *alternate; first one, then the other* 376.
áltum, -ī, n., *the deep sea, the deep.* (subst. of áltus)
áltus, -a, -um, adj., *high, lofty;* alta

petens 508, *aiming (at) high* (*places, standards, or results*). (part. of **álō**)
Amazónius, -a, -um, adj., *of or belonging to Amazons.*
ámbedō, ambédere or **ambésse, ambédī, ambésum,** tr., *to eat or gnaw around;* **ambésa** 752 *charred.* (**ámbō** + **édō**)
ambíguus, -a, -um, adj., *drifting here and there;* hence *doubtful.* (**ámbō** + **ágō**)
ámbō, -ae, -ō, adj. and pron., *both.*
amíctus, -ūs, m., *dress, garment.*
amícus, -a, -um, adj., *friendly, kind;* m. subst. *friend.* (**ámō**)
āmíttō, -míttere, -mísī, -míssum, tr., *to let go, send away, lose.*
ámnis, -is, m., *river.*
ámō, -áre, -ávī, -átum, tr., *to love; to hug the shore,* 160.
amoénus, -a, -um, adj., *pleasing* (*to the senses*)
ámor, -óris, m., *love, affection;* pl. **amóres, amórum,** *beloved friend* (*whether boy or girl*) 334. (**ámō**)
ampléctor, -pléctī, -pléxum, dep., *to twine* (*oneself*) *around; embrace, clasp.* (**ámbō**)
ámplius, adv. (comp. only), *more, longer, further.*
Ámycus, -ī, m., *the king of the Bébryces.* (373 n.)
an, adv. and conj. (interrog.), *or* (28 n.)
ánceps, -cípitis, adj., (lit. *double-headed*); *doubtful.* (**cáput**)
Anchísēs, -sae; acc. –**sēn,** m., *a Trojan hero, consort of Venus and father of Aeneas.*
Anchīséus, -a, -um, adj., *of or belonging to Anchises.*
Anchīsíadēs, -dae, m. (patronymic*),

a son or descendant of Anchises; hence, *Aeneas.*
ánguis, -is, m. and f., *a snake or serpent.*
anhélitus, -ūs, m., *a gasp; gasping or panting for breath.*
anhélō, -áre, -ávī, -átum, intr., *to gasp or pant; to be out of breath.*
anhélus, -a, -um, adj., *gasping or panting.*
ánima, -ae, f., *spirit* in the sense of *breath;* hence *life.*
ánimus, -ī, m., *spirit* in the sense of *emotion,* esp. *courage* or *intellect;* hence *mind.*
ánnus, -ī, m., *a year.*
ánnuus, -a, -um, adj., *yearly, annual.*
ánte, adv. , *in front, beforehand, ahead, first* (of time and place); prep. with acc., *before* (of time and place)
antíquus, -a, -um, adj., *of former times, of old, ancient.*
apériō, aperíre, apéruī, apértum, tr., *to open;* perf. part.
appéllō, -áre, -ávī, -átum, tr., *to call by name; to salute* as or *declare* 540.
apértus, -a, -um, , adj., *open.* (perf. part. of **apériō**)
aprícus, -a, -um, adj., *sunny.* (128 n.)
áptō, -áre, -ávī, -átum, tr., *to make something fit; to provide as equipment* 753.
áptus, -a, -um, adj., *fit or suitable* (perf. part. of **áptō**)
ápud, prep. with acc., *at, near.*
áqua, -ae, f., *water.*
Áquilō, -ónis, m., *the name of the North Wind.*
ára, -ae, f., *an altar.*
arátrum, -ī, n., *a plow.* (**árō**)
árbor, árboris, f., *a tree;* **árbor málī** 504, *the mast-tree.*

Arcádius, -a, -um, adj., *of or from Arcadia, a district in the center of Peloponnese; Arcadian.*
árceō, arcére, árcuī, (no supine stem), tr., *to shut off, ward off, keep at a distance;* hence, *hinder, restrain from.*
arcéssō, arcéssere, arcessívī, arcessítum, tr., *to cause to come; to summon.*
árcus, -ūs, m., *bow; rainbow.*
árdens, -éntis, adj., *glowing; fiery, eager.* (pres. part. of the following)
árdeō, ardére, ársī, ársum, intr., *to glow, burn, blaze, catch* or *be on fire.*
árduus, -a, -um, adj., *steep;* hence *rearing* or *rising up* (to one's full height); **árdua, -órum,** n. pl. *heights.*
aréna, -āe, f., *sand, seashore; arena.*
argéntum, -ī, n., *silver.*
Argívus, -a, -um, adj., *of or from Argos, one of the chief cities of the Peloponnese; kingdom of Agamemnon; Argive.*
Argólicus, -a, -um, adj., *of or from the district around Argos (i.e. the Argolid); Argive.*
áridus, -a, -um, adj., *dry, parched.*
árma, -órum, n. pl., *equipment,* especially *weapons, armor, arms,* but also *ship's tackle.* (15 n.)
ármiger, armígera, armígerum, adj., *arms bearer;* of the eagle that carries Jupiter's thunderbolts 255.
arréctus, -a, -um, adj., *upright; aroused, excited, eager;* **in dígitōs . . . arréctus** 426, *raised up on tiptoe.* (perf. part. of **árrigō**)
ars, ártis, f., *skill; workmanship; craft.*
ártus, -ūs, m., *a joint* or *limb.*
árvum, -ī, n., *plowed land, farmland, field.*

Ascánius, -ī, m., *the son of Aeneas and Creusa; also called* **Iū̯lus.**
aspéctō, -áre, -ávī, -átum, tr. *to look hard at.* (freq. of **aspíciō**)
ásper, áspera, ásperum, adj., *rough,* either (of objects) to the touch 267; (of the sea) with respect to traveling 767; (of people) in terms of culture 730, hence *wild* or *uncivilized.*
aspíciō, -spícere, -spéxī, -spéctum, tr., *to look at.*
ast, conj., *but* (a stronger form of **at**)
ástrum, -ī, n., *a star.*
at, conj., *but.*
áter, átra, átrum, adj., *black* or *dark.*
Átius, -a, -um, adj., and subst.
Átius, -ī, m., *the name of a Roman gens supposedly descended from the Trojan hero* **Átys.**
átque, see **āc.**
attíngō, attíngere, áttigī, attáctum, tr., *to reach to; to attain.* (**tángō**)
attóllō, attóllere (no perf. or supine stem), tr., *to lift up; to raise;* in pass. often with middle sense, *to rise, raise oneself,* or *stand* 127.
attónitus, -a, -um, adj., *thunderstruck.* (**tónō**)
Átys, Átyos, m., *a grandson of Priam, friend to* **Ascánius,** *and legendary Trojan ancestor of the Roman* **Átiī,** *the family to which Augustus' mother belonged.* (568 n.)
áuctor, -óris, m., *originator; guarantor; witness* 17; *adviser* 418. (**áugeō**)
áudax, audácis, adj., *bold.*
áudeō, audére, áusus sum, semidep. *to dare* or *venture.*
áudiō, audíre, áudiī, audítum, tr., *hear.*
áugeō, augére, áuxī, áuctum, tr., *produce, increase.*

augúrium, -ĭī, n., *the art of divination by omens;* hence *a portent* 7; *import* 523.
aúra, -ae, f., *air, breeze.*
aurátus, -a, -um, adj., *gilt, gilded, gold-plated.* (**aúrum** + part. suffix **-átus**)
aúreŭs, -a, -um, adj., *golden.* (**aúrum**)
auríga, -ae, m., *a charioteer.*
aúris, -is, f., *an ear.*
Auróra, -ae, f., *the goddess of the morning; the dawn.*
aúrum, -ī, n., *gold.*
Ausónius, -a, -um, adj., *of or belonging to the Aúsonēs,* hence *Italian;* subst. **Ausónia, -ae,** f. *the country of the Aúsonēs,* i.e. *Italy.*
auspícium, -ī, n., *the art of divination by observing the flight of birds;* hence *an omen.* (**ávis**)
Aúster, -trī, m., *the name of the South Wind.*
aut, conj. (disjunctive), *or;* **aut . . . aut,** *either . . . or.*
aútem, conj. (adversative and continuative), *but; moreover, in addition.*
auxílium, -ĭī, n., *aid, help.* (**aúgeō**)
Avérnus, -a, -um, adj., *of or belonging to Lake Avernus;* subst. **Avérna, -órum,** n. pl. *places around Lake Avernus,* and so, *the region of Lake Avernus.*
ávis, -is, f., *a bird.*
ávus, -ī, m., *a grandfather.*
áxis, -is, m., lit. *axle;* fig. *chariot.*
Bácchus, -ī, m., *Dionysus, son of Jupiter and Semele and god of wine;* hence (by metonymy*), *wine.*
bálteus, -ī, m.; pl. **báltea, -órum,** n. *swordbelt, baldric.*
Bebrýcius, -a, -um, adj., *of or belonging to the Bébrycēs.* (372-3 n.)

béllum, -ī, n., *a war; a fight.*
Bérŏē, -ēs, f., *the wife of Doryclus of Epirus.*
bícolor, -colóris, adj., *dappled.*
bídens, -déntis, f., *a two-year-old sheep, fit for sacrifice.*
bígae, -árum, f. pl., *a pair of yoke horses, oxen, etc.* (contracted from **bi̯ugae:** cf. the following)
bíi̯ugus, -a, -um, adj., (having to do with **bígae;** hence) *a race for two-horse chariots.* (**bīs** + **i̯úgum**)
bíni, -ae, -a, adj., (distributive num.) *two apiece.*
bipénnis, -is, f., *a double-edged axe.*
bīs, adv., *twice.*
blándus, -a, -um, adj., *flattering.*
bónus, -a, -um, adj., *good.* (comp. **mélior,** superl. **óptimus**) .
bōs, bŏvis, gen. pl. **bŏum,** m. and f., *a beeve; an ox.*
brácchium, -ĭī, n., *the forearm; a yardarm, sailyards* 829.
brévis, -e, adj., *short; shallow.*
Bútēs, -ae, m., (1) *the son of* **Ámycus,** *slain by Dares* 372; (2) *an Argonaut, consort of Venus and father of Éryx.* (23-4 n., 864 n.)
cádō, cádere, cécĭdī, cásum, intr., *to fall.*
caécus, -a, -um, adj., *blind; hidden, unseen.*
caédō, caédere, cecídī, caésum, tr., *to cut; to slaughter.*
caélō, -áre, -ávī, -átum, tr., *to emboss, carve,* or *chisel.*
caélum, -ī, n., *the sky; heaven.*
caérulus, -a, -um, adj., *intensely blue in color,* like the sea or sky.
caéstus, -ūs, m., *a boxing glove.* (**caédō**)
calx, cálcis, f., *the heel.*
cámpus, -ī, m., *a flat, open plain.*

cándeō, candḗre, cánduī, no supine stem, intr., *to be white; to glisten; to shine.*

cándidus, -a, -um, adj., *white, glistening, shining; fair.*

cáneō, canḗre, cánuī, no supine stem, intr., *to be gray.* (**cánus**)

cánis, -is, gen. pl. **cánum,** m. and f., *a dog.*

cánō, cánere, cécinī, cántum, intr. and tr., *to sing;* of a trumpet, *to sound* 113; of a prophet, *to interpret omens* 524.

cánus, -a, -um, adj., *white- or gray-haired.* (**cán(d)eō, cándidus**)

capéssō, -ere, -ívī, -ítum, tr., *to catch at; strive to reach,* 703.

cápiō, cápere, cḗpī, cáptum, tr., *to take, seize; receive;* **cápit lócum** 185, *to take a favorable position.*

cáput, cápitis, n., *head; head of cattle* 62.

cárcer, cárceris, m., *a jail; a cage;* in a race, esp. in pl., *the starting cage.*

carchḗsium, -iī, n., *a two-handled goblet.*

cáreō, carḗre, cáruī, cáritum, intr. with abl. of separation, *to go without, be deprived of, lack; to have nothing to do with* 651.

carína, -ae, f., *a ship's keel;* by synecdoche*, *a ship.*

Carpáthius, -a, -um, adj., *from or having to do with Cárpathus* (mod. Scarpontō, an island between Crete and Rhodes); *mostly referring to the Carpathian Sea.*

cárus, -a, -um, adj., *dear.*

Cassándra, -ae, f., *a daughter of Priam;* see 636 n.

castéllum, -ī, n., *a castle or fortress.* (diminutive of **cástrum**)

cástigō, -áre, -ávī, -átum, tr., *to chastise or rebuke.* (**cástus**)

cástrum, -ī, n., mostly pl. **cástra,** *a camp, encampment.*

cástus, -a, -um, adj., *chaste, holy.*

cásus, -ūs, m., *a fall; an accident or mischance.* (**cádō**)

catérva, -ae, f., *a troop.*

Caúrus, -ī, m., *the name of the Northwest Wind.*

caúsa, -ae, f., *a cause or reason.*

caútēs, -is, f., *a rock or cliff.*

cávea, -ae, f., (lit. *a hollow area*); *the part of a theatre where the spectators sit* 340.

cávus, -a, -um, adj., *hollow.*

cḗdō, cḗdere, céssī, céssum, intr. and tr., *to withdraw, retreat, step back, make room; to give in or grant.*

célebrō, -áre, -ávī, -átum, tr., *to frequent; to celebrate.*

céler, céleris, célere, adj., *swift.*

célerō, -áre, -ávī, -átum, tr., *to traverse speedily.*

célsus, -a, -um, adj., *elevated, uplifted, lofty, high.*

Centaúrus, -ī, m., *a ship in Aeneas' fleet commanded by the Trojan hero* **Sergéstus** *and named for the mythical creature, half man and half horse.*

cérebrum, -i, n., *the brain.* (accent and pronunciation: cf. 413 n.)

cérnō, cérnere, crḗvī, crḗtum, tr., *to see clearly, discern.*

certámen, certáminis, n., *a contest, struggle, or race.*

certátim, adv., *with effort.*

cértō, -áre, -ávī, -átum, intr., *to contend or strive.* (freq. of **cérnō**)

cértus, -a, -um, adj., *decided,*

determined, settled, sure. (perf. part. of **cérnō**)
cérvus, -ī, m., *a deer.*
céterus, -a, -um, adj., normally pl., *the rest, remaining.*
cétus, -ī, m.; **cétē,** n. pl. (822 n.), *sea creatures; whales, sharks, dolphins,* etc.
ceū, conj., *like* or *as.*
Chimaéra, -ae, f., *a ship in Aeneas' fleet commanded by the Trojan hero* **Gýas** *and named for the mythical creature, part lion, part goat, and part snake, that was slain by Bellerophon.*
chlámys, chlámydis, f., *a cloak* or *mantle.*
chórus, -ī, m., *a dance in a ring; a group* (of nymphs 581)
cíeō, ciére, cívī, cítum, tr., *to rouse* or *set in motion.* (**cítō, cítus**)
cíngō, cíngere, cínxī, cínctum, tr., *to encircle, wreath,* or *gird.*
cínis, cíneris, m., *ash.*
círculus, -ī, m., (lit. *a small circle*); *a necklace* (diminutive of **círcus**)
círcum, adv. and prep. with acc., *about* or *around.*
circumfléctō, -fléctere, -fléxī, -fléxum, tr., *to turn* (something) *around.*
círcus, -i, m., *a circle* or *circuit; esp. a racecourse.* (109–10 n., 288–9 n.)
Císseūs, -eī, m., *a king of Thrace, father of Hecuba.* (537 n.)
cítō, comp. **cítius,** adv., *quickly; more quickly.*
cítus, -a, -um, adj., *quick, speedy, swift.* (perf. part. of **cíeō**)
cívis, -is, m. and f., *a citizen.*
clámor, -ṓris, m., *a shout* or *cry; shouting.*
clárus, -a, -um, adj., *clear,* i.e. (to the ear) *loud* or *shrill;* (to the eye) *distinct* or *bright;* (to the mind) *evident,* hence, *renowned.*
clássis, -is, f., *an army* or, more commonly, *a fleet.*
claúdus, -a, -um, adj., *crippled, maimed, lame.*
clávus, -i, m., *a rudder handle* or *tiller.*
clípeus, -ī, m., and **clípeum, -ī,** n., *the bronze shield of a Roman soldier.*
Cloánthus, -ī, m., *legendary Trojan ancestor of the* **Cluéntiī,** *captain of the* **Scýlla,** *one of the ships in Aeneas' fleet, and a contestant in the boat race.*
Cluéntius, -a, -um, adj. and subst.
Cluéntius, -iī, m., *the name of a Roman gens, supposedly descended from the Trojan hero* **Cloánthus.**
coétus, -ūs, m., *a gathering* or *assembly.*
cognóscō, cognóscere, cognṓvī, cógnitum, tr., *to learn; to perceive.* (**nóscō**)
cṓgō, cṓgere, coḗgī, coáctum, tr., *to drive together; to pack; to force.* (**ágō**)
cólligō, collígere, collḗgī, colléctum, tr., *to get together; to collect.* (**légō**)
cóllis, -is, m., *a hill.*
cóllum, -ī, n., *a neck.*
cólō, cólere, cóluī, cúltum, tr., *to inhabit; to tend* or *keep,* esp. (in agriculture) *to till the ground;* (in religion) *to worship;* (in grooming) *to dress* or *adorn.*
cólor, -ṓris, m., *a color.*
colúmba, -ae, f., *a dove* or *pigeon.*
cóma, -ae, f., *the hair* or *a lock of hair.*
cómes, cómitis, m. and f., *an attendant, comrade,* or *companion.*

cómitor, -ári, -átus sum, dep., *to accompany.*
comméndō, -áre, -ávī, -átum, tr., *to entrust* (mandō)
commíttō, -míttere, -mísī, -míssum, tr., *(to bring together; hence) to begin;* púgnam commíttere, *to join battle* 69; lúdī commíssī, *the opening of the games* 113 n.
commóveō, -movére, -móvī, -mótum, tr., *to rouse or set in motion.*
compéllō, -áre, -ávī, -átum, tr., *to address.*
compléctor, -pléctī, -pléxus sum, dep., *(to twine oneself with, hence) to embrace.*
cómpleō, -plére, -plévī, plétum, tr., *to fill up; of time, to pass* 46. (plénus)
compléxus, -ūs, m., *embrace.* (compléctor)
cómprimō, -prímere, -préssī, -préssum, tr., *(to press together or compress; hence) to restrain.* (prémō)
cóncavus, -a, -um, adj., *hollow.* (cávus)
concédō, -cédere, -céssī, -céssum, intr. and tr. *to go away; to yield or grant.*
cóncidō, concídere, cóncidī, no supine stem, intr., *to fall down, tumble down, collapse.* (cádō)
concílium, -iī, n., *an assembly; a council.*
concípiō, -cípere, -cépī, -céptum, tr., *to conceive.* (cápiō)
conclámō, -áre, -ávī, -átum, intr., *to shout (of a group, all together)*
concúrsus, -ūs, m., *(a running together; hence) a gathering or concourse.* (cúrrō)
concútiō, -cútere, -cússī, -cússum, tr., *to shake up.* (quátiō)
condō, cóndere, cóndidī, cónditum, tr., *to put together; to put away, hide or bury; to found, build (e.g. a city)*
confíciō, -fícere, -fécī, féctum, tr., *to make completely; to finish.* (fáciō)
confídō, -fídere, -físus sum, semidep. *to trust completely.* (fídēs)
confúndō, -fúndere, -fúdī, -fúsum, tr., *(to pour together; hence) to disturb, disconcert, confound.*
congrédior, cóngredī, congréssus sum, dep., *(to go in step with; hence) to encounter.*
congréssus, -ūs, m., *(a walking or coming together; hence) a meeting or an encounter.*
coníciō, -ícere, -iécī, -iéctum, tr., *to throw together; to throw with force.* (iáciō)
coniúngō, -iúngere, -iúnxī, -iúnctum, tr., *to join together; to unite.*
coniunx, cóniugis, m. and f., *spouse; husband or wife.* (iúgum)
conlúceō, -lucére, no perf. or supine stem, intr., *to shine brightly.*
cōnítor, -nítī, -níxus sum, dep., *to struggle with all one's might.*
consanguíneus, -a, -um, adj., *of the same blood; related by blood.* (sánguis)
cónscius, -a, -um, adj., *aware of; conscious of* (scíō)
cónsequor, cónsequī, consecútus sum, dep., *to follow, follow up, or overtake.*
cónserō, -sérere, -séruī, -sértum, tr., *to weave together.*
conséssus, -ūs, m., *(a sitting together, hence) an assembly; a gathering or concourse.*
consídō, -sídere, -sédī, -séssum, intr., *to seat oneself; to settle down.* (sédeō)

consílium, -iī, n., *counsel, advice, debate.*

consístō, consístere, cónstitī, cónstitum, intr., *to stand still; to come to a halt.* (**stō**)

cónsonō, -sonáre, -sónuī, no supine stem, intr., *to resound.* (**sónus**)

conspíciō, -spícere, -spéxī, -spéctum, tr., *to get a general view* or *a glimpse* (of something); *to catch sight* (of something). (**spéctō**)

constítuō, -stitúere, -stítuī, -stitútum, tr., *to station, set, place,* or *set up; to settle once and for all; to determine.*

cónstō, constáre, cónstitī, (fut. part. **constātúrus**), intr., *to take a stand; to stand fast;* (of ideas or plans) *to be determined* or *settled* 748.

consū́mō, -sū́mere, -súmpsī, -súmptum, tr., *to destroy entirely; to consume.*

consúrgō, -súrgere, -surréxī, -surréctum, intr., *to rise up in a group* or *in groups.*

conténdō, -téndere, -téndī, -téntum, intr. and tr. *to stretch* or *extend; to strain, strive, contend; to draw* or *aim* (in archery, 520); *to direct* (one's course, 834). (**cum** intensive + **téndō**)

conténtus, -a, -um, adj., (*held together* or *kept whole;* hence) *satisfied, content.* (perf. part. of **contíneo** = **cum** + **téneō**)

contíngō, contíngere, cóntigī, contáctum, intr. and tr., (*to touch upon;* hence) *to reach* a destination; *to hit* a goal or target. (**tángō**)

contínuō, adv., , *immediately.* (**téneō**)

cóntrā, adv. and prep. with acc., *opposite; against.*

cóntus, -ī, m., *a pole* or *pike.*

convéllō, -véllere, -véllī -vúlsum, tr., *to tear up, pluck; to pull apart.*

convéniō, -veníre, -vénī, -véntum, intr., *to come together; to meet.*

convértō, -vértere, -vértī, -vérsum, tr., *to turn around; to change.*

cṓpia, -ae, f., *an abundance; a supply; an opportunity* or *ability.*

cor, córdis, n., *the heart;* by synecdoche*, *a brave man* (729 n.).

córneus, -a, -um, adj., *made of cornelwood.*

córnū, -ūs, n., *a horn; the end of a sailyard* (antenna)

corṓna, -ae, f., *a wreath* or *a crown.*

córpus, córporis, n., *a body;* by synecdoche*, *a person* 318 n.; *a defensive boxing maneuver* 445 n.; *a complete set* of something, e.g. *an entire fleet of ships* 683 n.

corrípiō, -rípere, -rípuī, -réptum, tr., *to grab up;* of movement over a course, *to traverse rapidly,* with **cámpum** 144–45 n.; with **spátia** 316 n. (**rápiō**)

corúscō, -áre, -ávī, -átum, tr., *to brandish.*

crássus, -a, -um, adj., *thick.*

crátēr, -ḗris, acc. sing. **crātḗra** 536, m., *a mixing bowl.* (= Greek κρατήρ)

crḗber, crḗbra, crḗbrum, adj., *frequent; thick; rapid; coming in quick succession.* (**crḗscō**)

crḗdō, crḗdere, crḗdidī, crḗditum, intr. and tr. *to put faith in; to trust.*

crépitō, -áre, no perf. or supine stem, intr., frequentive of **crépō, crepáre, crépuī, crépitum**, intr. and tr., *to make a creaking, cracking, scraping,* or *rattling sound.*

Créssa, -ae, f., *a Cretan woman.*

Crḗta, -ae, f., *the island of Crete.*

Crīmísus, -ī, m., *a river of Sicily; the god of that river, father of* **Acéstēs.**
crínis, -is, m., *hair; the trail of a meteor or comet.* (528 n.)
crūdus, -a, -um, adj., *(raw, unrefined; hence) primitive, wild, savage.*
crúor, -ŏris, m., *blood (after it has flowed from a wound); gore.*
cúlmen, cúlminis, n., *roof or housetop.*
cúltus, cúltūs, m., *way of life.* **(cólō)**
cum[1], conj., *when; since, because; although.*
cum[2], prep. with abl., *together with or along with.*
cúmulō, -áre, -ávī, -átum, tr., *to pile up or load.*
cúnctor, -ári, -átus sum, dep., *to dawdle, delay, or hesitate.*
cúnctus, -a, um (found mostly in pl.), adj., *all together.* (perhaps contracted from **coniúnctus,** perf. part. of **coniúngō**)
cúněŭs, -ēī, m., (lit. *a wedge;* hence) *a triangular section of seats in a theatre.*
cupídō, cupídinis, f., *a desire or longing.*
cúpiō, cúpere, cúpiī (or **-ívi**), **cupítum,** tr., *to desire or long for.*
cúra, -āe, f., *care, anxiety.*
cúrrō, cúrrere, cucúrrī, cúrsum, intr., *to run.*
cúrrus, cúrrūs, m., *a chariot.*
cúrsus, cúrsūs, m., *(a run; running; hence) a race; a racecourse; a chase.*
cúrvus, -a, -um, adj., *bent, crooked, or curved.*
cúspis, cúspidis, f., *a point.*
cústos, custódis, m. and f., *a keeper, guard, guardian,* or *watchman.*
cýmbium, -iī, n., *a small drinking cup.* (κυμβίον)

Cȳmódocē, -āe or **-ēs,** f., *Cymódoce, a* **Nēréis.** (Κυμοδόκη)
Cytheréus, -a, -um, adj., *of or having to do with the island of Cythēra;* usually found as a subst., **Cytheréa, -āe,** f. *a cult title of Venus* (Aphrodite), *who was born from the sea near that island.*
Dánăŭs, -a, -um, adj., *of or belonging to Danaus, an early king of Argos;* subst. **Dánăī, -ŏrum,** m. *the Danaans or Argives;* fig. *the Greeks.*
daps, dápis, f., *a formal banquet, generally of ritual nature and involving animal sacrifice;* usually pl.
Dardánidāe, Dardánidum or **-idárum,** m. pl. (patronymic*), *sons or descendants of Dardanus;* hence, *the Trojans.*
Dardánius, -a, -um, adj., *of or belonging to* **Dárdanus;** hence, *Trojan.*
Dárdanus, -a, -um, adj., *of or belonging to* **Dárdanus;** hence, *Trojan.*
Dárdanus, -ī, m., *son of Zeus and Electra and the mythical ancestor of the Trojans.*
Dárēs, Darétis (acc. **-ēn** and **-ēta**), m., *a Trojan; one of the contestants in the boxing match.*
dē, prep. with abl., *down from; from, of, concerning;* idiom, **dē móre,** *according to custom, duly, ritually.*
déa, -āe, f., *a goddess.*
dēbéllō, -belláre, -ávī, -átum, tr., *to vanquish in war.*
débeō, -ēre, débuī, débitum, intr. (with complementary inf.) *to be obligated* to do something; tr. with dir. obj. *to owe* something.
débilis, -e, adj., *unhandy; feeble, disabled.*

dēcḗdō, -cḗdere, -céssī, -céssum, intr., *to withdraw; depart.*
décet, decḗre, décuit, no supine stem, intr., impers., *it is becoming; it is suitable.* (**décus**)
dḗcidō, dēcídere, dḗcidī, no supine stem, intr., *to fall down.* (**cádō**)
dēcípiō, -cípere,-cḗpī, -céptum, tr., *to take in, beguile, or deceive.* (**cápiō**)
dēclā́rō, -ā́re, -ā́vī, -ā́tum, tr., *to make clear; declare.*
decṓrus, -a, -um, adj., *comely; becoming; adorned.* (**décus**)
dēcúrrō, -cúrrere, -cúrrī, -cúrsum, intr., *to run down; speed down; race home.*
decus, décoris, n., *ornament, beauty; glory, renown; appearance to others* 174. (**décet, decṓrus**)
déferō, dēférre, détulī, dēlā́tum, tr., *to bear away; to ship off; to bring to harbor* 57.
dĕhínc, adv., *of place, hence, from here; of time, henceforth; then.* (accent: cf. Allen (1978) 87)
dĕhíscō, -híscere, -hī́vī, no supine stem, intr., *to yawn; to gape open.*
dēíciō, -ícere, -i̯ḗcī, -i̯éctum, tr., *to hurl down; to bring down* with a weapon 542; *to cast lots* 490. (**i̯áciō**)
deīndĕ (two syllables, with synezesis* of **ei**: cf. 14 n.), adv., (of place and time) *thereafter, then, next.*
dēlā́bor, -lā́bī, -lā́psus sum, dep., *to glide; to slide; to slip and fall down.*
dḗligō, -lígere, -lḗgī, -léctum, tr., *to choose out* or *select.* (**légō**)
délphin, -ī́nis, m., *a dolphin.*
dēméntia, -ae, f., *madness.* (**mens**)
dēmíttō, -míttere, -mī́sī, -míssum, tr., *to send down; to bring* a boat *to harbor* 29.

Dēmóleos, -ī, m., *a Greek warrior slain by Aeneas.*
dens, déntis, m., *a tooth.*
dénsus, -a, -um, adj., *closely packed, crowded, crowding, dense,* or *thick.*
dēpā́scō, -pā́scere, -pā́vī, -pā́stum, tr., *to feed upon* or *from.*
dēpéllō, dēpéllere, dḗpulī, -púlsum, tr., *to drive away.*
dēpṓnō, -pṓnere, -pósuī, -pósitum, tr., *to put down; to put ashore* (cf. 751 n.).
dēpréndō, -préndere, -préndī, -prénsum, tr., *to snatch away;* hence *to catch, surprise.*
dēprṓmō, -prṓmere, -prómpsī, -prómptum, tr., *to draw out of.*
dēscéndō, -scéndere, -scéndī, -scénsum, intr., *to climb down; to sink; to descend.* (**dē + scándō**)
dḗserō, -sérere, -séruī, -sértum, tr., *to abandon, desert, leave behind.*
dēsī́gnō, -signā́re, -signā́vī, -signā́tum, tr., *to mark down; to trace out.* (**sígnum**)
dētórqueō, -torquḗre, -tórsī, -tórtum, tr., *to twist aside; to steer away from land* (165); *to shift aside* or *haul down* (cf. 832 n.).
dḗtrahō, -tráhere, -trā́xī, -tráctum, tr., *to drag down* or *strip off.*
dētúrbō, -turbā́re, -turbā́vī, -turbā́tum, tr., *to throw down.*
déus, -ī, voc. déus, nom. pl. dī, abl. dīs, m., *a god.*
déxter, -tra, -trum, adj., *on the right hand, to* or *on the right;* subst. déxtra, -ae, f. *the right hand* (for **mánus déxtra**).
dī́cō, -ā́re, -ā́vī, -ā́tum, tr., *to proclaim;* hence *consecrate.*

dī́cō, dī́cere, dī́xī, dī́ctum, tr., *to say* or *speak; to call* or *name.*

dī́ctum, -ī, n., *a saying;* n. pl. **dī́cta, -ṓrum,** *words;* **dā́re dī́cta,** *to speak* (cf. 32 n.). (perf. part., subst. of **dī́cō, dī́cere**)

Dī́dō, Elíssāe (3 n.), f., *daughter of Belus, king of Tyre; legendary founder of Carthage.*

dīdū́cō, -dū́cere -dū́xī, -dū́ctum, tr., *to pull apart; to separate.*

Didymā́ōn, -ŏ̆nis, m., *a metalworker* (otherwise unknown).

dīēs, diḗī, m. and f. sing., m. pl., *a day; daylight;* fig. **lónga díes,** *a great length of time,* hence, *the passage of time* (783).

diffícilis, -e, adj., *difficult; dangerous.* (**fácilis**)

diffū́giō, -fū́gere, -fū́gī, no supine stem, intr., *to flee in different directions; to disperse.*

dígitus, -ī, m., *a finger* or *toe.*

dígnus, -a, -um, adj., *worthy;* with abl. of specification, *worthy of* (AG §418b).

digrédior, -gredī, -gréssus sum, dep., *to step away.* (**grádior**)

dī́ligō, -lígere, -léxī, -léctum, tr., *(to single out, set apart,* or *choose;* hence) *to love.* (**légō**)

dimóveō, -movḗre, -mṓvī, -mṓtum, tr., *to move* (something) *away.* (**móveō**)

Diṓrēs, -is, m., *a Trojan follower of Aeneas, a son of Priam, and one of the contestants in the footrace.*

dī́rigō, -rígere, -réxī, -réctum, tr., *to steer.* (**régō**)

dī́rimō, -ímere, -ḗmī, -ḗmptum, tr., *to take apart* or *separate.* (**emō**)

Dīs, Dī́tis, m., *the Roman god of the underworld.*

dī́scō, dī́scere, dī́dicī, no supine stem, tr., *to get to know; to learn* (*how*)

discrī́men, discrī́minis, n., *a difference* or *distinction;* hence *a contest* (*to make a distinction*); *a distance* (154). (**cérnō**)

discúrrō, -cúrrere, -cúrrī, -cúrsum, intr., *to run away* or *in different directions; to veer off* (580)

dispéllō, dispéllere, dispulī, dispúlsum, tr., *to drive away; to scatter.*

divérberō, -ā́re, -ā́vī, -ā́tum, tr., *to break through, cleave,* or *pierce.*

divérsus, -a, -um, adj., *turned aside;* hence *off course* (166) or *different, various* (676). (**vértō**)

divī́nus, -a, -um, adj., *divine, godlike.*

dī́vus, -a, -um, adj., *divine;* subst., **dī́vus, -ī,** m. or **dī́va, -āe,** f. *a god(dess)*

dō, dā́re, dédī, dā́tum, tr., *to give, grant,* or *allow;* poetic idioms: **dā́re dī́cta,** *to speak* or *say* 32 n.; **dā́re sónitum,** *to make noise* 139 n., 435 n.; **dā́re tórtūs,** *to writhe* 276 n.; **dā́re vḗla,** *to set sail* 796 n.; **dā́re lḗtō,** *to put to death* 806 n.

dóceō, docḗre, dócuī, dóctum, tr., *to teach; to disclose the meaning of something* 523; with acc. + inf., *to teach* someone *how* to do something 598.

dólor, -ṓris, m., *pain, grief, resentment, rage, indignation.* (**dóleō**)

dólus, -ī, m., *guile* or *treachery; cheating* 342; *a puzzle* 590.

dómitor, -ṓris, m., *a tamer* or *conqueror.* (**domō**)

dómus, dómūs (acc. **dómōs** 732 n., 756, f., *house,* as in English, in the sense of both *dwelling* and *family.*

dónec, conj., *as long as; until.*
dónō, -áre, -ávī, -átum, tr., *to give something* (acc.) *to someone* (dat.); *to present someone* (acc.) *with a gift* (abl.) 282, 361; AG § 364); perf. part. **donátī,** (*those*) *having been presented* with prizes 268.
dónum, -ī, n., *a gift; a prize.* (**dō, dónō**)
Dóryclus, -ī, m., *king of Thrace and husband of Beroë.* (accent and pronunciation: cf. 620 n., 647 n.)
dūcō, dúcere dúxī, dúctum, tr., *to lead; to take away; to trace,* in different senses: **crínem dúcere,** *to trace a "hairy" trail across the sky* 528; **génus dúcere,** *to trace one's ancestry* 801.
dúctor, -óris, m., *leader; captain.*
dúdum, adv., *long since; long ago.*
dúlcis, -e, adj., (lit. *sweet to the taste*); fig. *dear, precious.*
dum, conj., *while, until.*
dúō, dúae, dúō, adj., cardinal num., *two.*
duplex, dúplicis, adj., *twofold; double.*
dūrus, -a, -um, adj., *hard; cruel, stern.*
ē or **ex,** prep. with abl., *out of, from.*
écce, interj., *look! behold!* .
édō, édere, édidī, éditum, tr., *to put forth; to give out; to utter.*
édō, ésse, édī, ésum, 3 sing. pres. ind. act. **est,** tr., *eat.*
ēdóceō, -docére, -dócuī, -dóctum, tr., *to explain clearly and thoroughly.*
éfferō, efférre, éxtulī, ēlátum, tr., *to bear out; bring out; raise up.*
effétus, -a, -um, adj., (lit. *of women*) *past the age of childbearing;* (fig. *of men or women*) *worn out.*
éffor, effárī, effátus sum, dep., *to speak out.*
effríngō, -fríngere, -frégī, -fráctum, intr. and tr., *to break out* or *break open.* (**frángō**)
effúgiō, -fúgere, -fúgī, no supine stem, intr. and tr., *to get away* or *escape from.*
effúlgeō, -fulgére, -fúlsī, no supine stem, intr., *to gleam; to blaze* or *shine forth.*
effúndō, -fúndere, -fúdī, -fúsum, tr., *to pour out; to spend; to utter;* (of reins) *to shake loose* 818.
égeō, egére, éguī, no supine stem, intr., *to need, crave,* or *lack.*
égo, méī, míhi, mē, mē, pron., 1st pers. sing., *I; sometimes intensified by the suffix* **-met** 650.
ēgrégius, -a, -um, adj., (lit. *standing out from the flock;* hence) *distinguished.* (**grex**)
ēi̯éctō, -áre, -ávī, -átum, tr., *to throw out.* (**i̯áctō**)
ēlábor, -lábī, -lápsus sum, dep., *to glide out, off,* or *away; to slip in front; to dodge* or *escape.*
Elíssa, -ae, f., *a name for* **Dídō.** (cf. 3 n.)
Elýsium, -ī, n., *the abode of the blessed souls in the underworld.*
ēmétior, -metírī, -ménsus sum, dep., *to measure out; to traverse, survey.*
émicō, -micáre, -mícuī, no supine stem, intr., *to glance; to spring out; to shoot forth.* (cf. 319 n.)
ēn, interj., *behold!.*
énim, conj., *for* or *indeed;* (in combinations) **sed énim,** *but the fact is; but indeed* 395; **quid énim,** *why indeed?* 850. (**nam**)
énsis, -is, m., *a sword.*
Entéllus, -ī, m., *an old Sicilian hero, one of the contestants in the boxing match.*
éō, íre, íī, ítum, intr., *to go.*

epulae, -arum, f. pl., *feast or banquet.*
Epýtidēs, -is, (acc. **-ēn**), m., *the name of a herald.* (cf. 547 n.)
éques, équitis, m., *a horseman.* (**équus**)
equéster, -tris, -tre, adj., *having to do with horsemen; of the cavalry.* (**éques**)
équidem, adv., *indeed; truly.*
équus, -ī, m., *a horse.*
érgō, adv., *therefore.*
érigō, -rígere, -réxī, -réctum, tr., *to set upright.* (**régō**)
ērípiō, -rípere, -rípuī, -réptum, tr., *to snatch out of or away from; to rescue.* (**rápiō**)
érrō, -āre, -āvī, -ātum, intr., *to lose one's way; to wander; to miss a target.*
érror, -ōris, m., (lit. *a wandering; a mistake*); fig. *a maze, trap, or snare.* (cf. 591 n.)
éruō, ērúere, éruī, érutum, tr., *to tear out or uproot.*
Erycínus, -a, -um, adj., *belonging to Mt. Eryx*; subst. **Erycína, -ae,** f. *a cult title of Venus.* (**Éryx**)
Erymánthus, -ī, m., *a mountain chain in Arcadia.*
Éryx, Érycis, m., (1) *a hero, son of Venus and Butes and half-brother to Aeneas* (cf. 24 n.); (2) *a mountain on the Northwestern tip of Sicily.*
est, 3rd pers. sing. pres. ind. act. of, (1) **édō** (2) **sum.**
et, conj., *and, also, too;* (in combination) **et ... et,** *both ... and;* (adverbial = **etsi**) *although, even though* (cf. 851 n.)
étiam, conj., *also; even, still.*
Eumélus, -ī, m., *one of Aeneas' Trojan followers.* (665 n.)
Eurýalus, -ī, m., *one of Aeneas' Trojan followers, the winner of the footrace.*

Eurytion, -ōnis, m., *one of Aeneas' Trojan followers; the archer who brought down the dove.*
ēvādō, -vādere, -vāsī, -vāsum, intr. and tr., *to escape from.*
ēvínciō, -vincíre, -vínxī, -vínctum, tr., *to bind or wind round.*
ēvólvō, -vólvere, -vólvī, -volútum, tr., *to unroll or roll out.*
ex, prep. with abl., *out from or of; made from or of*; idioms **ex mōre,** *according to custom,* 244; **ex órdine,** *in due order,* 773; **ex quō,** *since,* 47. (**ē**)
exanimátus, -a, -um, adj., (lit. *unsouled;* hence) *deprived of all spirit.* (**ánima/ánimus** + part. suffix **-átus**)
exánimis, -e, adj., (lit. *soulless;* hence) *lifeless, dead.*
exardéscō, -ardéscere, -ársī, -ársum, intr., incohative, *to begin burning.*
excédō, -cédere, -céssī, -céssum, intr., *to withdraw.*
excélsus, -a, -um, adj., *elevated; very lofty.* (perf. part. of **excéllō**).
excídium, -iī, n., (lit. *a cutting off;* hence) *utter destruction.* (**scíndō**)
éxciō, excíre, éxciī, excítum, tr., *to rouse up; excite.* (**ex + cíeō / cíō**)
excípiō, -cípere, -cēpī, -céptum, tr., *to take out of, take away from; to except; to receive.* (**cápiō**)
excútiō, -cútere, -cússī, -cússum, tr., *to shake or knock out.* (**ex + quátiō**)
éxedō, exésse, exédī, exésum, tr., *to eat up or devour.* (**édō**)
éxeō, exíre, éxiī, éxitum, intr., *to go or come out;* tr. *to avoid* 438.
exérceō, exercére, exércuī, exércitum, tr., *to drive out; to harass or worry.*
exércitus, -ūs, m., *an army.*

éxigō, exígere, exḗgī, exáctum, tr., (*to drive out; to push all the way,* hence) *to complete, take to completion,* or *fulfil.* (**ágō**)

exíguus, -a, -um, adj., *scanty* or *few.*

exítium, -iī, n., (*a going out;* hence) *destruction.*

éxitus, -ūs, m., (*a going out;* hence) *outcome.* (**éxeō**)

exódī, exōdísse, exósus sum, semidep., *to hate utterly.* (**ódium**)

exórior, -orírī, -órtus sum, dep., *to rise.*

expédiō, -pedíre, -pḗdiī, -péditum, tr., (lit. *to free one's foot;* hence) *to disentangle; to get out of storage* 209. (**pēs**)

exsaturábilis, -e, adj., *capable of being satisifed.* (**sátis**)

éxsequor, éxsequī, exsecútus sum, dep., (lit. *to follow all the way*); *to perform according to tradition.* (**séquor**)

éxsors, exsórtis, adj., *extraordinary, special.*

exspéctō, -áre, -ávī, -átum, tr., *to look out for; to await.*

éxstruō, exstrúere, exstrúxī, exstrúctum, tr., *to pile up.*

éxsul, éxsulis, m. and f., *an exile.*

exsúltō, -áre, -ávī, -átum, intr., (lit. *to leap out;* hence) *to throb; to exult.* (**sáltō,** freq. of **sáliō**)

éxta, extórum, n. pl., *the upper internal organs* (i.e. heart, lungs, etc., as opp. to the **víscera,** *intestines*)

extémplō, adv., *immediately.*

exténdō, -téndere, -téndī, -téntum, tr., *to stretch* something *to its full length.*

extérreō, -terrḗre, -térruī, -térritum, tr., *to frighten completely.*

extrḗmus, -a, -um, adj., *outermost, utmost, last, end of.*

éxuō, exúere, éxuī, exútum, tr., *to remove* or *strip off* clothing or armor. (**exúviae**)

exū́rō, -úrere, -ússī, -ústum, tr., *to burn up.*

fáciēs, faciḗī, f., (lit. *the make* or *shape* of something; hence) *face, look, appearance; ghost* or *phantom,* 722.

fáciō, fácere fḗcī, fáctum, intr. and tr., *to make* or *do;* in religious language, *to make sacrifice* 763; in nautical language, **vḗla fácere** *to set sail* 281; **pédem fácere** *to make fast the sail* 830; pass. *to be made,* (hence) *to become* (perf. system only; pres. system supplied by **fíō**).

fállax, -ácis, adj., *deceptive, treacherous.*

fállō, fállere, feféllī, fálsum, tr., (lit. *to cause to stumble;* hence) *to deceive, baffle, cheat.*

fáma, -āe, f., *report; rumor, tradition, reputation.* (**for**)

fámulus, -ī, m., *a slave, servant,* or *attendant; an attendant spirit,* 95.

far, fárris, n., *spelt,* a kind of grain.

fās, n. indecl., *what is right, permissable,* or *ordained by the gods.*

fātális, -e, adj., *according to fate; destined, fated.* (**for**)

fátigō, -áre, -ávī, -átum, tr., *to tire* (someone) *out.*

fátum, -ī, n., (*that which is / has been spoken* or *decreed;* hence) *fate.* (**for, fárī, fátus sum**)

fáveō, favḗre, fávī, faútum, intr., *to show favor* to someone (dat.), hence *to favor* or *support;* in religious language, **óre favḗre,** *to show favor in speaking,* hence *to keep silent* 71

n.; pres. part. **favéntēs**, m. subst. *those who show favor,* hence *backers, supporters* of a contestant or a team 148. (**fávor**)
favílla, -āe, f., *ash.*
fávor, -óris, m., *friendliness;* hence *partisanship, applause, acclamation.* (**fáveō**)
fax, fácis, f., *a firebrand* or *torch.*
fémina, -āe, f., *a lady; a woman.*
fére, adv., *nearly* or *almost.*
fériō, feríre, no perf. or supine stem, tr., *to strike, smite,* or *beat.*
férō, férre, túlī, látum, tr., irreg., *to bear* or *carry; to bring* or *take;* idioms, *to make sacrifice* 763; **férre mánum**, *to engage in battle at close quarters* 402; **sē férre**, *to carry* or *take oneself,* hence *to go* 290; with abl. of manner, *to carry* or *comport oneself* in a certain way 373; pass. *to be borne along, to travel, sail, ride,* or *speed away;* impers. **fértur**, *it is said* 588.
férox, -ócis, adj., *fierce.* (**férus**)
ferrátus, -a, -um, adj., *plated* or *tipped with iron.* (**férrum** + part. suffix *-ātus*)
férrum, -ī, n., lit. *iron* or *steel;* fig. *sword, spear, arrowhead.*
férus, -a, -um, adj., *wild, untamed;* subst. **férus, -ī**, m. and **féra, -āe**, f. *wild beast.* (**férox**)
féssus, -a, -um, adj. *weary, tired out.* (= perf. part. of *fatígeor; cf.* **fátigō**, *fatíscō*)
fíbula, -āe, f., *a pin, brooch,* or *buckle.* (contr. from archaic *figíbula;* cf. **fígō**)
fídēs, fídeī, f., *faith, truth, honesty, reliability.*
fídō, fídere, físus sum, semidep., *to trust; to trust in* someone or something (with dat. or abl.); *to have the confidence* to do something (with inf.)
fídus, -a, -um, adj., *trustworthy; faithful; safe.*
fígō, fígere, fíxī, fíxum, tr., *to fasten; to pierce.*
fímus, and **-um, -ī**, m. and n., *filth; slime.*
fínis, -is, m. and f., *the end; a boundary; a territory;* in a race, *the finish* or *starting line* 139.
fínitimus, -a, -um, adj., *bordering, neighboring;* **fínitimī, -ōrum**, m. subst. *neighbors.*
fíō, fíerī, intr., *to become;* as pass. of **fáciō** in the pres. system, *to be made.*
flagéllum, -ī, n., *a whip.*
flámen, fláminis, n., *a breeze.*
flámma, -āe, f., *a blaze; a flame.*
flāvus, -a, -um, adj., *a rich, bright yellow, ranging in hue between gold and straw.* (cf. **fúlvus**)
fléctō, fléctere, fléxī, fléxum, tr., *to bend; to turn* or *steer;* perf. part. **fléxus, -a -um**, *bent* or *curving.*
fléō, flére, flévī, flétum, intr., *to weep;* tr. *to weep for, bewail.*
flétus, -ūs, m., *weeping.*
fléxilis, -e, adj., *pliant.* (**fléctō**)
flōs, flóris, m., *a flower.*
flúctus, -ūs, m., (*a flowing;* hence) *a wave.*
flúitō, -áre, -ávī, -átum, intr., *to float about at random.*
flúmen, flúminis, n., (*a flowing;* hence) *a stream* or *river.*
flúō, flúere, flúxī, flúctum, intr., *to flow.*
fócus, -ī, m., *a hearth.* (**fóveō**)
foédē, adv., *foully.* (**foédus, -a, -um**)

foedus, foederis, n., *a league; an alliance or treaty*. (**fīdus**).
fólium, -ī, n., *a leaf*.
for, fárī, fátus sum, dep., def., *to say or speak*.
fórem, fóre. See **sum**.
fórma, -ae, f., *bearing; shape or beauty*.
fors, fórtis, f., *chance, luck;* (used adverbially in nom. and abl.) *perhaps* 232 n. (**fortúna**)
fórtis, fórte, comp. **fórtior**, superl. **fortíssimus.**, adj., *strong; brave*.
fortúna, -ae, f., *luck, whether good or bad; chance;* personified, *the goddess Fortune*. (**fors**)
fórum, -ī, n., *an open, outdoor place of assembly; a marketplace;* **in foró**, *in assembly* 758. (*fóras* and *fóris*)
frágor, fragóris, m., *a sudden, loud noise; applause* 228.
frángō, frángere, frḗgī, fráctum, tr., *to break* or *smash*.
fráter, frátris, m., *a brother*.
fratérnus, -a, -um, adj., *brotherly*.
fraus, fraúdis, f., *guile, deception*.
frémitus, -ūs, m., *a roaring; applause; hubbub*.
frémō, frémere, frémuī, frémitum, intr., *to roar; to applaud*.
frēnátus, -a, -um, adj., *bridled*. (perf. part. of *frḗnō*)
frḗnum, -ī, n., *a bit* or *bridle*.
frétum, -ī, n., lit. *a narrow channel between two larger bodies of water; a strait;* fig. *the sea; a body of water*.
frḗtus, -a, -um, adj., *leaning on, relying on*, with abl. of place where (AG §431a).
frígeō, frigére, no perf. or supine stem, intr., *to freeze, to be stiff with cold; to fail in strength* or *fighting spirit* 396.

fróndeō, frondḗre, no perf. or supine stem, intr., *to bear leaves;* pres. part. **fróndens, -éntis**, *leafy*.
frondósus, -a, -um, adj., *full of leaves, leafy*.
frons, fróndis, f., *leaf* or *leaves; foliage*.
frons, fróntis, f., *the forehead; the prow* of *a ship*, 158.
frústrā, adv., *in vain*.
fúga, fúgae, f., *flight*.
fúgiō, fúgere, fūgī, fugītum, intr., *to flee* or *escape;* tr. *to avoid* or *shun*.
fugō, -áre, -ávī, -átum, tr., *to put to flight*.
fúlgeō, fulgḗre, fúlsī, no supine stem, intr., *to shine* or *glisten*.
fulgor, -óris, m., *a glow*.
fulmen, fúlminis, n., *a lightning bolt* or *thunderbolt*.
fúlvus, -a, -um, adj., *a rich, dark yellow ranging in hue from amber to olive*. (*cf*. **flávus**)
fúmus, -ī, m., *smoke*.
fúndō, fúndere, fúdī, fúsum, tr., *to pour, pour out; of speech, to utter; of opponents in battle, to rout*.
fúndō, -áre, -ávī, -átum, tr., *to found* or *establish; to lay the foundation of something*.
fúndus, -ī, m., *the bottom*.
fúnis, -is, m., *a cable, rope,* or *cord*.
fúrō, fúrere, fúruī, no supine stem, intr., *to rage* or *rave;* pres. part. **fúrens, -éntis**, *frantic* or *mad*.
fúror, -óris, m., *a rage; raving* or *madness*.
fúror, fūrárī, fūrátus sum, (tr., dep.), *to steal*.
fúrtim, adv., *by stealth, stealthily*.
futúrus, -a, -um, fut. part. of **sum**.
Gaetúlus, -a, -um, adj., *of* or *from Gaetulia in northwest Africa*.

gálea, -ae, f., *a helmet.*
gaúdeō, gaudḗre, gavīsus sum, semidep., *to be glad; to rejoice.*
gaúdium, -iī, n., *joy.*
gáza, -ae, f., *treasure.* (a Persian loan word)
gélidus, -a, -um, adj., *icy, cold.* (*gélū*)
géminus, -a, -um, adj., *twin, double, paired.*
gémma, -ae, f., (lit. *a bud* of a plant; hence) *a jewel.*
gémō, gémere, gémuī, gémitum, intr., *to groan* or *sigh;* tr. *to bemoan.*
géna, -ae, f., *a cheek.*
génerō, -áre, -ávī, -átum, tr., *to beget;* perf. part. **generátus** with abl. of source, *son of* 61.
génitor, -óris, m., *begetter,* (hence) *father.*
génius, -iī, m., *a tutelar deity, familiar spirit,* see 95 11.
gens, géntis, f., *a clan; race, tribe, nation.* (**génus, gígnō**)
génu, génūs, n., *a knee.*
génus, géneris, n., *birth; race, family, pedigree.* (**gens**)
germánus, -a, -um, adj., *of the same parents;* subst. **germánus, -ī,** m. *brother;* **germána, -ae,** f. *sister.*
gérō, gérere, géssī, géstum, tr., *to wear; carry, carry on.*
gígnō, gígnere, génuī, génitum, tr., *to beget* or *bear* children. (**gens**)
Glaúcus, -ī, m., *a minor god of the sea.*
glória, -ae, f., *pride* or *self-esteem; renown.*
Gnósius, -a, -um, adj., *of* or *from the city of Cnossus* on Crete.
grāmíneŭs, -a, -um, adj., *grassy.* (*grámen*)
grándō, grándinis, f., *hail; a hailstorm.*
grátor, -árī, -átus sum, dep., *to make oneself agreeable to;* hence *to welcome,* usually with the dat., but cf. 40 n.
grátus, -a, -um, adj., *agreeable; pleasing; welcome.*
grávis, -e, adj., *heavy; burdensome; disagreeable; harsh.*
gráviter, adv., *heavily.*
grémium, -iī, n., *lap* or *bosom.*
gressus, -ūs, m., *step, pace,* or *gait.* (*grádior*)
gubernáclum, -ī, n., *a rudder.*
gubernátor, -óris, m., *a helmsman.*
gúrgēs, gúrgitis, m., lit. *a whirlpool;* fig. *the deep sea.*
Gýas, -ae, acc. **Gýan,** m., *a Trojan hero, captain of the* **Chimaéra,** *one of the ships in Aeneas' fleet, and a contestant in the boat race.*
gỹrus, -ī, m., *a ring* or *circle.*
habḗna, -ae, f., (lit. *a device for holding onto something;* hence) *a rein* (for a horse)
hábeō, habḗre, hábuī, hábitum, tr., *to hold; to have* or *possess; to wear; to consider.*
hāc, adv., (*by*) *this way;* (with **ténus,** for **háctenus**) *thus far.*
haéreō, haerḗre, haésī, haésum, intr., *to stick fast; to stop dead* 529; *to cling to one's post* 852.
hámus, -ī, m., (*a hook,* hence) *a link of chain armor.*
harúndō, harúndinis, f., *a reed; the shaft of an arrow.*
hastīle, hastīlis, n., *a spearshaft.* (*hásta*)
haud, adv., *not; in no way* (emphatic)
haúriō, haurīre, haúsī, haústum, tr., *to drain* or *empty.*
hébeō, hebḗre, no perf. or supine stem, intr., *to be blunt* or *dull.*

Héctor, Héctoris, m., *the eldest son of Priam and chief defender of Troy, slain by Achilles.*

Hectórĕŭs, -a, -um, adj., lit. *of or belonging to* **Héctor;** fig. *Trojan.*

Hélymus, -ī, m., (1) *one of Aeneas' Trojan followers* 73 n.; (2) *one of Acestes' Sicilian followers, a participant in the footrace.*

hérba, -āe, f., *grass; pasture.*

Hércŭlēs, -is, m., *a Greek hero, the son of Iuppiter and Alcmena.*

hḗrōs, hērṓis, m., *a hero.*

heu, interj., *alas!*

hibérnus, -a, -um, adj., *wintry, stormy.*

hic, haec, hoc, pron. and adj., demonst., 1st pers. deixis, *this; he, she, it;* the latter *in combination with* **ílle,** *the former.*

hīc, adv., *here, hereupon.*

híems, híemis, f., *winter; storm.*

hinc, adv., *from this place; hence, from there, from here.* (**hic, haec, hoc**)

Hippócŏōn, -óntis, m., *a Trojan follower of Aeneas, one of the contestants in the archery contest.* (cf. **Hyrtácidēs**)

honōrā́tus, -a, -um, adj., *honored; sacred.* (perf. part. of hónōrō)

hónor and **hónos, -ṓris,** m., *honor; prize; ritual* (58 n.)

hṓra, -āe, f., *an hour; a season.*

hórridus, -a, -um, adj., *bristling, rough.* (**horréscō**)

hórtor, -ā́rī, -ā́tus sum, dep., *encourage; exhort; urge; cheer on.*

hóspēs, hóspitis, m., (lit. *a stranger;* hence) *a guest* or *a host.*

hóstis, -is, m. and f., (lit. *a stranger;* hence) *a foe.*

hūc, adv., *to this place; hither.* (**hic, haec, hoc**)

humā́nus, -a, -um, adj., *human.* (**hómō**)

húmerus, -ī, m., *the shoulder.*

húmidus, -a, -um, adj., *moist, damp.*

húmus, -ī; loc. **húmī,** f., *the ground.*

Hyrtácidēs, -āe, m. (patronymic*), *son of Hyrtacus,* i.e. **Hippócŏōn.**

Īásidēs, -āe, m. (patronymic*), *son of Iasius,* i.e. **Palinū́rus.** (cf. 843 n.)

íctus, -ūs, m., *a stroke* of an oar; *a blow* of a fist or stone.

Ī́da, -āe, f., *a mountain near Troy.*

Īdálius, -a, -um, adj., *of* or *from Idalium, a town and mountain on Cyprus, sacred to Venus.*

idcírcō, conj., *because of that; therefore.*

ídem, éadem, ídem, pron. and adj., *the same.* (accent: Allen 1987: 87–88)

ignā́rus, -a, -um, adj., *unknowing; ignorant of,* with gen. (**ignṓrō**)

ígnis, -is, m., *fire.*

ignṓrō, -ā́re, -ā́vī, -ā́tum, tr., *to overlook* or *fail to notice;* intr. *to be unaware.* (**ignā́rus**)

ignṓtus, -a, -um, adj., *unknown.* (**nóscō**)

ī́lex, ī́licis, f., *a type of evergreen oak tree, native to Europe but similar to the American live oak.*

Īlíacus, -a, -um, adj., *of Ilium; Trojan.*

Īliās, Īlíadis, f. (patronymic*), *a daughter* or *descendant of Ilus;* hence, *a Trojan woman.*

Ī́lium, -iī, n., *the city of Ilus,* i.e. *Troy.*

ílle, ílla, íllud, pron. and adj., demonst. with 3d pers. deixis, *he, she, it;* used to indicate a change of subject 39 n.; *that famous . . .* (391 n.); **hīc . . . ílle,** *the latter . . . the former.*

íllīc, adv., *to that place; over there.*

imā́gō, imā́ginis, f., *a likeness; a phantom.*

ímber, -bris, m., *rain; a rain shower; a rain cloud.*

immā́nis, -e, adj., *enormous; huge.*
ímmemor, immémoris, adj., *forgetful;* with gen. *forgetful of.*
imménsus, -a, -um, adj., *unmeasured; immeasurable; immense.* (**métior**)
immísceō, -miscḗre, -míscuī, -míxtum, tr., *to mix together.*
immíttō, -míttere, -mī́sī, -míssum, tr., *to send on* or *let go;* idiom **immíttere habḗnās**, *to give free rein to*, 662 n.; cf. 146 n.
immṓtus, -a, -um, adj., *unmoved.* (**móveō**)
immúndus, -a, -um, adj., *unclean; dirty; filthy.*
impédiō, -pedī́re, -pédiī, -pedī́tum, tr., (lit. *to get by the foot;* hence) *to hinder, stop,* or *block.* (**pēs**)
impéllō, impéllere, ímpulī, impúlsum, tr., *to drive on; to shove along.*
impérium, -iī, n., *command; ruling authority; empire.* (**ímperō**)
ímpetus, -ūs, m., *forward motion; momentum.* (**ímpetō**)
impíngō, -píngere, -pḗgī, -páctum, tr., *to press someone or something onto* or *against someone or something.* (**pángō**)
ímpius, -a, -um, adj., *undutiful; wicked.*
ímpleō, -plḗre, -plḗvī, -plḗtum, tr., *to fill up.*
impṓnō, -pṓnere, -pósuī, -pósitum, tr., *to place upon;* **impṓnere fī́nem**, *to put an end to.*
ímprimō, -prímere, -préssī, -préssum, tr., *to press upon, stamp* or *emboss.* (**prémō**)
ímprobus, -a, -um, adj., *immoderate, excessive; shameless.*
impū́bēs, -bis, adj., *beardless; youthful.*
ímus, -a, -um, adj., *bottommost, lowest, bottom of, inmost;* subst. **ab ī́mō** 810 *from the bottom, from its foundations.* (contr. of **ínfimus**, superl. of **ínferus**, *low, below,* comp. **inférior**, *lower;* cf. **inférnus**)
in, prep., with abl. *in, on;* with acc. *into, to, for, on to;* idioms **in vérbera péndunt**, *they* (chariot drivers) *hang over* (or) *lean into blows* (from the whip) 147; **in vṓta vocā́re**, *to call someone to witness* or *hear one's vows* 234, 514; **in mṓrem**, *in* (proper) *fashion* 556.
inā́nis, -e, adj., *empty; vain.*
incḗdō, -cḗdere, -céssī, -céssum, intr., *to process; to bear oneself proudly.*
incéndium, -iī, n., *a conflagration.*
incéndō, -céndere, -céndī, -cénsum, tr., *to set on fire, light up.*
incéptum, -ī, n., (lit. *something begun;* hence) *an attempt, an undertaking.* (perf. part. of **incípiō**)
incértus, -a, -um, adj., *uncertain; doubtful.* (**cérnō**)
incípiō, -cípere, -cḗpī, -céptum, tr., (lit. *to take something in hand;* hence) *to begin.* (**cápiō**)
inclū́dō, -clū́dere, -clū́sī, -clū́sum, tr., *to shut in.* (**claúdō**)
incúmbō, -cúmbere, -cū́buī, -cúbitum, intr., *to lean on* or *against; to put one's weight into; to press upon.*
incúrvō, -ā́re, -ā́vī, -ā́tum, tr., *to bend sharply.*
índe, adv., *next, then.*
indēprénsus, -a, -um, adj., *undiscovered; undiscoverable* (**préndō**)
indī́cō, -dī́cere -dī́xī, -díctum, tr., *to proclaim.*
indígnor, -dignā́rī, -dignā́tus sum, dep., *to think something unworthy of oneself; to be offended.* (**dígnus**)

indómitus, -a, -um, adj., *untamed.*
(**dómō**)
indū́cō, -dū́cere -dū́xī, -dúctum,
tr., *to lead in; to draw onwards.*
(**dū́cō**)
índuō, indúere, índuī, indū́tum, tr.,
to put on (clothing, armor, etc.)
íneō, iníre, íniī, ínitum, intr. *to enter,
go in;* tr. *to go into* or *enter upon
something.*
infaū́stus, -a, -um, adj., *unlucky; ill-
omened.* (**fáveō**).
infḗctus, -a, -um, adj., *stained.* (perf.
part. of *inficiō* from **fáciō**)
infḗlix, infēlī́cis, adj., *unhappy;
luckless.*
infḗnsus, -a, -um, adj., *hostile.*
inférnus, -a, -um, adj., *having to do
with the underworld.* (strengthened
form of ínferus; cf. **ímus**)
ínferō, inférre, íntulī, illā́tum, tr.,
to bring in; to take to; **sḗ inférre,**
to go forward, advance.
inféstus, -a, -um, adj., *hostile.*
infī́gō, -fī́gere, -fī́xī, -fī́xum, tr., *to
fix in(to)*
infíndō, -fíndere, -fī́dī, -físsum, tr.,
to cut into; to cleave.
ínfit, def., *to begin speaking.*
infrā́ctus, -a, -um, adj., *broken.* (**frángō**)
infúndō, -fúndere, -fū́sī, -fū́sum, tr.,
to pour over, on, or *in.*
ingéminō, -ā́re, -ā́vī, -ā́tum, intr. and
tr., *to double, redouble,* or *repeat.*
(**géminus**)
íngens, -géntis, adj., *huge; mighty;
monstrous* or *unnatural.* (**gens**)
ingrédior, íngredī, ingréssus sum,
dep. *to enter; to step into* with dat.
ingréditur dōnī́s 543 *he comes
upon the prizes,* i.e. "finishes in
the money." (**grā́dior**)

inhorrḗscō, -horrḗscere, -hórruī,
no supine stem, incohative, *to
begin to bristle, to grow rough.*
(**hórridus**)
inhóspitus, -a, -um, adj., *inhospitable.*
(**hóspēs**)
inimī́cus, -a, -um, adj., *unfriendly.*
(**amī́cus**)
inī́quus, -a, -um, adj., *unequal; unfair,
mischievous, spiteful, luckless.*
(**aḗquus**)
inlī́dō, -lī́dere, -lī́sī, -lī́sum, tr., *to
crash into* or *against.* (**laḗdō**)
innéctō, -néctere, -néxuī, -néxum,
tr., *to bind; to tie on.* (**néctō**)
innóxius, -a, -um, adj., *harmless.*
(**nóceō**)
Ī́nō, Ī́nūs, f., *Ino, daughter of Cadmus;
identified with a sea goddess called
by the Romans Mater Matuta.*
inopī́nus, -a, -um, adj., *unexpected.*
(**opīnor**)
Ī́nóus, -a, -um, adj., *of* or *having to
do with* **Ī́nō;** *used of Ino's son*
Palaḗmon 823.
ínquam, ínquit, def., *I said, he* or *she
said.*
inrī́sus, -a, -um, adj., *scorned* or *jeered
at.* (perf. part. of inrídeō)
ínritus, -a, -um, adj., *ineffectual, in
vain, baffled.*
ínsequor, ínsequī, insecū́tus sum,
dep., intr. *to follow, come next;*
tr. *to pursue, persecute.*
insígnis, -e, adj., *marked; remarkable*
or *preeminent.* (**sígnum**)
ínsonō, insonā́re, insónuī, insónitum,
intr., *to make a loud sound.*
ínsons, -sóntis, adj., *guiltless.*
instaū́rō, -ā́re, -ā́vī, -ā́tum, tr., *to
renew* or *repeat a sacrifice* or
religious ceremony.

instígō, -áre, -ávī, -átum, tr., *to goad; to spur on.*
ínstō, instáre, ínstitī, ínstitum, intr., *to stand upon; to press close upon.*
ínstruō, -strúere, -strúxī, -strúctum, tr., *to build into; arrange.*
ínsuō, insúere, ínsuī, insútum, tr., *to sew into.*
insúrgō, -súrgere, -surréxī, -surréctum, intr., *to arise* or *rise to.*
inténdō, -téndere, -téndī, -téntum, tr., *to stretch* something *over* something; *to draw tight, bind tight, stiffen; to spread* sails; *to exert* oneself.
inténtus, -a, -um, adj., *straining; eager.* (perf. part. of **inténdō**)
ínter, prep. with acc., *among, amid,* or *between.*
intéreā, adv., *meanwhile.*
intérior, -ōris, adj., *inner, on the inner side* (as if from positive degree *ínterus,* which does not occur; cf. superl. **ímus** and *íntimus*)
intérritus, -a, -um, adj., *unalarmed, fearless.* (**térreō**)
intervállum, -ī, n., *the distance between two things; an interval.* (**vállum**)
intéxō, -téxere, -téxuī, -téxtum, tr., *to weave* something *into* something.
intremíscō, -tremíscere, -trémuī, no supine stem, inchohative, *to shudder violently.* (**trémō**)
íntrō, -áre, -ávī, -átum, tr., *to enter.*
inválidus, -a, -um, adj., *powerless; weak.*
ínvehō, -véhere, -véxī, -véctum, tr., *to carry upon;* pass. *to ride upon* (a ship, horse, etc.)
invídeō, -vidére, -vídī, -vísum, intr. and tr., *to look upon with envy* (cf. 541 n.)

invítō, -áre, -ávī, -átum, tr., *to invite; to tempt.*
Īónius, -a, -um, adj., *of, from,* or *having to do with Ionia; Ionian.*
ípse, ípsa, ípsum, pron. and adj., (intensive), *oneself;* idioms, *nothing other than . . . ,* e.g. **ípse cásus,** *mere chance* 201; **succéssū ípsō,** *sheer success* 210; cf. 323 n., 332 n., 861 n.
ira, -ae, f., *wrath; anger.*
Īris, Īris or **Īridis,** acc. **Īrim** 606 n., *Iris, Juno's messenger; the rainbow.*
irremeábilis, -e, adj., *irretraceable.* (**méō, meáre**)
is, éa, id, pron. and adj., demonst., unemphatic, *he, she, it.*
íste, ísta, ístud, pron. and adj. demonstrative with 2d pers. deixis, *you there! that* (of yours), *your;* sometimes contemptuous (397 n.)
íta, adv., *thus.*
Ītália, -ae, f., *Italy, the land of the* **Ítalī.** (18 n.)
Ítalus, -a, -um, adj., *Italian.* subst. **Ítalī, -ōrum,** *the peoples of ancient Italy.* (18 n.)
íter, itíneris, n., *a going; journey, voyage, route, way, course.* (**éō, íre**)
íterum, adv., *for the second time; again.*
iáceo, iacére, iácuī, iáctum, intr., *to lie down; to sprawl.*
iáciō, iácere iēcī, iáctum, tr., *to throw* or *hurl; to lay* (e.g. foundations); *to build.*
iáctō, -áre, -ávī, -átum, tr., lit. *to throw* or *toss repeatedly;* fig. *to boast.* (freq. of **iáciō**)
iáculum, -i, n., *something that is thrown; a spear.* (**iáciō**)
iam, adv., *so far, by this time, already; now; soon, presently;* with negative, **nec iam,** *no longer.*

i̯amdū́dum, adv., *long ago.*
i̯úbeō, i̯ubḗre, i̯ússī, i̯ússum, tr., *to command; to order; to tell (someone to do something)*
i̯úgum, -ī, n., *a yoke.* (i̯úngō)
Ī́ulus, -ī, m., *son of Aeneas and Creusa, legendary ancestor of the* **gens Ī́ulia**; *also called* **Ascánius.**
i̯úngō, i̯úngere, i̯únxī, i̯únctum, tr., *to join or yoke.* (i̯úgum)
Ī́ūnō -ṓnis, f., *Juno, queen of the gods, sister and wife of Jupiter, goddess of marriage, and Aeneas' divine antagonist.*
Ī́úppiter, Ī́óvis, m., *Jupiter, king of the gods.*
i̯ū́s, i̯ū́ris, n., *law, justice; a right.*
i̯ússum, -ī, n., *a command.* (perf. part. of i̯úbeō)
i̯uvenā́lis, -e, adj., *youthful* (i̯úvenis)
i̯uvéncus, -ī, m., *a young ox, steer.*
i̯úvenis, -e, adj., *young, youthful.* subst. m. and f. *a young man* or *woman*; pl. *youths, the young.*
i̯uvénta, -ae, f., *youth.*
i̯uvéntās, -tā́tis, f., *youth.*
i̯uventū́s, -tū́tis, f., *youth;* (collectively) *the youth; the young.*
lábō, -ā́re, -ā́vī, -ā́tum, intr., *to totter.*
lā́bor, lābā́rī, lā́psus sum, dep. *to slip; to slip down; to fall; to glide.*
lábor, -ṓris, m., *work, toil, trouble.*
Labyrínthus, -ī, m., *in Greek myth, a great maze built to house the Minotaur in the palace of Minos, king of Cnossus on Crete, by the brilliant artist and inventor Daedalus.*
lāc, láctis, n., *milk.*
lácer, lácera, lácerum, adj., *mangled.* (lacéssō)
lacértus, -ī, m., *the upper arm.*

lacéssō, lacéssere, lacéssiī, lacessī́tum, tr., *to provoke.* (lácer)
lácrima, -ae, f., *a tear.*
lácrimō, -ā́re, -ā́vī, -ā́tum, intr., and lácrimor, -ā́rī, -ā́tus sum, dep., *to shed tears.*
laétus, -a, -um, adj., *glad; joyful.*
laévus, -a, -um, adj., *left, on the left; left-handed;* subst. **laéva, -ae**, f. *the left hand* (for **mánus laéva**)
Lar, Láris, m., *the Lar, the chief household god.*
lā́tē, adv., *far and wide; widely.* (from **lā́tus, -a, -um**)
latebrṓsus, -a, -um, adj., *full of hiding places.*
láteō, latḗre, látuī, no supine stem, intr., *to lie hidden;* impers. **látet**, *it is uncertain, it is a mystery.*
Latī́nus, -a, -um, adj., *of* **Látium**; *Latin*; subst. **Latī́nī, -ṓrum**, m. pl. *the Latin peoples; the inhabitants of* **Látium.**
Látium, -iī, n., *a district of central Italy including Rome and the surrounding hill towns; home of the Latin peoples.*
latrā́tus, -ūs, m., *a barking* or *baying*, lit. *of dogs, but also used figuratively.* (*látrō, -ā́re*)
látus, láteris, n., *a side* or *the side* (of something)
lā́tus, -a, -um, adj., *wide; broad.* (perf. part. of **férō**)
Laúrens, -éntis, adj., *of or belonging to Laurentum, a town of* **Látium.**
laúrus, -ī, f., *the bay* or *laurel tree.*
laūs, laúdis, f., *praise; renown; merit.*
láxō, -ā́re, -ā́vī, -ā́tum, tr., *to loosen* or *relax.*
lébēs, lebḗtis, m., *a cauldron.* (a Greek loan word, λέβης)

légō, légere, légī, léctum, tr., *to gather up; to choose.*
léntus, -a, -um, adj., *pliable; tough; slow* or *leisurely.*
léō, leónis, m., *a lion.*
Lēthaéus, -a, -um, adj., *of* or *having to do with Lethe, a river of the underworld.*
létum, -ī, n., *death.*
lḗvis, -e, adj., *smooth; polished, slippery.* (lḗvō)
lĕ́vis, -e, adj., *light* (in weight)
lḗvō, -áre, -ávī, -átum, tr., *to polish.* (lḗvis)
líbō, -áre, -ávī, -átum, tr., *to pour out as an offering; to sip* or *taste.*
líbrō, -áre, -ávī, -átum, tr., *to balance* or *poise.* (líbra)
Líbycus, -a, -um, adj., *of, from,* or *having to do with Libya,* or *by extension with northern Africa in general.*
Libýstis, Libýstidis, *f.* adj., = Líbycus. (a Greek loan word, Λιβυστίς).
lícet, licére, lícuit, lícitum, impers., *it is allowed,* with inf. 82, 796–7; with inf. + subj. acc. 350.
límen, líminis, n., *a threshold; starting line,* 316.
línea, -ae, f., *a line of string.* (subst. of línĕus)
línĕus, -a, -um, adj., *made of flax.* (línum)
línquō, línquere, líquī, líctum, tr., *to leave.*
líquens, -éntis, adj., *fluid; clear.* (pres. part. of líqueō)
líquidus, -a, -um, adj., *flowing; clear, limpid, liquid.* (líqueō; líquor)
lítus, lítoris, n., *shore, coast.*
lócō, -áre, -ávī, -átum, tr., *to place.*
lócus, -ī, m.; also lóca, -órum, n. pl., *a place; places.*

longaévus, -a, -um, adj., *long-lived, aged.*
lóngē, comp. lóngius, adv., *far, afar, by far; far off.* (*from* lóngus)
lóngus, -a, -um, adj., *long* (of space or time)
loquéla, -ae, f., *gentle speech.*
lóquor, lóquī, locútus sum, dep., *to speak; to say* something (acc.)
lōríca, -ae, f., *a breastplate* or *coat of chain armor;* originally perhaps made of leather; see the following entry.
lórum, -ī, n., *a leather thong;* pl. *reins.*
lúbricus, -a, -um, adj., *slimy; slippery.*
lúceō, lucére, lúxī, no supine stem, intr., *to gleam* or *shine.*
lúcidus, -a, -um, adj., *gleaming.* (lux)
lúctor, -árī, -átus sum, dep., *to wrestle; to struggle.*
lúcus, -ī, m., *a sacred area defined by a stand of trees.* (cf. 761 n.)
lúdō, lúdere, lúsī, lúsum, intr. and tr., *to play.*
lúdus, -ī, m., *a game* or *sport.*
lúmen, -minis, n., lit. *light* or *a light;* fig., usually pl., *eye(s).* (lux)
lústrō, -áre, -ávī, -átum, tr., *to survey* or *review;* in ritual, *to purify.*
lux, lúcis, f., *light; daylight.* (lúceō; lúmen)
mactō, -áre, -ávī, -átum, tr., *to sacrifice* (a victim)
mácula, -ae, f., *a spot* or *blemish.*
maculósus, -a, -um, adj., *spotted.*
madefáciō, -fácere, -fécī, -fáctum, tr., *to moisten.*
mádeō, -ére, no perf. or supine stem, intr., *to be wet.*
madéscō, madéscere, máduī, no supine stem, incohative *to become wet.*
mádidus, -a, -um, adj., *wet.*

Maeánder, -drī, m., lit. *a river of Asia Minor, famous for its winding course;* fig. *a decorative winding pattern* or *design.* (cf. 251 n.)
maéstus, -a, -um, adj., *mournful.*
mágis, adv., *more; rather.*
magíster, -trī, m., *master; teacher, tutor;* in sailing, *pilot* or *captain.*
magnánimus, -a, -um, adj., *greathearted.*
mágnus, -a, -um, comp. **májor,** superl. **máximus,** adj., *great, big, mighty.*
mála, -ae, f., *cheek; jaw.*
Málea, -ae, f., *a promontory of Laconia in south central Greece, treacherous to sailors.*
malígnus, -a, -um, adj., *ill-natured.*
málus, -ī, m., *the mast of a ship.*
máneō, manére, mánsī, mánsum, intr. and tr., *to await; to remain.*
Mánēs, Mánium, m. pl., *the spirits of the dead.*
mánus, -ūs, f., *a hand; a band of men, especially soldiers;* idiom **mánum férre in proélia,** *to do battle at close quarters.*
máre, -is, n., *sea.*
máter, -tris, f., *mother.*
matérnus, -a, -um, adj., *of one's mother; motherly.*
matúrus, -a, -um, adj., *ripe.*
máximus -a, -um, adj., *greatest; eldest.* (superl. of **mágnus**)
mécum, pron. + prep. = **cum mē,** *with me.*
médius, -a, -um, adj., *middle; in the midst of; midway; between.*
Meliboéus, -a, -um, adj., *of, from,* or *having to do with Meliboea in Thessaly; therefore, Thessalian.*
mélior, mélius, adj., *better.* (comp. of **bónus**)

Mélitē, -ēs, f., *Melite, a sea-nymph.*
mémbrum, -ī, n., *a limb.*
Mémmius, -a, -um, adj. and subst. **Mémmius, -iī** m., *name of a Roman gens, supposedly descended from the Trojan hero* **Mnésthēus.**
mémor, mémoris, adj., *mindful.*
mémorō, -áre, -ávī, -átum, tr., *to call to mind; to relate; to say.*
Menoétēs, -ae, acc. **-ēn,** voc. **-ē,** m., *Menoetes, pilot of the ship* **Chimaéra.**
mens, méntis, f., *mind; intellect; thought* or *purpose.* (**méminī; móneō;** etc.)
ménsis, -is, m., *a month.*
méreō, merére, méruī, méritum, tr., and **méreor, merérī, méritus sum,** dep., *to deserve* or *earn.*
mérgus, -ī, m., *a seagull.*
mérus, -a, -um, adj., *unmixed* (of wine)
méta, -ae, f., *a turning post on a race course.*
métuō, metúere, métuī, metútum, intr., *to fear;* pres. part. **métuens,** *fearful.*
métus, -ūs, m., *fear* or *dread.*
méus, -a, -um, adj., poss., 1st pers. sing., *my* or *mine.*
mília, mílium, n. pl., *thousands.*
mílle, adj., indecl., *one thousand.*
Minérva, -ae, f., *Minerva, the Roman goddess of mind;* in Greek *Athena.* (**Pállas; Trītónia**).
ministrō, -áre, -ávī, -átum, tr., *to furnish* or *supply.*
mínor, mínus, gen. **minóris,** adj., *less.* (comp. of **párvus**)
mīror, -árī, -átus sum, dep., *to wonder; to wonder at* or *admire.*

mísceō, miscére, míscuī, míxtum, tr., *to mix together.*
míser, mísera, míserum, adj., *miserable; wretched.*
miséreō, miserére, misérúī, misér(i)tum, impers., *to feel pity for; to have pity for.* (cf. 350 n.)
míseror, -árī, -átus sum, dep. *to pity;* gerundive **miserándus,** *to be pitied; pitable.*
mítigō, -áre, -ávī, -átum, tr., *to soothe* or *assuage.* (**mítis**)
míttō, míttere, mísī, míssum, tr., *to send; to let go; to dispatch* or *finish.*
Mnésthēus, -ēī, m., *a Trojan hero, eponymous ancestor of the* **gens Mémmia,** *captain of the* **Prístis,** *one of the ships in Aeneas' fleet and a contestant in the boat race.*
módō, adv., *only; just; lately.*
módus, -ī, m., *a measure; manner, way.*
moénia, -ium, n. pl., *the defensive walls of a city.* (**múniō, múrus**)
móles, -is, f., *any kind of bulky* or *massive object.* (**mólior**)
mons, móntis, m., *a mountain.*
mónstrum, -ī, n., *a portent; a monster.* (**móneō**)
montánus, -a, -um, adj., *of* or *having to do with mountains.* (**mons**)
moniméntum, -ī, n., *a reminder; a memorial.* (**móneō**)
móra, -ae, f., *delay;* idiom **haūd** or **nec móra (est),** *there is no delay,* i.e. *without delay, at once, instantly.*
moribúndus, -a, -um, adj., *doomed; on the point of death.* (**mors**)
móror, -árī, -átus sum, dep., *to delay, tarry, lag behind;* with acc. **nec dóna móror** *nor do I stop for* (i.e. *care about*) *gifts* 400. (**móra**)
mors, mórtis, f., *death.*

mortális, -e, adj., *having to do with death; mortal;* subst. *a mortal; a human being.*
mos, móris, m., *manner* or *custom;* idioms, **de** or **ex móre,** *according to custom, duly, ritually;* **síne móre,** *without* (*observance of*) *normal behavior,* i.e. *without restraint.*
mótus, -ūs, m., *motion, movement.*
móveō, movére, móvī, mótum, tr., *to set in motion; to move; to change* or *alter; to plot,* 608.
mox, adv., *soon.*
múlceō, mulcére, múlsī, múlsum, tr., *to smooth, soothe.*
múltiplex, multíplicis, adj., *manifold.*
múltus, -a, -um, adj., sing. *much;* pl. *many.* (comp. **plūs,** superl. **plúrimus**)
múnus, múneris, n., *a duty* or *obligation; a gift* or *prize; bounty; a spectacle* (652 n.)
múrex, múricis, m., *a shellfish from which purple was obtained; a bed of such shellfish forming an underwater ridge.*
múrmur, múrmuris, n., *a murmur* or *hubbub.*
múrus, -ī, m., *the defensive wall of a town.* (**múniō, moénia**)
mútō, -áre, -ávī, -átum, tr., *to change; to give* or *take in exchange.*
Mycéna, -ae, f.; *more commonly* **Mycénae, -árum,** pl., *Mycenae, the ancient capital of the Argolis.*
mýrtus, -ī and **-ūs,** f., *the myrtle tree.*
nam, conj., *for.*
námque, conj., *for indeed.*
náscor, náscī, nátus sum, dep., *to be born;* **náte déā,** cf. 383 n.
nátō, -áre, -ávī, -átum, intr., *to swim about.* (freq. of **nō**)

nátus, -ūs, m., *birth*, found only in idiom **máximus nátū** *greatest by birth*, i.e. *eldest*.

nátus, -ī, m., *one who was born*, therefore, *a son*. (perf. part. of **náscor**)

naúta, -ae, m., *a sailor*.

Naútēs, -is, m., *a Trojan follower of Aeneas*.

naúticus, -a, -um, adj., *having to do with sailors; naval*.

nāvális, -e, adj., *having to do with ships; naval*.

nāvígium, -iī, n., *a ship*.

návis, -is, f., *a ship*.

-ne, interrog. suffix, **-ne . . . -ne**, *whether . . . or*.

nec, adv. and conj., *and not, nor;* **nec . . . nec**, *neither . . . nor;* **nec non et**, also, *moreover* 100 n. (**néque**)

nécdum, adv. and conj., *not yet*.

néctō, néctere, néxuī, nexum, tr., *to bind*.

nefándus, -a, -um, adj., *unutterable; wicked*.

néfās, n. indecl., *unutterable wickedness; disgrace*. (**fās**)

némō, néminis, m. and f., *no one, nobody*. (ne + **hómō**)

némus, némoris, n., *a grove of trees*.

Neptúnus, -ī, m., *Neptune, Roman god of the sea* (=Greek Poseidon).

néque, adv. and conj., *and not, nor*. (see **nec**)

nēquíquam, adv., *by no means; in vain*.

Nēréis, Nēréidis, f. (patronymic*), *a daughter of Nereus* (a Greek god of the sea); *Nereid; sea-nymph;* esp. in pl. *the Nereids*.

nérvus, -ī, m., *a bow string*.

nī or **nísī**, conj., *if not; unless*.

nídus, -ī, m., *a nest*.

níger, -gra, -grum, adj., *black*. (comp. nígrior, superl. **nigérrimus**)

nígrans, -ántis, adj., *black*. (pres. part. of **nígrō**)

nīl or **níhil**, n. indecl., *nothing;* adverbial *in no way, not at all*.

nímbus, -ī, m., *a cloud*, such as a *stormcloud* or *a cloud of smoke*.

nímium, adv., *too much*. (n. acc. sing. of **nímius -a, -um**)

Nīsaéē, -ae or **ēs**, f., *Nisaéa*, a Nēréis.

nísī, conj., *if not; unless*.

nísus, -ūs, m., *attitude* or *position; stance*. (perf. part. of **nītor**; cf. **obnítor**)

Nísus, -ī, m., *one of Aeneas' Trojan followers, a contestant in the footrace*.

nitéscō, nitéscere, nítuī, no supine stem, incohative, *to grow bright; to shine*. (**níteō**)

níxor, -árī, -átus sum, dep., *to struggle hard*. (freq. of **nītor**; cf. **obnítor**)

nō, náre, návī, intr., *to swim*.

nóceō, nocére, nócuī, nócitum, intr., *to harm; be be harmful* or *hurtful, do mischief* (to).

noctúrnus, -a, -um, adj., *of* or *having to do with night; by night*. (**nox**)

nódus, -ī, m., *a knot*.

nómen, nóminis, n., *a name*. (**nóscō**)

non, adv., *not*. (**nec, néque**)

nóndum, adv., *not yet*. (**nécdum**)

nónus, -a, -um, adj., ordinal num., *ninth*. (= no(vé)nus; **nóvem**)

nóscō, nóscere, nóvī, nótum, inchoative, *to get to know; to recognize;* perf. **nōvísse**, *to have (already) got to know*, therefore *to know* (with present force); **nótus**, *known, well-known, familiar;* perf. part. **nótum**, *a thing that is known; the knowledge* (6 n.)

nóster, -tra, -trum, adj. and pron., possess, 1st pers. pl., *our; ours.* **(nōs)**
nŏta, -ae, f., *a distinguishing mark or spot.* **(nóscō)**
nŏtō, -áre, -ávī, -átum, tr., *to mark.* **(nŏta)**
Nŏtus, -ī, m., *name of the south wind.*
nóvem, adj., cardinal num., *nine.* **(nŏnus)**
nóvō, -áre, -ávī, -átum, tr., *to make new; to reverse; to throw into confusion;* **nováre fídem,** *to break faith* (604 n.)
nóvus, -a, -um, adj., *new.*
nox, nóctis, f., *night.*
nūbes, -is, f., *a cloud.*
nūbilum, -ī, n., *cloudy weather, cloudy sky;* pl. *the clouds.* (subst. of nūbilus, -a, -um)
nūdō, -áre, -ávī, -átum, tr., *to lay bare; to strip.*
nūdus, -a, -um, adj., *bare* or *naked.*
núllus, -a, -um, gen. **nullíus** and **núllīus,** dat. **núllī,** adj., *no, none, not any.* (ne + **úllus**)
nūmen, nūminis, n., literally, *a nod,* and so, *divine will* or *influence; a deity.* **(núō)**
númerus, -ī, m., *a number.*
nunc, adv., *now.*
núntius, -iī, m., *a messenger.*
núper, adv., *recently.*
núsquam, adv., *nowhere.* (ne + **úsquam)**
nūtrix, nūtrícis, f., *nurse.*
o, interj., *oh!*
ob, prep. with acc., *over, upon; towards, over, against; on account of.*
obíciō, -ícere -iếcī, -iéctum, tr., *to throw in front of; to display to.* **(ob + iácio)**

oblíquō, -áre, -ávī, -átum, tr., *to slant, turn slantwise.* **(oblíquus)**
oblíquus, -a, -um, adj., *slanting.*
oblivíscor, oblivíscī, oblítus sum, dep., *to forget;* perf. part. **oblítus,** *forgetful;* with gen. *forgetful of.*
obnítor, -nítī, -níxus sum, tr. dep., *to strive against.*
óbruō, obrúere, óbruī, óbrutum, tr., *to overwhelm.*
obscúrus, -a, -um, adj., *covered over; overshadowed, dim.*
obstipéscō, -stipéscere, -stípuī, no supine stem, incohative, *to become dazed;* perf. *to be amazed.* **(stúpeō)**
obtórqueō, -torquére, -tórsī, -tórtum, tr., *to bend* or *twist into a circle.*
óccubō, -cúbere, no perf. or supine stem, intr., *to lie down upon.* **(cúmbō)**
occúrrō, -cúrrere, -cúrrī, -cúrsum, intr., *to run against* or *upon; to meet, hasten to meet; to meet the view of.*
ócior, ócius, adj., *swifter.*
ócius, adv., *more swiftly.*
óculus, -ī, m., *an eye.*
ódium, -iī, n., *hatred; spite.* **(exŏdī)**
ófferō, offérre, óbtulī, oblátum, tr., *to bring towards; to offer.*
óleŭm, -ī, n., *olive oil.* **(olíva)**
ólim, adv., *at some distant time, past* or *future; sometimes.*
olíva, -ae, f., *the olive tree.* **(óleŭm)**
óllī, pron., archaic for **íllī.** (cf. 10 n.).
Olýmpus, -ī, m., *a mountain of Thessaly; home of the gods.*
ŏmen, óminis, n., *a sign from the gods; an omen.*
omnípotens, -poténtis, adj., *all-powerful.* **(ómnis + póssum)**
ómnis, -e, adj., *whole, entire;* sing. *every;* pl. *all.*
ónerō, -áre, -ávī, -átum, tr., *load.*

onerṓsus, -a, -um, adj., *burdensome; heavy; weighty.* (**ónus**)

oppṓnō, -pṓnere, -pósuī, -pósitum, tr., *to place against* or *in the way of.*

oppúgnō, -ā́re, -ā́vī, -ā́tum, tr., *to fight against; to blockade* or *besiege.*

ops, ópis, f., *power, ability, aid;* pl. *means, wealth, resources.*

óptimus, -a, -um, adj., *best.* (superl. of **bónus**)

óptō, -ā́re, -ā́vī, -ā́tum, tr., *to wish; to choose.*

ópus, óperis, n., *a work, toil;* **úrbis ópus,** *as big as a city.* (cf. 119 n.)

óra, -ae, f., *coast; region.*

órbis, -is, m., *circle, cycle; wheel; turning; the world.*

órdō, órdinis, m., *a row; a series; a bank of oars,* 271; *the order of fate,* 707; abl. **órdine,** *in due order* (53). (**órdior**)

Óriens, Oriéntis, m., *the Rising* (Sun), *therefore the East.* (**órior**)

ṓrō, -ā́re, -ā́vī, -ā́tum, tr., *to beseech; to pray for.* (**ōs, ṓris**)

ōs, ṓris, n., *mouth; face, countenance; lips;* idiom, **ṓre favḗre,** *to maintain silence.* (cf. 712 n.)

ōs, óssis, n., *a bone,* usually pl. *bones.*

osténdō, -téndere, -téndī, -téntum, tr., (lit. *to spread* something *out before* someone; therefore) *to show.* (**ob** + **téndō**)

osténtō, -ā́re, ā́vī, -ā́tum, tr., *to display; show off.* (freq. of **osténdō**)

óstium, -iī, n., *the mouth of a river* or *harbor* (**ōs, ṓris**)

óstrum, -ī, n., *a kind of shellfish; the purple dye obtained from that shellfish; Tyrian purple.*

óvō, -ā́re, -ā́vī, -ā́tum, intr., *to rejoice;* especially *to exult in victory.*

pacíscor, pacíscī, páctus sum, tr., dep., incohative, *to bargain for; to stake* (as in a wager)

Palaémōn, -ŏnis, m., *Palaemon, a Greek sea god identified with the Roman god Portunus.* (cf. 823 n.)

Palinū́rus, -ī, m., *Palinurus, the pilot of Aeneas' flagship.*

Pallās, Pálladis, f., *an epithet of* **Minérva.**

pálma, -ae, f., *the palm of the hand; a palm tree, leaf,* or *branch; the prize for victory.*

pálmula, -ae, f., *an oarblade.* (diminutive of **pálma**)

pálor, -ā́rī, -ā́tus sum, dep., *to wander about; to straggle.*

Pándarus, -ī, m., *a Trojan warrior, son of Lycaon, famous as an archer.* (cf. 496 n.)

Panopéa, -ae, f., *Panopéa, a* **Nēréis.**

Pánopēs, -ae, m., *one of* **Acéstēs'** *Sicilian followers, a contestant in the footrace.*

par, páris, adj., *well matched; equal* (in age, number, etc.); *balanced.*

Párcae, -ā́rum, f. pl., *the Fates.*

párens, -éntis, m. and f., *a father* or *mother; parent.* (**páriō**)

páreō, -ḗre, -uī, -itum, intr., *to obey* (with dat.)

páriēs, párietis, m., *the wall of a house.*

páriō, párere, péperī, pártum, tr., *to bear, bring forth,* or *give birth to; to acquire* or *gain.* (**párens**)

Páris, Páridis, m., *Paris, son of Priam, also known as Alexander.*

páriter, adv., *equally, evenly; at the same time, at once, together.* (**par**)

párō, -ā́re, -ā́vī, -ā́tum, tr., *to make ready; to prepare;* perf. part. **parā́tus,** *ready.*

pars, pártis, f., *a part;* collectively, *some.* (cf. 108 n.)
pártio, -íre, -ívī, -ítum, tr., and **pártior, -írī, -ítus sum,** dep., *to share; to divide.*
párvus, -a, -um, adj., *small* or *little; young.* (comp. **mínor,** superl. **mínimus**)
pássim, adv., *here and there.* (from *pássus,* perf. part. of *pándō*)
pátens, -éntis, adj., *lying open; open; unobstructed.* (pres. part. of *páteō*)
páter, pátris, m., *a father* or *a more distant male ancestor; a leader; an honored figure, human* or *divine;* pl. *elders.*
pátera, -ae, f., *a flat dish* or *bowl; a plate.*
patérnus, -a, -um, adj., *fatherly; ancestral.* (**páter**)
pátiens, -éntis, adj., *enduring; capable of endurance.* (pres. part. of the following)
pátior, pátī, pássus sum, dep., *to suffer* or *endure; to allow.*
pátria, -ae, f., *fatherland.*
pátrius, -a, -um, adj., *having to do with one's father, ancesters,* or *country.* (**páter**)
Pátrōn, -ónis, m., *a follower of Aeneas from* **Tegéa** *in Arcadia, one of the contestants in the footrace.*
paulísper, adv., *for a little while.*
pávidus, -a, -um, adj., *timid; nervous* or *excited.*
pávor, -óris, m., *fear; nervousness* or *excitement.*
pax, pácis, f., *peace.*
péctus, péctoris, n., *the breast; the heart* or *soul.*
pécus, pécudis, f., *a farm animal, especially a sheep.*
pélagus, -ī, n., *the open sea.*

Pēlídīs, -ae, m. (patronymic*), *the son of Peleus,* i.e. **Achíllēs.**
péllis, -is, f., *the pelt, skin,* or *hide of an animal.*
péllō, péllere, pépulī, púlsum, tr., *to drive; to drive away; to rout.*
Penátēs, -ium, m. pl., *the ancient Latin household gods.* (744 n.)
péndeō, -ére, pepéndī, no supine stem, intr., *to hang* or *lean.*
penetrális, -e, adj., *inmost* (**Penátēs**)
pénna, -ae, f., *a feather* or *a wing.*
per, prep. with acc., *through,* of space, time, or cause.
péragō, -ágere, -ḗgī, -áctum, tr., *to drive through; to accomplish* or *finish.*
percéllō, percéllere, pérculī, percúlsum, tr., *to smite thoroughly; strike to the ground.*
perérrō, -áre, -ávī, -átum, intr., *to wander through; to roam all over.* (**érror**)
pérferō, perférre, pértulī, perlátum, tr., *to carry to the end; to endure; to bring a message.*
perfíciō, -fícere -fḗcī, -féctum, tr., *to finish off;* perf. part. **perféctus,** *finished, highly wrought.* (**fáciō**)
perfúndō, -fúndere, -fúdī, -fúsum, tr., *to pour over; to anoint well; to dye thoroughly.*
Pergáměŭs, -a, -um, adj., *of, from,* or *having to do with Pergamus, the citadel of Troy.*
períclum, -ī, n., *danger, peril.*
périmō, -ímere, -ḗmī, -émptum, tr., *to destroy utterly.* (**émō**)
periū́rus, -a, -um, adj., *lying, deceitful.* (**iū́rō**)
permíttō, -míttere, -mísī, -míssum, tr., *to send through; to allow; to grant.*

permúlceō, -mulcére, -múlsī, -múlsum, tr., *to stroke down; to soothe completely.*
persólvō, -sólvere, -sólvī, -solútum, tr., *to give in full payment.*
pérstō, perstáre, pérstitī, perstátum, intr., *to stand fast; to continue.*
pertaédet, pertaēdére, pertaésum est, impers., *to be utterly sick of something.*
pertémptō, -áre, -ávī, -átum, tr., *to make a determined attempt on something.*
pēs, pédis, m., *a foot; a paw or claw of an animal; the bottom of a sail* (830 n.)
péstis, -is, f., (lit. *a plague*); fig. *a disaster of any kind.*
pétō, pétere, pétiī, petítum, tr., *to go after something*, in any sense; *to seek or aim at.*
Phăĕthōn, Phăĕthóntis, m., *a name for the sun god; the sun.*
pháleraē, -árum, f. pl., collectively, *the bridles, saddles, etc.* used to ready a horse for riding.
pháretra and **pharétra, -aē**, f., *a quiver.* (accent and pronunciation: cf. 311 n.)
Phégeūs, Phégeī, m., *a household slave of Aenéās.*
Phólŏĕ, Phólŏēs, f., *a Cretan slave in the possession of Aenéās.*
Phórbas, -bántis, m., *a Trojan follower of Aenéās.* (842 n.)
Phórcus, -ī, m., *a Greek sea god.*
Phryx, Phrýgis, m., (lit. *Phrygian*, a people of Asia Minor); fig. *Trojan.*
píetās, -átis, f., *devotion.* (**píus**)
píget, pigére, píguit, impers., *it makes someone weary* of something, with acc. of person affected and gen. of the cause of feeling (AG §354b).
pígnus, pígnoris, n., *a pledge.*
píngō, píngere, pínxī, píctum, tr., *to paint.*
pínus, -ūs, f., (lit. *a pine tree*); fig. *a ship.*
píus, píī, adj., *dutiful.*
plácidē, adv., *calmly.* (adv. from **plácidus**)
plácidus, -a, -um, adj., *calm.* (**pláceō**)
plaúdō, plaúdere, plaúsī, plaúsum, intr. and tr., *to clap or applaud; to beat* (e.g. *wings*, 516).
plaúsus, -ūs, m., *clapping; applause.* (**plaúdō**).
plĕnus, -a, -um, adj., *full.*
plícō, -áre, -ávi, -átum, tr., *to fold.*
plúmbus, -ī, m., *lead.*
plūs, plúris, n., *more, very much.* (comp. of **múltus**; cf. **plúrimus**)
póculum, -ī, n., *a drinking cup or goblet.*
poéna, -aē, f., *a fine, penalty, or punishment.*
Polítēs, -aē, m., *a son of Priam.*
pólluō, pollúere, pólluī, pollútum, tr., *to defile.* (**lúō**)
pólus, -ī, m., *the celestial North Pole;* (by metonymy*) *the sky.*
pómpa, -aē, f., *a procession.*
póndus, pónderis, n., *a weight.* (**péndō**)
pónō, pónere, pósuī, pósitum, tr., *to put down; to lay aside; to found* (a city); *to hold or institute* (a ceremony)
póntus, -ī, m., *the sea.*
populĕŭs, -a, -um, adj., *of poplar.*
pópulus, -ī, m., *a people.*
pórrō, adv., *further; in succession.*
porténdō, -téndere, -téndī, -téntum,

tr., (*to hold out* or *indicate*; therefore) *to predict* or *foretell*. (**pro** + **téndō**)

pórtō, -áre, -ávī, -átum, tr., *to carry*.

Portúnus, -ī, m., *the Roman god of harbors, in Greek* **Palaémōn**. (**pórtus**)

pórtus, -ūs, m., *a harbor*.

póscō, póscere, pepóscī, no supine stem, tr., *to demand; to ask for* or *pray for*.

póssum, pósse, pótuī, no supine stem, intr., *to be able*. (*pótis* + **sum**)

post, prep. with acc. and adv., *after, afterwards*, of space and time; *behind*.

pósterus, -a, -um, adj., *coming behind; following*. (**post**)

póstis, -is, m., *a doorpost*.

póstquam, conj., *after* (introducing a temporal clause)

praéceps, praecípitis, adj., *headlong; with great haste*. (*prae* + **cáput**)

praecéptum, -ī, n., *an instruction*. (*praecípiō*)

praecípuus, -a, -um, adj., *first chosen; chief, special*. (*prae* + **cápiō**)

praécō, praecónis, m., *a crier; a herald*.

praéeō, praeíre, praeiī, praéitum, intr. and tr., *to go in front* or *before; to lead*.

praéferō, praéferre, praétulī, praelátum, tr., *to bear before; to prefer*. (*prae* + **férō**)

praefígō, -fígere, -fíxī, fíxum, tr., *to attach at the front of something*.

praémium, -iī, n., *prize, reward*. (*prae* + **émō**)

praépēs, praépetis, adj., *swift*. (*prae* + **pétō**)

praésens, -éntis, adj., *at hand; present; prompt*. (pres. part. of praésum)

praéstans, -ántis, adj., *standing first; excellent*. (pres. part. of *praéstō*)

praetéreā, adv., *besides, moreover*.

praetéreō, praeteríre, praetériī, praetéritum, intr. and tr., *to go beyond; to pass*.

praevídeō, -vidére, -vísī, -vísum, tr., *to foresee* or *forestall*.

précēs, précum, f. pl., *prayers*. (**précor**)

précor, -árī, -átus sum, dep., with acc. *to beseech* someone.

prémō, prémere, préssī, préssum, tr., *to press; tread; rub* or *grind*.

prétium, -iī, n., *price; value; prize* or *present*.

Príamus, -ī, m., (1) *the last king of Troy*; (2) *his grandson*.

prímō and prímum, adv., *first; at first; firstly*. (**prímus**)

prímus, -a, -um, adj. (ordinal num.), *first; foremost*. (superl. of **príor**)

prínceps, príncipis, adj., *foremost*; (m. subst.) *a preeminent person*.

princípium, -iī, n., *beginning*; abl. princípiō, *in the beginning; to begin with; first of all*. (**prínceps**)

príor, -óris, adj., *the former; in the lead*. (comp. of **prímus**)

príscus, -a, -um, adj., *extremely ancient*. (**príor**; **prímus**)

Prístis, -is, f., *a ship in Aeneas' fleet commanded by the Trojan hero* **Mnéstheus** *and named for a sea monster*.

prō, prep. with abl., *before; for; instead* or *in place of*.

próbō, -áre, -ávī, -átum, tr., *to approve*. (**próbus**)

prōcédō, -cédere, -céssī, céssum, intr., *to go forth; advance*.

procélla, -ae, f., *a storm*. (**procéllō**)

prōclā́mō, -ā́re, -ā́vī, -ā́tum, intr., *to announce* or *proclaim*.
prócul, adv., *far off; from afar; away from*.
prōcúmbō, -cúmbere, -cúbuī, -cúbitum, intr., *to tumble forwards; lean forwards*.
prōcúrrō, -cúrrere, -cúrrī, -cúrsum, intr., *to run forwards; to jut out*.
prōcúrvus, -a, -um, adj., *bent forwards; winding*.
prōdígium, -iī, n., *a prophetic sign* or *omen*.
proélium, -iī, n., *a battle*.
profúndus, -a, -um, adj., *extremely deep*.
prōgéniēs, prōgeniéī, f., *offspring*.
prohíbeō, -hibḗre, -híbuī, -híbitum, tr., *to restrain* or *forbid; to forestall* or *avert*. (**pro + hábeō**)
prōíciō, -ícere, -i̯ḗcī, -i̯éctum, tr., *to cast away*. (**pro + i̯áciō**)
prōmíssum, -ī, n., *a promise*. (perf. part. of **prōmíttō**)
prōmíttō, -míttere, -mī́sī, -míssum, tr., *to promise*.
prṓmō, prṓmere, prṓmpsī, prṓmptum, tr., *to put forward*.
prṓnus, -a, -um, adj., *forward; bent forwards; inclining towards*.
propínquō, -ā́re, -ā́vī, -ā́tum, intr., *to draw near to* something (with dat.)
própior, -ius; gen. **propiṓris,** adj. (comp.), *nearer*. (positive adv. *prope*, superl. **próximus**)
prōpṓnō, -pṓnere, -pósuī, -pósitum, tr., *to put forth; to propose*.
próprius, -a, -um, adj., *one's own*.
prṓra, -ae, f., *a ship's prow*.
prōrípiō, -rípere, -rípuī, -réptum, tr., *to seize, tear away from*. (**prō + rápiō**)

prṓsequor, prṓsequī, prōsecū́tus sum, dep., *to follow closely* or *pursue*.
prōsíliō, -silī́re, -sílui, no supine stem, intr., *to leap forth*. (**prō + sáliō**)
prṓsum, prōdésse, prṓfuī, no supine stem, intr., *to be for;* therefore, *to be of use*.
prōténdō, -téndere, -téndī, -ténsum and **-téntum,** tr., *to stretch* something *forwards*.
prṓtinus, adv., *forthwith; immediately*. (**prō + ténus**)
próximus, -a, -um, adj. (superl.), *next*. (positive adv. própe, comp. adj. própior)
prū́na, -ae, f., *a live coal*.
pū́bēs, -is, f., *the time of manhood; as a collective, all the young men* or *youth*.
púdet, pudḗre, púduit, no supine stem, impers., *it makes* someone *ashamed* of something (with acc. of person affected and gen. of the cause of feeling, AG §354b).
púdor, -ṓris, m., *sense of shame; self-respect*.
púer, púerī, m., *a boy*.
puerī́lis, -e, adj., *of* or *having to do with boys; composed of boys*.
púgna, -ae, f., *a fight* or *battle*.
púlcher, -chra, -chrum, adj., *beautiful* or *handsome; fine* or *excellent*. comp. **púlchrior,** superl. **pulchérrimus.**
púlsō, -ā́re, -ā́vī, -ā́tum, tr., *to beat*. (freq. of **péllō**)
púmex, pū́micis, m., *pumice stone;* (by metonymy*) *a cliff full of holes and caves*.
pūnī́ceŭs, -a, -um, adj., *of a red color*.
púppis, -is, f., *the stern of a ship;* (by synecdoche*) *a ship*.

púrpura, -ae, f., *purple dye.*
purpúrĕus, -a, -um, adj., *purple-colored.*
pútō, -áre, -ávī, -átum, tr., *to think.*
Pýrgō, Pýrgūs, f., *one of the Trojan women among* **Aēnēās'** *followers, formerly nurse to Priam's children.*
quā, adv. (rel. and interrog.), *where; by which way.*
quaérō, quaérere, quaesívī, quaesítum, tr., *look for; seek.*
quális, -e, adj. (rel. and interrog.), *of which kind; of what kind? such as, like.* (correlative of **tális**)
quam, adv., *than; how, as.* (correlative of **tam**)
quámquam, conj., *although, and yet.*
quámvis, conj., *although.* (**quam** + **vis** *from* **vólō, vélle**)
quántus, -a, -um, adj. (rel. and interrog.), *as big; how big?* (correlative of **tántus**)
quássō, -áre, -ávī, -átum, tr., *to shake hard; to shatter.* (freq. of **quátiō**)
quátiō, quátere, no perf. stem, **quássum,** tr., *to shake.*
quáttuor, adj. (cardinal num., indecl.), *four.*
-que, conj. (enclitic), *and;* **-que . . . -que** or **-que . . . et,** *both . . . and.*
quéstus, -ūs, m., *a complaint.* (**quéror**)
quī, quae, quod, pron. and adj. (rel.), *who* (or *whom*), *which* (or *that*)
quī, quae, quod, adj. (interrog.), *which? what?*
quía, conj., *because.*
quíanam, adv. (*interrog.*), *why?*
quicúmque, quaecúmque, quodcúmque, pron. and adj. (rel.), *whoever* (or *whomever*), *whichever, whatever.*
quiēs, -étis, f., *rest, repose.*

quiéscō, -éscere, -évī, -étum, intr. (incohative), *to become quiet.*
quiḗtus, -a, -um, adj., *peaceful, at rest, quiet.*
quīn, conj., *how not?* (adverbial, 635) *but instead.*
quis, quae, quid, pron. (interr.), *who* (or *whom*)? *which? what?*
quísquam, quaéquam, quícquam, pron. (indef.), *any one at all.*
quísque, quaéque, quódque (subst. **quídque** or **quícque**), pron. and adj. (indef.), *each, every.*
quísquis, quísquis, quídquid, pron. (indef.), *whoever* (or *whomever*), *whichever, whatever.*
quō, adv. (rel. and interrog.), *where* or *where?* i.e. *to which* (or *what*) *place* (?); *to what purpose?* i.e. *why?* 384.
quod, conj., *because.*
quóndam, adv., *once upon a time; back in the day.* (**cum** + indef. suffix -**dam**)
quóniăm, adv. and conj., *since; seeing that.* (**cum** + **iam**)
quóque, conj., *also.*
quotánnīs, adv. (indecl.) *annually; every year.* (**quot** + **ánnīs,** from **ánnus;** abl. of time)
rábiēs, acc. **rábiem,** f., *rage.*
rádius, -ī, m., (lit., *a rod; a spoke of a wheel;) a sunbeam.*
rādix, rādícis, f., *a root.*
rádō, rádere, rásī, rásum, tr., *to scrape; to shave* or *skim.*
rámus, -ī, m., *a bough.*
rápidus, -a, -um, adj., *irresistible* (of a river whose current carries off everything in its path: cf. **rápiō**); *swift, eager.*
rápiō, rápere, rápuī, ráptum, tr., *to seize; to carry off; to rob; to rescue.*

rátis, -is, f., *a raft, boat,* or *ship.*
raúcus, -a, -um, adj., *rough-sounding, hissing and crashing loudly.*
recédō, -cédere, -céssī, -céssum, intr., (lit. *to withdraw*); *to vanish.*
recípiō, -cípere, -cḗpī, -céptum, tr., *to take back; to recover; to rescue.* (**re** + **cápiō**)
recóndō, -cóndere, -cóndidī, -cónditum, tr., *to put away; to hide; to keep secret.* (**re** + **cóndō**)
réctor, -ōris, m., *a guide* or *pilot.* (**régō**)
recúrsus, -ūs, m., *a return; a retreat.* (**re** + **cúrrō**)
recū́sō, -ā́re, -ā́vī, -ā́tum, tr., *to decline* or *refuse.*
réddō, réddere, réddidī, rédditum, tr., *to give back* or *to render* (as what is owed).
rédeō, redíre, rédiī, réditum, intr., *to go back; to return.*
redū́cō, -dū́cere, -dū́xī, -dū́ctum, tr., *to lead back; to draw back.*
rédux, redúcis, adj., *led* or *brought back; returned.*
réferō, reférre, réttulī, relā́tum, tr., *to bring back; to repeat; to utter in reply; to offer; to repay.*
refī́gō, -fī́gere, -fī́xī, fī́xum, tr., *to unfasten; to take down.*
régius, -a, -um, adj., *royal.*
régnum, -ī, n., *kingdom; realm.*
régō, régere, rḗxī, réctum, tr., (lit. *to keep straight*); *to steer, guide,* or *rule.*
rēíciō, rēícere, rēiḗcī, rēiéctum, tr., *to throw back.* (**iáciō**)
relínquō, -línquere, -líquī, -líctum, tr., *to leave behind; to abandon.*
rēlíquiae, -ā́rum, f. pl., *the leavings; the remains.*
remḗtior, -mētī́rī, -mḗnsus sum, dep., (lit. *to measure again*); *to travel again.* (**mḗtior**)
rḗmex, rḗmigis, m., (*a rower;*) as a collective, *rowers* or *crew.*
rēmígium, -iī, n., *oars, oarage; rowing equipment.*
remíttō, -míttere, -mī́sī, -míssum, tr., (lit. *to send back*); *to forego* or *dispense with.*
rḗmus, -ī, m., *an oar.*
réor, rḗrī, rắtus sum, dep., *to think* or *believe.*
repéntē, adv., *suddenly.*
repériō, reperī́re, répperī, repértum, tr., *to discover.*
répleō, -plḗre, -plḗvī, -plḗtum, tr., *to fill up.*
repṓnō, -pṓnere, -pósuī, -pósitum, tr., *to replace; to put aside.*
réquiēs, -ḗtis, f., *rest, respite, pause.*
rēs, réī, f., (lit. *thing,* but with many more specific meanings in different contexts); pl. *fortunes, endeavors.*
resérvō, -ā́re, -ā́vī, -ā́tum, tr., *to keep back; to reserve.*
resī́dō, -sī́dere, -sḗdī, -séssum, intr., (lit. *to sit down*); *to settle down.* (**sédeō**)
résonō, -ā́re, -ā́vī, no supine stem, intr., *to resound.*
rēspíciō, -spícere, -spḗxī, spéctum, tr., *to look back at; to behold; to have regard for* or *respect* (**spíciō**)
respónsum, -ī, n., (lit. *an answer*); *an interpretation of an oracle, a prodigy,* etc.
restínguō, -stínguere, -stínxī, -stínctum, tr., *to extinguish.*
resúltō, -ā́re, no perf. stem, **-ā́tum,** intr., *to rebound; to echo.* (freq. of resíliō from **sáliō**)
rétegō, -tégere, -téxī, -téctum, tr., *to uncover* or *disclose.*

reténtō, -áre, -ávī, -átum, tr., *to hold back.* (freq. of **retíneō**)
retíneō, -tenére, -ténuī, -téntum, tr., *to hold back; to hold in check.* (**téneō**)
rétrahō, -tráhere, tráxī, tráctum, tr., *to drag* or *draw back; to do so again and again* (see 709 n.).
rétrō, adv., *backwards.*
réus, -a, -um, adj., *liable for* (see 237 n.)
revéllō, -véllere, -véllī, -vúlsum, tr., *to tear out, tear off,* or *dislodge from.*
revértor, -vértī, -vérsus sum, dep., *to turn oneself back; to go back* or *return.*
révocō, -áre, -ávī, -átum, tr., *to call back.*
revólvō, -vólvere, -vólvī, -volútum, tr., *to roll over.*
révomō, -vómere, -vómuī, no supine stem, tr., *to belch back.*
rex, régis, m., *ruler, king.* (**régō**)
Rhoetéiŭs, -a, -um, adj., *from Rhoeteum, a promontory on the Hellespont near Troy; therefore, by metonymy*, Trojan.*
rídeō, rīdére, rísī, rísum, intr. and tr., *to laugh at; to laugh.*
rígeō, rigére, ríguī, no supine stem, intr., *to be stiff.*
ríte, adv., *duly; ritually.*
rívus, -ī, m., *a brook* or *stream.*
róbur, róboris, n., *oak* or *timber* (met. *strength*).
Róma, -ae, f., *Rome.*
Rōmánus, -a, -um, adj., *Roman.*
rōs, róris, m., *dew.*
róstrum, -ī, n., (lit. *a beak); the prow of a ship.*
róta, -ae, f., *a wheel.*
rúdens, -éntis, m., *a cable.*
rúmpō, rúmpere, rúpī, rúptum, tr., *to break open* or *apart.*

rúō, rúere, rúī, rútum, intr. and tr., *to rush, rush upon; to push* or *hurry.*
rúpes, -is, f., *a rock* or *rock formation.*
rúrsus, adv., *back again.* (contr. reversus from **revértō**)
sácer, -cra, -crum, adj., *holy, sacred;* n. pl. subst. *sacred rites, sacrifice, worship.*
sacérdos, -dótis, m. and f., *priest* or *priestess.*
sácrō, -áre, -ávī, -átum, tr., *to consecrate.*
saépe, adv., *often.*
saéviō, saevíre, saéviī, saevítum, intr., *to be furious; to rage.*
saévus, -a, -um, adj., *furious; savage, fierce, cruel.*
Ságaris, -is, m., *a household slave of Aenéās.*
sagítta, -ae, f., *an arrow.*
sal, sális, m., (lit. *salt*); met. *the sea.*
Sálius, -ī, m., *a follower of Aeneas from Acarnania, one of the contestants in the footrace.*
sálsus, -a, -um, adj., *salty.*
sálūs, -útis, f., *health; safety.*
sálvē, salvére, intr. (def., only in imperat. and inf.), *be well!* commonly used as a greeting, *hail!* or *hello!*
sánctus, -a, -um, adj., *holy.*
sánguis, sánguinis, m., *blood.*
sátis, pron. (indecl.), *enough.*
Satúrnius, -a, -um, adj., *of* or *having to do with Saturn;* subst. *child of Saturn:* **Satúrnius, -iī,** m. *Neptune* (799 n.); **Satúrnia, -ae,** f. *Juno* (606 n.).
sáturō, -áre, -ávī, -átum, tr., *to satisfy; to appease.*
sátus, -a, -um, adj., *begotten of,* with abl. of source: **sátus Anchísā,** *son*

of Anchises. (perf. part. of **sérō,
sérere, sévī, sátus,** *to sow*)
sáxum, -ī, n., *a stone; rock.*
scélus, scéleris, n., *wickedness; guilt.*
scílicet, adv., *to be sure; of course.* (**scíre**
+ **lícet**)
scíō, scíre, scívī, scítum, intr., *to know.*
scópulus, -ī, m., *a crag or rock.*
Scýlla, -āe, f., *a ship in Aeneas' fleet
commanded by the Trojan hero*
Cloánthus *and named for the
mythical sea monster, a woman
with rabid dogs about her waist.*
sē, see **súī.**
sécō, secáre, sécuī, séctum, tr., *to cut
or cleave.*
sēcrétus, -a, -um, adj., *separated, kept
apart; secret.* (perf. part. of sēcérnō)
sécum, pron. + prep. = **cum sē,** *with
himself, herself, itself, themselves.*
secúndus, -a, -um, adj., (lit. *following,
and so*) as an ordinal num., *second;
of the wind, favorable* for sailing;
of comment or applause, *friendly,
supportive.* (**séquor**)
sed, conj. (adversative), *but; still.*
sédeō, sedére, sédī, séssum, intr., *to
sit down;* impers. **sédet,** *it is settled,*
with dat. of reference (418).
sédēs, -is, f., *a seat; a home.*
sĕdíle, -is, n., *a seat or bench.*
ségnis, -e, adj., *slow; listless.*
semínecem, adj., *half dead.* (acc. sing.;
nom. and gen. sing. are unattested),
adj. *half dead.*
semústus, -a, -um, adj., *half burnt.*
(semi- + perf. part. ústus from **úrō**)
sémper, adv., *forever; always.*
senécta, -āe, f., *old age.*
senéctūs, -tútis, f., *old age.*
sénex, sénis, adj., *old;* subst. *an old
man or woman.*

sénī, -āe, -a, adj. (distributive num.),
six apiece.
sénior, -ōris, adj. (m. and f. only),
older; rather old; elderly. (comp.
of **sénex**)
senténtia, -āe, f., *an opinion.*
séntiō, sentíre, sénsī, sénsum, tr.,
to feel; perceive.
séptem, adj. (cardinal num., indecl.),
seven.
septénī, -āe, -a, adj. (distributive num.),
seven apiece; seven; sevenfold.
séptimus, -a, -um, adj. (ordinal num.),
seventh.
séquax, -ácis, adj., *pursuing.*
séquor, séquī, secútus sum, dep.,
to follow or pursue.
serénus, -a, -um, adj., *clear; bright,
calm.*
Seréstus, -ī, m., *a Trojan hero, captain
of one of the ships in Aeneas' fleet.*
Sergéstus, -ī, m., *a Trojan hero,
eponymous ancestor of the* **gens
Sérgia,** *captain of the* **Centaúrus,**
*one of the ships in Aeneas' fleet
and a contestant in the boat race.*
Sérgius, -a, -um, adj. and subst.
Sérgius, -iī, m., *name of a Roman
gens, supposedly descended from
the Trojan hero* **Sergéstus.**
sérpens, -éntis, f. (sometimes m.),
(lit. *a crawler); a snake.*
sérus, -a, -um, adj., (lit. *late* or *too late);*
with adverbial force, *belatedly,
afterwards* (524 n.)
sérva, -āe, f., *a female slave.*
sérvō, -áre, -ávī, -átum, tr., *to save* or
rescue; to observe or *keep watch
over; to preserve* or *maintain* (a
custom).
sésē, see **súī.**
sétius, adv., *otherwise.* (comp. of **sécus**)

sēu, conj., *or if;* **sēu** ... **sēu**, *whether* ... *or.* (= **sī́ve**)
sī, conj., *if.*
sī́bī or **sī́bi**, see **súī**.
sī́bilus, -a, -um, adj., *hissing.*
Sibýlla, -ae, f., *the Sibyl of Cumae, a prophetic priestess of Apollo.*
sīc, adv., *in this way; so; thus; just so.*
Sicā́nus, -a, -um, adj. and subst. **Sicā́nī, -ṓrum**, m., (lit.) *the most ancient settlers of western Sicily;* (therefore) *Sicilian.*
sí́ccus, -a, -um, adj., *dry.*
sī́cubi, conj. + adv. (indef.), *if anywhere.* (**sī** + alicubi; see 677 n.)
Sí́culus, -a, -um, adj., *Sicilian.*
Sīdónius, -a, -um, adj., *from Sidon, a city of Phoenicia also known as Tyre.*
sī́dus, sī́deris, n., *a star* or *constellation of stars.*
sígnō, -ā́re, ā́vī, -ā́tum, tr., *to mark.*
sígnum, -ī, n., *a mark, sign,* or *signal;* also, *embossed figures* or *designs* (267, 536).
sī́leō, silḗre, sí́luī, no supine stem, intr., *to be silent.*
sí́lva, -ae, f., *a forest.*
sí́milis, -e, adj., *like*, with dat. (but see 594 n.).
Sī́mŏĭs, Simŏéntis, m., *the Simois, a tributary of the river Scamander near Troy.*
sí́mul, adv., *at the same time; at once, as soon as.*
simulā́crum, -ī, n., *a likeness, image* or *representatation.*
sí́ne, prep. with abl., *without; apart from.*
siní́ster, -tra, -trum, adj., *left, left-handed;* subst. **siní́stra, -ae**, f. *the left hand.*

sī́nō, sínere, sī́vī, sī́tum, tr., *to leave alone; to let* or *allow.*
sí́nus, -ūs, m., (lit. *a curve*); *the billowing* of sails.
Sīrḗnēs, -um, f., *the Sirens* (see 864 n., 865–6 n.).
sócius, -a, -um, adj., *allied;* subst. **sócius, -iī**, m. *a companion* or *ally.*
sōl, sṓlis, m., *the sun.*
sōlā́cium, -iī, n., *comfort, consolation.*
sóleō, solḗre, sólitus sum, semidep., *to be in the habit of doing; to do habitually* or *usually.*
sollémnis, -e, adj., *traditional, ceremonial;* subst. **sollémnia, -ium**, n. pl. *customary rites.*
sólor, -ā́rī, -ā́tus sum, dep., *to console.*
sólum, -ī, n., *the ground* (199 n.).
sṓlus, -a, -um, gen. **sōlī́us**, dat. **sṓlī**, adj., *alone, only, solitary.*
sólvō, sólvere, sólvī, solū́tum, tr., *to loosen; to release* or *dismiss; to relax.*
sómnium, -iī, n., *a dream.*
sómnus, -ī, m., *sleep;* **Sómnus, -ī**, m. *the Roman god of sleep* (= Greek *Hypnos*)
sónitus, -ūs, m., *a sound.*
sónō, sonā́re, sónuī, sónitum, intr. and tr., *to make a sound* or *resound; resound.*
sónus, -ī, m., *sound.* (**sónō**)
sópiō, -ī́re, -ī́vī, -ī́tum, tr., *to put to sleep;* perf. part. **sopī́tus**, *asleep.*
sopṓrō, -ā́re, -ā́vī, -ā́tum, tr., (lit. *to put to sleep.*) perf. part. **sopōrā́tus**, *endowed with soporific properties* (855 n.).
sors, sórtis, f., *a lot,* for choosing places along a starting line, etc. (132 n.); **sórte suprḗmā** 190, *in the final hour* (i.e. *last chance*).

sórtior, -íri, -ítus sum, dep., *to cast lots; to assign by lot.*
spárgō, spárgere, spársī, spársum, tr., *to scatter* or *sprinkle.*
spátium, -iī, n., *space, room, area.*
spéctō, -áre, -ávī, -átum, tr., *to look at.*
spéculor, -árī, -átus sum, dep., *to scout; to observe.*
spēlúnca, -ae, f., *a cave* or *cavern.*
spérō, -áre, -ávī, -átum, tr., *to hope; to hope for.*
spēs, spéī, f., *hope.*
spículum, -ī, n., *the pointed tip* (of an arrow, spear, etc.)
Spíō, Spíūs, f., *Spio, a* **Nēréis.**
spíritus, -ūs, m., *breath; spirit.*
spírō, -áre, -ávī, -átum, intr., *to breathe; to blow.*
spíssus, -a, -um, adj., *thick.*
spóliō, -áre, -ávī, -átum, tr., *to strip; to rob of, deprive of.*
spólium, -iī, n., *that which is stripped from a dead animal* or *foe; spoil.*
spóndeō, spondére, spopóndī, spónsum, tr., *to vouch for; to pledge one's word for.*
spúmō, -áre, -ávī, -átum, intr., *to foam.*
squáma, -ae, f., *the scale of a fish* or *serpent.*
státiō, -ónis, f., *a place for standing* or *resting.*
stélla, -ae, f., *a star.*
stérnō, stérnere, strávī, strátum, tr., *to strew; to knock down, level,* or *flatten.*
stirps, stírpis, f., (lit. *the trunk of a tree); family, lineage.*
stō, stáre, stétī, státum, intr., *to stand.*
strídeō, strídēre, strídī, no supine stem, and **strídō, strídere, strídī,** no supine stem, intr., *to creak* or *whistle.*

stríngō, stríngere, strínxī, stríctum, tr., *to graze.*
strúō, strúere, strúxī, strúctum, tr., *to pile together, pile up; build.*
stúdium, -iī, n., *favor, eagerness, excitement.*
stupefáciō, -fácere, -fécī, -fáctum, tr., *to astonish* or *amaze.*
stúpeō, stupére, stúpuī, no supine stem, intr., *to be astonished* or *amazed.*
stúppa, -ae, f., *a kind of coarse flax used to fill gaps in the hulls of ships.*
Stýgius, -a, -um, adj., *Stygian,* i.e. *having to do with the river Styx, one of the rivers of the underworld; so, infernal, hellish.*
sub, prep., (1) with acc. of place to which, *under, up towards, close upon; approaching;* (2) with abl. of place where, *under, beneath; down among; at the foot of; behind;* idioms, **sub úbere** 285, *at her breast;* **sub ármīs** 440, *armed, at arms.*
súbeō, subíre, súbiī, súbitum, intr. and tr., *to come up upon, approach,* or *enter; succeed* or *replace.*
súbigō, -ígere, -égī, -áctum, tr., *to drive under; subdue; compel.* (**ágō**)
subíciō, -ícere, -iécī, -iéctum, tr., *to throw under; to place beneath.* (**iáciō**)
súbitō, adv., *suddenly.*
súbitus, -a, -um, adj., *sudden.* (= perf. part. of **súbeō**)
sublímis, -e, adj., *elevated; aloft; up high.*
summérgō, -mérgere, -mérsī, -mérsum, tr., *to plunge under; to sink.*
subnéctō, -néctere, -néxuī, -néxum, tr., *to attach* or *fasten underneath.*
subsídiō, -sídere, -sédī, -séssum, intr., *to settle* or *sink down.* (**sédeō**)

súbtrahō, -tráhere, -tráxī, -tráctum, tr., *to draw out from underneath* (199 n.)

subúrgeō, -ére, no perf. or supine stem, tr., *to push* or *drive close up to.*

súbvehō, -véhere, -véxī, -véctum, tr., *to carry up from below.*

succédō, -cédere, -céssī, -céssum, intr., *to come up to, withdraw to.*

successus, -ūs, m., *success.*

súdor, -óris, m., *sweat.*

suéscō, suéscere, suévī, suétum, intr. (incohative) *to grow used to something.*

súfferō, sufférre, sústulī, sublátum, tr., *to bear from below; to lift; to remove; to undergo.* **(tóllō)**

suffíciō, -fícere, -fécī, -féctum, intr., *to hold out; to suffice* or *be able.* **(fáciō)**

suī (gen.), **síbī** or **síbĭ** (dat.), **sē** or **sésē** (acc. and abl.), pron. (ref., no nom., sing. and pl. identical), *himself, herself, itself, themselves.*

súlcō, -áre, -ávī, -átum, tr., *to furrow; to plow.*

súlcus, -ī, m., *a furrow.*

sum, ésse, fúī, futúrum, intr., *to be.*

súmmus, -a, -um, see **súperus, -a, -um.**

sűmō, súmere, súmpsī, súmptum, tr., *to remove* or *take away.*

súper, prep. with acc. and abl., *above, over, upon;* adv. *over, above, from above.*

supérbus, -a, -um, adj., *overbearing, proud.*

súperō, -áre, -ávī, -átum, intr. and tr., *to survive; to remain; to abound* or *be in excess; to overcome, win, pass,* or *surmount.*

supérsum, superésse, supérfuī,

superfutúrum, intr., *to survive; to remain.*

súperus, -a, -um, adj., *high up, above;* subst. **súperī, -ōrum,** m. *the gods above.* (comp. **supérior, -ius,** *higher;* superl. **suprémus, -a, -um** and **súmmus, -a, -um,** *highest; last* or *final*).

súpplex, súpplicis, adj., *suppliant.*

súprā, prep. with acc., *above.*

suprémus, -a, -um, see **súperus, -a, -um.**

súrgō, súrgere, surréxī, surréctum, intr., *to arise.*

sūs, súis, m. and f., *pig; sow; boar.*

súscitō, -áre, -ávī, -átum, tr., *rouse up.*

suspéndō, -péndere, -péndī, -pénsum, tr., *to hang aloft;* perf. part. **suspénsus,** *doubtful.* **(sub + péndō)**

súus, -a, -um, adj. (poss. and ref.), *his own, her own, its own, their own; appropriate* or *suitable;* subst. **súī, -órum,** m. *one's own people (friends, children, etc.)*

Sýrtis, -is, f., *a shoal* or *sandbank,* especially *Syrtis major and minor,* off the northern coast of Africa.

taédet, taedére, taéduit or **taésum est,** impers., *one is sick and tired of.*

taénia, -ae, f., *a headband.*

taléntum, -ī, n., *a weight* of precious metal, such as silver or gold (112 n.).

tális, -e, adj., *of such kind; such.*

tam, adv., *so.*

támen, adv. and conj., *yet, still, nevertheless.*

tándem, adv., *finally; at last.*

tángō, tángere, tétigī, táctum, tr., *to touch.*

tántum, adv., *so much; only; enough.*

tántus, -a, -um, adj., *so big; so much.*

tárdō, -áre, -ávī, -átum, tr., *to slow something down.*

tárdus, -a, -um, adj., *slow.*
Tártarus, -ī, m. and **Tártara, -ōrum,** n. pl., *the abode of the damned in the underworld.*
taúrus, -ī, m., *a bull.*
téctum, -ī, n., *a roof; a dwelling.*
técum, pron. + prep. = **cum tē,** *with you.*
Tegĕaéus, -a, -um, adj., *of* or *from Tegea in Arcadia,* and so, *Arcadian.*
téllus, -ūris, f., *earth, land* (9 n.).
télum, -ī, n., *a weapon,* particularly one that is thrown, such as a *spear* or *arrow.*
tempéstas, tempestátis, f., *weather; season; storm.*
témplum, -ī, n., *a sacred precinct; a temple.*
témptō, -áre, -ávī, -átum, tr., *to try; to attempt.*
témpus, témporis, n., *time; a period of time; time.*
témpora, témporum, n. pl., *the temples* (of the head)
téndō, téndere, teténdī, ténsum *and* **téntum,** intr. and tr., *to stretch* or *strain; to strive; to aim at, direct one's course towards, go towards.*
ténebrae, -árum, f. pl., *gloom; darkness.* (accent and pronunciation: cf. 11 n.)
tenebrósus, -a, -um, adj., *gloomy.*
téneō, tenére, ténuī, téntum, tr., *to hold* or *grasp; to keep back, check, restrain.*
ténuis, -e, adj., *thin, slender.*
ténus, prep. with abl. (postpositive), *as far as, up to;* **háctenus,** *thus far, up to this point.*
téres, téretis, adj., *round and smooth, polished.*
térgum, -ī or **térgus, térgoris,** n., *the back; a hide.*

térnus, -a, -um, adj. (distributive num.), *three apiece; in three groups; triple.*
térō, térere, trívī, trítum, tr., *to rub* or *chafe.*
térra, -ae, f., *earth; land; a country.*
térreō, terrére, térruī, térritum, tr., *to frighten.*
terríficus, -a, -um, adj., *frightening, terrible.*
tértius, -a, -um, adj. (ordinal num.), *third.*
téstis, -is, m. and f., *a witness.*
téstor, -árī, -átus sum, tr., *to attest; to call to witness.*
Teúcrī, Teūcrórum or **Teúcrum,** m. pl., *the Trojans, descendants of the hero Teucer, son of Scamander and father-in-law of Dardanus.*
téxō, téxere, téxuī, téxtum, tr., *to weave.*
Thalía, -ae, f., *Thalía, a* **Nēréis.**
theátrum, -trī, n., *a theatre.*
Thétis, Thétidis, f., *Thetis, a* **Nēréis** *and the mother of* **Achíllēs.**
Thrácius, -a, -um, adj., *of Thrace, Thracian.*
Thrēícius, -a, -um, adj., *of Thrace, Thracian.*
Thýbris, Thýbridis, acc. **Thýbrim,** m., *the name of the river Tiber in Greek.*
tímeō, timére, tímuī, no supine stem, intr. and tr., *to be afraid; to fear.*
tímor, -óris, m., *fear.*
títubō, -áre, -ávī, -átum, intr., *to totter.*
Tmárius, -a, -um, adj., *from Tmaros,* a mountain in Epirus.
tolerábilis, -e, adj., *bearable.*
tóllō, tóllere, sústulī, sublátum, tr., *to lift up; to remove, take away.* (**súfferō**)
tóndeō, tondére, tetóndī, tónsum, tr., *to shear; to clip.*

tónitrus, -ūs, m. and **tonítrua, -uum,** n. pl., *thunderclap.*
tónō, tonáre, tónuī, tónitum, intr. and tr., *to thunder.*
tórqueō, torquḗre, tórsī, tórtum, tr., *to twist; to send spinning; to hurl.*
tórreō, torrḗre, tórruī, tóstum, tr., *to scorch; to roast.*
tórtus, -ūs, m., *a twisting or writhing.*
tórus, -ī, m., (lit. *a bulge,* and so, *a muscle*); *a bed or couch.*
tot, adj. (indecl.), *so many;* **tot . . . quot,** *as many . . . as.*
tótidem, adj. (indecl.), *just as many; the same number of.* (**tot;** *-dem*)
tótiens, adv., *so often;* **totiens . . . quotiens,** *as often . . . as.*
tṓtus, tōtī́us, dat. **tṓtī,** adj., *whole; entire.*
trā́dō, trā́dere, trā́didī, trā́ditum, tr., *to hand over; to hand down* (over time).
trā́hō, trā́here, trā́xī, trā́ctum; trā́xe by syncope* for **traxísse** (786 n.), tr., *to drag or draw.*
trāíciō, -ícere, -i̯ḗcī, -i̯ḗctum, tr., *to put through, across,* or *around.* (**iáciō**)
trā́mes, trā́mitis, m., *a path.*
tranquíllus, -a, -um, adj., *calm, still.*
transcrī́bō, -scrī́bere, -scrī́psī, -scrī́ptum, tr., *to enroll* or *enlist* (750 n.).
transcúrrō, -cúrrere, -cúrrī, -cúrsum, intr., *to speed across.*
tránseō, transī́re, tránsiī, tránsitum, intr. and tr., *to go across; to pass.*
tránstrum, -ī, n., (lit. *a crossbeam*); *a bench across a ship,* for rowers.
transvérsus, -a, -um, adj., *across, athwart.*
trā́xe, see **trā́hō.**
treméscō, treméscere, no perf. or supine stem, intr. (incohative), *to start trembling; to shudder.* (**trémō**)
trémō, trémere, trémuī, trémitum, intr., *to tremble; to quiver.*
trēs, tría, adj. (cardinal num.), *three.*
trídens, tridéntis, adj., *three-pronged.*
trílix, trilī́cis, adj., *triple-laced.*
Trīnácrius, -a, -um, adj., *of* or *from* **Trīnácria, -ae,** f. *a name for Sicily* (the three-cornered island)
tríplex, tríplicis, adj., *triple; threefold.*
trípūs, trípodis, m., *a tripod,* (a three-legged or three-footed utensil)
trīs, = **trēs,** acc., m. and f. of **trēs, tría.**
trístis, -e, adj., *sad.*
Trítōn, -ṓnis, m., *a minor god of the sea, subordinate to Neptune* (pl. **Trītṓnēs,** cf. 824 n.).
Trītónia, -ae, f., *an epithet of* **Minérva** (704 n.).
Trṓas, Trṓadis, f. adj. (patronymic*, lit. *daughter of* **Trōs**); *Trojan woman.*
Trōi̯a, -ae, f., *Troy* (the city of **Trōs**).
Trōi̯ā́nus, -a, -um, adj., *Trojan.*
Trōï̯us, -a, -um, adj., *Trojan.*
Trōs, Trṓis, m., *grandson of Dardanus, who gave his name to Troy.*
trúdis, -is, f., *a pointed pole; a boathook.*
tu, túī, tíbī or **tíbĭ, tē, tē,** pron. (2d pers. sing.), *you.*
túba, -ae, f., *a horn.*
túeor, tuḗrī, túitus sum, dep., *to watch, gaze at,* or *guard.*
tum, adv., *then; next.*
túmeō, tumḗre, túmuī, no supine stem, tr., *to swell.*
túmidus, -a, -um, adj., *swelling* or *swollen.*
túmulus, -ī, m., *a swelling* or *rising of the ground; a mound.*
tunc, adv., *then, next.*

túndō, túndere, tútudī, túnsum or **túsum**, tr., *to thump* or *beat*.
túrba, -ae, f., *a crowd* or *mob*.
túrbidus, -a, -um, adj., *thick, murky*.
túrbō, -áre, -ávī, -átum, tr., *to confuse, throw into confusion*.
túrma, -ae, f., *a squadron of cavalry*.
túrpis, -e, adj., *ugly; foul; disgraceful; base*.
tūtámen, tūtáminis, n., *a safeguard; protection*.
tútor, -árī, -átus sum, dep., *to guard well; back up*.
tútus, -a, -um, adj., *protected, safe*.
túus, -a, -um, adj. (poss., 2d pers. sing.), *your*.
úber, úberis, n., *the breast*.
úbi, adv. and conj., (rel. and interrog.), *where, when; where? when?*.
údus, -a, -um, adj., *wet*.
úllus, -a, um, gen. **ullíus**, dat. **úllī**, adj., *any*.
últimus, -a, -um, adj. (superl., cf. ultrā and ultrō, comp. *ultérior*), *farthest; last*.
últrō, adv., *beyond; more than is required* or *expected; even more; voluntarily, spontaneously*.
úmbra, -ae, f., *shade, shadow, darkness*; pl. **úmbrae, -árum**, f. *shades* or *ghosts of the dead*.
únā, adv., *all together; all at once*.
úncus, -a, -um, adj., *hooked*.
únda, -ae, f., *a wave; water*.
únde, adv. (rel. and interrog.), *from whom, which, what*, or *where*.
úndique, adv., *on every side; from all directions*.
úndō, -áre, -ávī, -átum, intr., *to move like a wave*.
únguis, -is, m., *a fingernail; a claw*.
únquam, adv., *at any time; ever*.

únus, -a, -um, gen. **ūníus** or **úníus**, dat. **únī**, adj. (cardinal num.) *one; only; unique*; idiom **ad únum**, *to a man*.
urbs, úrbis, f., *a city*.
úrgeō, urgére, úrsī, no supine stem, tr., *to push, press on*.
úrō, úrere, ússī, ústum, tr., *to burn*.
úrsa, -ae, f., *a she-bear*.
úsquam, adv., *anywhere at all*.
úsque, adv., *all the way; for ever; constantly*.
ut or **útī**, adv. and conj., *when* or *as; where; that, so that, in order that*.
utérque, útraque, utrúmque, adj. and pron. *both one and the other; each of two*. (accent: cf. Allen (1978) 88)
útor, útī, úsus sum, dep., *to use* or *employ* (with abl.).
ūtróque, adv., *in both directions; on this side and on that*.
vácuus, -a, -um, adj., *empty; void*.
vádō, vádere, no perf. or supine stem, intr., *to go* or *walk*.
vádum, -ī, n., (specifically) *a shoal* or *shallow part of a body of water, where one might walk* or *a ship might run aground*; (in general) *the sea*.
vágor, -árī, -átus sum, intr. dep., *to roam*. (**vágus**)
váleō, valére, váluī, valítum, intr., *to be strong; to excel*; with complementary inf. *to have the power* or *be able* (*to do something*); imper. **válē** and **valéte**, *farewell*.
válidus, -a, -um, adj., *strong*. (**váleō**)
válles (also **vállis**), **-is**, f., *a valley*.
vápor, -óris, m., *heat*.
várius, -a, -um, adj., *various, varying; different*.
vástus, -a, -um, adj., *vast, immense; mighty*.

vătes, -is, m. and f., *a prophet(ess) or seer; an interpreter of omens.*
-ve, conj., enclitic, *or.* (**vel; vélō, vélle**)
véhō, véhere, véxī, véctum, tr., *to carry, bear, transport.*
vel, conj., *or;* **vel . . . vel,** *either . . . or.* (**vólō, vélle; -ve**)
vélō, -áre, -ávī, -átum, tr., *to cover; to veil.* (**vélum**)
vélox, -ócis, adj., *swift.*
vélum, -ī, n., *a sail.* (**vélō**)
vélut, adv. and conj., *even as.* (**vel + ut**)
véneror, -árī, -átus sum, tr. dep., *to worship, venerate.*
véniō, veníre, vénī, véntum, intr., *to come.*
véntus, -ī, m., *the wind,* or *a particular wind blowing from a particular direction.* (**Áuster, Córus, Zéphyrus**)
Vénus, Véneris, f., *Venus, the Roman goddess of love* (= Greek *Aphrodite*), *mother of Aeneas.*
vérber, -eris, n., *a whip* or *lash.* (**vérberō**)
vérberō, -áre, -ávī, -átum, tr., *to whip* or *beat.* (**vérber**)
vérō, adv. and conj., *but, in fact, to be sure.* (n. abl. sing. of **vérus, -a, -um**)
vérrō, vérrere, vérrī, vérsum, tr., *to sweep, sweep over.*
vérsō, -áre, -ávī, -átum, tr., *to turn suddenly* or *repeatedly; to consider carefully; to meditate* or *ponder.* (freq. of **vertō**)
vérsus, -ūs, m., *a line* or *row; a tier* or *bank (of oars).* (*originally, a furrow, from turning the plow at the end of the field; cf.* **vértō**)
vértex, vérticis, m., *specifically, the narrowest point of a cone, therefore, the bottom (of a whirlpool)* or *top (of a mountain); more generally, head, summit, zenith;* (**vértō** or **vórtō**)
vértō, vértere, vértī, vérsum, tr., *to turn (something); to change, overturn, turn up;* pass. *to turn (oneself).*
véru, -ūs, n., *a spit.*
vésper (or **Vésper**), **-eris,** m., *the evening star; therefore, the evening (when Vesper appears);* or, *the west (where it appears).* (**Hésperus, Hespéria**)
Vésta, -ae, f., *Vesta, the Roman goddess of the hearth* (= Greek *Hestia*); cf. 744 n.
véster, -tra, -trum, pron., poss., *your, yours.* (**vōs**)
vestígium, -iī, n., *a footstep; track; a foothold, footing.*
véstis, -is, f., *a garment; clothing.* (**véstiō**)
vétus, véteris, adj., *old, aged.*
vía, víae, f., *a way, road,* or *course.*
viátor, -óris, m., *a wayfarer* or *traveler.* (**vía**)
vīcínus, -a, -um, adj., *neighbouring.* (**vīcus**)
vicíssim, adv., *in turn; by turns.* (**vícis**)
víctor, -óris, m., *a conqueror; a winner.* (**víncō**)
vídeō, vidére, vídī, vísum, tr., *to see;* pass. *to seem;* **vidérī síbī,** *to seem to oneself, i.e. to think that . . .* (231 n.).
vígilans, -ántis, adj., *watchful, watching.* (pres. part. of **vígilō**)
víllus, -ī, m., *shaggy hair* or *bristles.*
víncō, víncere, vícī, víctum, tr., *to conquer* or *win.* (**víctor**).
vínclum (also **vínculum**), **-ī,** n., *something used for binding; in boxing, the gloves* (or **cáestus**). (**vínciō**)
vínum, -ī, n., *wine.*

vir, vírī, m., *a man* (as opp. to ***homō***, *a person*); *gentleman; hero.*
vī́rēs, -ium, f. pl., *of* **vis.**
vírgō, -inis, f., *a young woman; a virgin, maiden.*
virgúltum, -ī, n., *a thicket of bushes, brushwood.* (**vírga**)
víridans, -ántis, adj., *green.* (perf. part. of **víridō**)
víridis, -e, adj., *green, blooming.* (**víreō**)
vírtūs, -tū́tis, f., *manliness; bravery; courage.* (**vir; vī́rēs**)
vis, acc. **vim,** abl. **vī.**; pl. **vī́rēs, vī́rium,** f., *force; violence;* pl. *strength; might; prowess; powers;* cf. 454 n.
víscera, -um, n. pl., specifically, *intestines;* more generally, *flesh* (103).
vī́sus, -ūs, m., *sight.* (**vídeō**)
vī́ta, -āe, f., *life.* (**vī́vō; vígeō;** *etc.*)
vítta, -āe, f., *a fillet* or *headband.*
vítulus, -ī, m., *a male calf.*
vī́vidus, -a, -um, adj., *full of life.* (**vī́vō**)
vī́vō, vī́vere, víxī, víctum, intr., *to live.* (**vígeō**)
vix, adv., *scarcely.*
Volcánus, -ī, m., *Vulcan, the Roman god of fire* (= Greek *Hephaestus*); by metonymy, *fire.*

vólitō, -ā́re, -ā́vī, -ā́tum, intr., *to flutter, flit about.* (*freq. of* **vólō, -ā́re**)
vúlnus, vúlneris, n., *a wound.*
vólō, -ā́re, -ā́vī, -ā́tum, intr., *to fly.*
vólō, vélle, vóluī, no supine stem, tr. and intr., irregular., *to want* or *wish; to be willing.*
vúltus, -ūs, m., *the face; a facial expression.*
vólucer, -cris, -cre, adj., *swift, winged.* subst. **vólucris, -is,** f., *a bird.* (**vólō, -ā́re**)
volū́men, -minis, n., *a roll* or *coil.* (**vólvō**)
volū́tō, -ā́re, -ā́vī, -ā́tum, intr. and tr., *to roll around; to roll* (*something*) *up.* (*freq. of* **vólvō**)
vólvō, vólvere, vólvī, volū́tum, tr., *to roll.*
vómō, vómere, vómuī, vómitum, tr. and intr., *to vomit; to spew.*
vōs, pron., 2d pers. pl., (*all of*) *you.* (*see* **tū**)
vótum, -ī, n., *a vow.* (subst. perf. part. of **vóveō**)
vox, vócis, f., *a voice; a word, speech,* or *statement.* (**vócō**)
Xánthus, -ī, m., *a river near Troy.*
Zéphyrus, -ī, m., *the west wind.*

Index

This index lists grammatical, metrical, and stylistic items mentioned in the commentary; numbers refer to lines in the Latin text and the corresponding commentary notes.

ablative
    absolute, 329, 331–2, 713–14, 793; *tranquillo*, 127; *modō* v. adverb *modŏ*, 25, 599; object (of *cum*), 733; (of *simul*), 357; (of *sub*), 323
    of attendant circumstance, 190, 338, 369
    of cause, 5, 11, 268, 337, 397–8, 445, 656, 865–6
    of description, 77, 118, 306, 609
    of manner, 18, 153–4, 200, 450, 610, 641
    of material, 307, 312–13; 663
    of means, 77–8, 116, 132, 275, 439, 454, 499, 610, 817
    of place where, 290, 473, 683, 762, 800, 821
    of price, 736
    of quality, 118, 372–3, 609
    of separation, 751
    of source, 61, 244, 383
    of specification, 61–2, 67–8, 267, 271, 274, 290, 295, 439
    of the gerund, 710
    of time when, 42, 190
    with *intendere*, 403.
accented and unaccented syllables: 11, 190, 318, 501, 647.
accusative
    + infinitive, with *gratari*, 40; adverbial, 21–2, 751
    cognate (or) internal, 6, 19–20, 168, 180, 194, 196, 235, 317, 335, 508, 608, 688, 695, 751, 825–6, 862, 865–6
    direct object, 36, 135, 298, 312–13, 345, 413, 420, 422–3, 429, 438, 499, 604, 677, 691, 701, 746–8, 750, 766, 787, 794–5, 834, 839, *see* omission; object (of *sub*), 327–8
    of duration of time, 762, 766
    of specification ("retained"), 96–7, 135, 309, 511, 604, 608
    of the person affected, with impersonal verbs, 354, 678–9, 713–14
    plural (fifth decelension), 690; (fourth declension), 16, 23–4, 350; (third declension), 359, 690, 750, 751
    predicate modifier, 50
    singular in -*im*, 606
    subject, 15, 18, 350, 413, 615–16, 800
    omitted but understood, 385, 794–5
    with *invideo*, 541
    with *secare*, 658.
adjectives
    attributive (participle) 565, (v. predicate modifier) 865, (replaced by prepositional phrases) 266, (v. ablative of quality) 609
    instead of adverb, 857
    instead of genitive, 141
    possessive, 538, 761, 823
    v. reflexive pronoun, 538

adjectives *(continued)*
    used as substantive, 244, 383, 397
    v. ablative of material, 663
    See predicate modifier: with adverbial force.
adverbial constructions
    ablative of manner, 641
    adverbial accusative, 21–2, 751
    appositives, 130
    cognate (or) internal accusative, 19–20, 608
    fors, 232
    hendiadys, 345; intensive pronoun, 332
    prepositional phrases, 266
    prepositions used adverbially, 21–2, 27, 312–13, 330, 339, 362
    relative clause, 289
    See predicate modifier: with adverbial force.
adverbs: indefinite, in conditions, 677
    instead of adjectives, 761
    modŏ v. ablative noun *modō*, 25.
aetiology: 545–603, 633, Appendix B.
agreement: *see* gender; number.
alliteration: 153–4, 278–9, 422–3, 458–60, 500, Appendix B.
antithesis: 509–10, Appendix B.
apo koinou construction: 21–2, 36, 604, Appendix B.
aposiopesis: 195, Appendix B.
apostrophe: 50, 840, Appendix B.
appositives: 52, 130, 359, 372–3, 664, 702–3, 754, 787.
arsis: 284, Appendix B.
assonance: 458, 505–6, Appendix B.
asyndeton: 509–10, Appendix B.
caesura: *see* meter and prosody.
causal clauses
    quod + subjunctive, 651
    relative, 621, 624.
chiasmus: 267, 299, Appendix B.

compound verbs: *see* verbs.
concessive constructions
    ablative absolute, 331–2
    cum clauses, 804–10, 810.
conditions, 325–6, 346–7
    indefinite pronouns and adverbs in, 363, 677
    relative clause, 291.
conjunctions
    coordinating v. subordinating, 857–9
    cum (v. preposition), 328
    emphatic, 858–9
    See *cum* clauses; postponement of conjunctions and pronouns.
connective relatives, 289, 296, 303, 323, 847.
cum clauses
    cum inversum, 84, 159–60, 857–9
    circumstantial, 804
    concessive, 804–10, 810
    temporal clauses, see *ut* temporal clauses.
dative
    ethic (or) ethical, 162, 305, 391, 646
    indirect object, 335, 346–7, 353, 616, 749, 794–5, 796–7, 800, (omitted but understood) 306
    of agent, 305, 360
    of end of motion, 34, 233, 451, (omitted but understood) 9
    of possession, 214, 353, 363, 621, 648–9, 804–5
    of purpose, 261–2, 685–6, 712
    of reference, 418, 548–51, 556, 646, 821
    of separation, 845
    with compound verbs, 9, 34, 233, 301, 346–7, 451, 691, 713–14, 847
    with *invideo*, 541
    with *licet*, 350
    with *similis*, 317.

diaeresis: 242, 643–4, Appendix B.
diphthongs: 105, 116, 183–4, 186, 294, 352, 493–8, 620, 664, 675, 690, 800.
ecphrasis: 250–7, 588–95, Appendix B.
elision: 261–2, 422–3, 710, Appendix B.
ellipsis: 355–5, 664, Appendix B.
emphasis: 5, 39, 52, 84, 104–603, 118, 191, 323, 334, 397–8, 467, 509–10, 545–603, 568–9, 569–70, 648–9, 691, 728, 761, 789, 823–6, 841, 848–9, 858–9.
enallage: 15, 23–4, 128, 274, 387, 663, 676–7, 761, 857, Appendix B.
enjambment: 5, 480, 841, Appendix B.
epanalepsis: 493–4, Appendix B.
epithet: 3, 556, 606, 704, 781, Appendix B.
etymology, 117, 369, 545–603, 547, 559, 568, 633, Appendix B.
gender: agreement, 122; common, 327–8.
genitive
    objective, 284, 296, 538, 712, 804–5, (with impersonal verbs) 713–14
    of apposition, 52, 288–89, 340
    of *domus*, 732
    of possession, 141, 190, 244, 349, 383, 823, *see* adjectives: possessive
    of specification, 73
    of the charge or penalty, 237
    of want, 751
    partitive, 695
    plural in *-um* instead of *-orum*, 45, 56, 148, 174, 369, 592, 622, 671, 675, 690, 707
    subjective, 369
    with *causā, gratiā*, etc., 337
    with *congressus*, 733
    with *similis*, 594
    with verbs and adjectives of feeling, 350, 354, 678–9
    with verbs of forgetting, 334.
genre: 6, 870–1.
gerund: 183–4, 618, 710.

golden line: *see* word order.
Greek forms
    Acestēn, 30
    Aenean, 708
    áēr, 20
    áĕrā, 839
    aethera, 13, 140
    Bĕrŏēn, 650
    Būtēn, 372
    cētē, 822
    crātéra, 536
    Daréta, 458–60
    Didūs gen. and *Dido* acc., 3
    Epytidēn, 547
    Iasidē, 843
    lebetas, 266
    Libystidis, 37
    Menoitē, 166
    Mnesthēi, 183–4, 190
    grammar and syntax, influence of, 751.
hendiadys: 36, 345, Appendix B.
hyperbaton: *see* word order.
hyperbole, 144–7, 391, 404–5, 439, 444, Appendix B.
imperative
    future, 310
    of deponents, 845of
    sino v. *sine* prep.163
    with jussive subjunctive, 548–51.
imperfect tense
    inceptive, 1–2, 159
    subjunctive, *see* sequence of tenses
    see conditions.
indicative v. historical infinitive, 655.
indirect commands: 342.
indirect questions: 4, 6, 648–9, 702–3, 746–8.
infinitive
    + *optem*, 29
    complementary, 21, 69, 155
    convértere v. *convertére*, 582

infinitive *(continued)*
   historical, v. indicative, 655
   in indirect discourse, 372–3
   in prose v. poetry, 21
   instead of gerund, 183
   of exclamation, 615
   of purpose, 247
   perfect passive, 413
   with *fas*, 800
   with *spero*, 18.
interrogatives
   adjectives, 648–9
   pronouns, 354, 648–9.
intransitive verbs: *see* verbs.
irony: 788, 870, Appendix B.
litotes: 39, 56, 100, 530–1, 618, Appendix B.
locative with verbs and adjectives of feeling, 202.
logic, poetic: 11.
logical (as opposed to grammatical) construction: 32–3, 278, 293, 325–6, 433–8, 480, 567, 728, 761, 764, 838.
metaphor, 31, 136–7, 141, 150, 228, 250–1, 316, 388, 396, 433–8, 440, 483–4, 528, 662, 762–871, Appendix B.
meter and prosody
   artificial lengthening of syllables, 11, 18, 47, 82, 117, 190, 338, 369, 413, 450, 480, 501, 565, 589, 620, 629, 730, 787
   caesura, 422–3, 458–60, 643–4, 841, Appendix B
   correption, 261–2, 735, Appendix B
   cretic, 266
   elision, 261–2, Appendix B
   expressive effects, 476–81, 568–9
   hiatus, 261–2, 735, Appendix B
   hypermetric elision (or) line, 422–3, 753
   monosyllable, final, 710

   nātus v. *sătus*, 244, 383
   shortening of diphthongs, 186
   spondaic, 320, 476–81, 614–15, 761, Appendix B
   trochee, 14, Appendix B
   see number: poetic plural; quantity, natural.
metonymy: 7, 19–20, 23–4, 71, 77–8, 286, 339, 433–8, 490–2, 493–8, 591, 626–7, 628, 646, 662, 721, 755–7, 758, Appendix B.
modifiers, multiple, with single nouns: 761.
neuter
   adjective *tranquillo*, *see* ablative: absolute
   impersonal verbs, 713–14
   pronoun, indefinite, for masculine and feminine, 716
   see accusative: cognate (or) internal; participle: used as a substantive
nominative
   predicate modifier, 176, (with adverbial force) 339, 521, 664
   subject, 670, (omitted but understood) 34, 136–37, 224, 330, 557, (of omitted but understood verb "to be") 677–8.
nouns
   abstract, 148
   collective, 108, 754
   common v. proper, 122, 250–1
   see adverbial constructions: *fors*.
number
   agreement, 87–8, 661–2
   poetic plural, 80–81, 98, 171, 194, 228, 238, 247–8, 277, 346–7, 350, 359, 659, 706–7, 733
   shades of meaning (singular v. plural), 19–20, 148, 233, 454, 473, 608, 641

singular, (collective) 116, 661–2,
678–9, (*Mycena* instead of *Mycenae*)
52, *talenta* v. *talentum*, 112
singular and plural grammatically
parallel, 334.
numbers: cardinal, ordinal, distributive,
61–2, 85, 120, 560–1
omission
of accusative, (direct object) 156,
741 413, (subject accusative) 15,
385, 794–5, (with *poscere*) 59
of dative, (indirect object) 306,
(of end of motion) 9, (*sibi*, with
videntur) 231
of demonstrative pronouns, 678–9;
of main verb, 822
of *pars*, 108
of subject, 34, 60, 224, 330, 480,
557
of verbs, 32, 322, ("to be") 23–4,
32, 40, 117, 136–7, 192, 214, 298–9,
299, 322, 334, 339, 362, 363, 370,
372–3, 391, 392, 400, 402–3, 412,
413, 529, 603, 616, 637–9, 644,
653, 670, 677–8, 698, 722, 749,
754, 763, 768, 804–5, 834, (of verbs
of speaking) 12, 26, 643–4, 645,
(in perfect system, passives and
deponents) 192, 296, 303, 643–4,
762, (in subjunctive) 643–4, 648–9.
onomatopoeia: 865–6, Appendix B.
oxymoron: 40, Appendix B.
parallelism: 299, 305, 334, 339, 677,
746–8.
parataxis, 163, 857–9, Appendix B.
participles
as predicate modifier, 136–7, 398,
413
circumstantial, 36, 336, 372–3,
521, 804–5
future active, (to express likelihood
or certainty) 565, (to express

purpose) 108
of *soporo*, 855–6; perfect passive,
(with "retained" accusative) 135,
(with dative of agent) 305
perfect, of deponents, 331–2, 708,
(equivalent to perfect active) 14,
493
present active, 181–2, (instead
of synonymous adjective) 96–7
used as substantive, 6, 290, 383,
678–9, (instead of synonymous
noun) 148.
pathetic fallacy: 23–4.
patronymic: 45, 547, 843.
perfect tense
alternate ending -*ēre* for -*ērunt*,
8, 140, 144–5, 147, 173, 181–2, 206,
404, 428, 490, 529, 568, 578, 582,
600, 681, 830–1
in narrative, 136–50, 243
see participles; subjunctive: in
indirect questions.
periphrasis: 29, 566, 695, Appendix B.
Persian: 40.
pleonasm: 39, 194, 334, 610, 761,
Appendix B.
pluperfect tense
indicative, instead of perfect, 397
subjunctive, *see* conditions.
polyptoton, 569–70, Appendix B.
postponement of conjunctions and
pronouns: 6, 117, 119, 178, 190, 264,
274, 303, 312–13, 320, 325–6, 329,
344, 355–6, 370, 388, 439, 475, 544,
563, 599, 651, 667, 713–14, 764, 814;
see prepositions.
predicate modifier
perfect passive participle, 136–7,
398, 413
with adverbial force, 34, 67–8,
136–7, 170, 278, 325–6, 480, 524,
567, 764, 838, 861, 865–6.

prepositions
   instead of attributive adjectives, 266
   omitted, with ablative of material, 307
   postponed, 512
   repetition of, 858; separation from object, 609; *simul,* used as, 357
   sine (v. imperative of *sino*) 163
   see adverbial constructions.
present tense
   in narrative, 136–50
   see infinitive; participles *and* participles: perfect, of deponents.
prolepsis: 80, 129, 255, 556, 816, 821, Appendix B.
pronouns
   demonstrative, (resumptive (or) pleonastic) 39, 90, 186, 334, 457, (to signal a change of subject) 75, 169, 242, 336, 394, 439, 482, 510, 609, 676–7
   distributive, in relative clauses, 100; *hic* nominative v. *hic* adverb, 331; indefinite, (in conditions) 363, 677, (neuter for masculine and feminine) 716
   intensive, 323, 332; *is,* infrequent in poetry, 708, personal, for emphasis, 691, 789
   quo ablative v. adverb, 29
   reflexive, v. possessive adjective, 538
   see postponement of conjunctions and pronouns.
pronunciation: 11, 38, 55, 61, 190, 194, 311–12, 663, 811.
purpose constructions
   circumstantial participle, 521
   dative, 261–2, 685–6, 712
   future active participle, 108

infinitive, 247–8
relative clause, 130, 590.
quantity, natural: 18, 647, 702–3.
redundancy. 163, 505–6..
relative clauses
   causal, 621, 624
   distributive pronouns in, 100
   of purpose, 130, 590
   omission of verb in, 117
   preceeding the antecedent, 397–8
   see connective relatives.
repetition, 8–11, 9, 11, 14, 32, 37, 77–8, 94, 96–7, 118, 136–7, 141, 153–4, 176, 228, 234, 237–8, 244, 259–60, 294, 303, 317, 318–26, 324, 334, 400, 426–7, 432, 468–73, 493–4, 505–6, 538, 553, 569–70, 572, 591, 606, 608, 626, 725, 738, 742, 767–9, 774–8, 774, 775–6, 777, 814, 821; of main verb, 181–2.
scansion: 194, 663.
sequence of tenses: 325–6, 804–10.
silver line: *see* word order.
simile: 136–50, 144–7, 199, 213–17, 273–81, 317, 432, 572–7, 582, 588–95, 594, Appendix B.
singular: *see* number.
style
   archaic, 8, 10, 15, 18, 40, 45, 197, 310, 383, 395, 468, 511, 594, 596–603, 622, 763
   coinages and first occurrences, 16, 40, 687, 765
   colloquial, 163, 334, 850
   epic, 8–11, 118
   exotic, 37, 40, 250–1, 311–12, 823–6
   grand (or) elevated, 6, 8, 9, 14, 17–18, 61–2, 67, 254, 310, 383, 566, 695, 870–1
   legal, 17–18, 310

parliamentary, 17–18; poetic, 6, 11,
16, 18, 21–22, 29, 34, 85, 96–7, 135,
139, 171, 194, 244, 261–2, 266, 277,
285, 286, 307, 342, 346–7, 350, 359,
383, 402–3, 466, 545–603, 609,
613, 659, 663, 706–7, 708, 728, 733,
762, 774–8, 870
prosaic, 14, 21–22, 29, 34, 117, 237,
276, 286, 330, 342, 362, 383, 394,
402–3, 467, 537, 560–1, 697, 728,
733
sacral (or) religious, 5, 7, 9, 94,
197, 254, 310, 761, 762, 763
technical, 25
vividness, 136–50.
sub
with ablative, 323
with accusative, 327–8.
subject, change of: *see* pronouns:
demonstrative.
subjunctive
in causal clauses, 651
in indirect commands, 342
in indirect questions, 4, 648–9
in relative causal clauses, 621, 624;
jussive, 163, 548–51, 788
omitted but understood, 643–4,
648–9
potential, 29
see concessive constructions;
conditions.
syncope: 42, 246, 785–6, Appendix B.
synecdoche: 51, 96–7, 307, 318, 340–1,
729, Appendix B.
synezesis: 14, 352, Appendix B.
synonyms: 16, 37, 67–8, 70, 85, 148,
244, 334, 340, 346–7, 383.
tmesis: 384, 603, 697, Appendix B.
transferred epithet: *see* enallage.
ut temporal clauses: 8.
variatio, 85, 104–761, Appendix A.

verbs
compounds, (of intransitives,
taking direct object) 438, (and
uncompounded forms) 233, 286,
330, 355–6, 402–3, 438, 451, 687
copulative, 176
deponent, 14
finite, in relation to circumstantial
participle, 36, 336
formed from adjectives, 16
frequentative, 458–60
impersonal, 4, 354, 678–9, 713–
14, (*fas est*) 800, (passive forms)
713–14
of desire, 155
of feeling, 678–9
with accusative instead of genitive,
350
of forgetting, 334, (omitted but
understood) *see* omission; tenses,
in narrative, 136–50
"to be" (omitted but understood),
see omission
see infinitive, gerund, imperative,
indicative, participles, subjunctive.
vocative
Iasidē, 843
Menoetē, 166
nate, 383
pueri, 349.
voice
active, *see* participles
passive, *see* omission: of verb "to
be", participles: perfect passive
passive, used with intransitive
or reflexive force, 19–20, 604
see verbs: impersonal, passive
forms; participles: perfect, of
deponents.
word order: 1–2, 5, 6, 14, 22–3, 117,
119, 178, 190, 264, 266, 274, 299,

word order *(continued)*
    303, 312–13, 320, 325–6, 329, 344,
    346–7, 349, 355–6, 370, 372–3, 388,
    439, 475, 509–10, 544, 563, 599,
    651, 663, 667, 698, 713–14, 764, 814
    golden line, 500, 524, 838,
    Appendix B
    hyperbaton, 664, Appendix B
    iconic, 1, 113, 556
    ille, following a noun, 391
    inversion, 397–8
    preposition and object, separation
    of, 609
    silver line, 38, 46, 134, 344, 516,
    Appendix B
    see postponement of conjunctions
    and pronouns.
zeugma: 53–4, 85, 136–7, Appendix B.